The Fabulous Future?

The Fabulous Future?

America and the World in 2040

EDITED BY

Gary Saul Morson and Morton Schapiro

NORTHWESTERN UNIVERSITY PRESS

EVANSTON, ILLINOIS

Northwestern University Press
www.nupress.northwestern.edu

Copyright © 2015 by Northwestern University Press. Published 2015.
All rights reserved.

Printed in the United States of America

10   9   8   7   6   5   4   3   2   1

Library of Congress Cataloging-in-Publication Data

The fabulous future? : America and the world in 2040 / edited by Gary Saul
Morson and Morton Schapiro.
     pages cm
     ISBN 978-0-8101-3196-5 (cloth : alk. paper) — ISBN 978-0-8101-3198-9
(pbk. : alk. paper) — ISBN 978-0-8101-3197-2 (ebook)
     1. United States—Forecasting. 2. Social prediction—United States.
3. Twenty-first century—Forecasts. I. Morson, Gary Saul, 1948– editor of
compilation. II. Schapiro, Morton Owen, editor of compilation.
     HN60.F33 2015
     973.930112—dc23
2015000068

For our children—

Emily and Alexander Morson and

Matthew, Alissa, and Rachel Schapiro—

and for everyone who will inherit the future

we are all making

Prediction is very difficult, especially about the future.
—OFTEN ATTRIBUTED TO NIELS BOHR

CONTENTS

Acknowledgments
xiii

Introduction: The Future of Prediction
Gary Saul Morson and Morton Schapiro
xv

Organization of the Volume and List of Contributors
xxxi

Part One: Wealth, Health, and Happiness

Chapter 1 **Wealth**
The Future of Economic Growth: Slowing to a Crawl
Robert J. Gordon
5

Chapter 2 **Health**
Longer and Healthier Lives?
Eileen M. Crimmins
23

Chapter 3 **Happiness**
A Happier World?
Richard A. Easterlin
33

Part Two: Politics, Religion, and Human Rights

Chapter 4   **Politics**
The World in 2040
Robert L. Gallucci
49

Chapter 5   **Religion**
The Future of American Religion
Eboo Patel
63

Chapter 6   **Human Rights**
Freedom's Future
Wendy Kaminer
79

Part Three: Science, Technology, and the Environment

Chapter 7   **Science**
Especially about the Future
Mark A. Ratner
99

Chapter 8   **Technology**
The Era of Answers
John Kelly III
113

Chapter 9   **The Environment**
Bridging the Gap between Knowing and Doing:
The New Environmental Governance
Mark R. Tercek and Jimmie Powell
129

Part Four: Education, Communication, and Society

Chapter 10 **Education**
The Future of Higher Education in the United States (and the World)
Gary Saul Morson and Morton Schapiro
155

Chapter 11 **Communication**
Media of the Future
Arianna Huffington
175

Chapter 12 **Society**
The Future of Fearmongering
Barry Glassner
183

Conclusion: The World To Be
Gary Saul Morson and Morton Schapiro
199

Index
205

ACKNOWLEDGMENTS

This book emerged from an undergraduate course we have been teaching together for several years—Alternatives: Modeling Choice Across the Disciplines. One of our favorite topics is the examination of different approaches to predicting the future and to understanding the past. We thank our students and our exceptionally talented teaching assistants for inspiring us to produce this volume.

We received great advice and assistance from the staff at Northwestern University Press, and we single out in particular its director, Jane Bunker, and assistant director, Henry Lowell Carrigan Jr., along with three anonymous referees who reviewed the volume with uncommon insight. We thank also the wonderful people in the Northwestern President's Office—Judi Remington, Lindsay Rathert, and Paula Peterson—for help in many ways, and especially Geneva Danko, who masterfully organized draft after draft in the most cheerful and efficient manner imaginable. Provost Dan Linzer provided helpful comments on our penultimate draft.

Finally, we thank the editors and authors of the classic 1955 book *The Fabulous Future: America in 1980.* While it is easy to scoff at so many of their predictions, we fully expect that, decades from now, much of what is written here will seem as hopelessly misguided. How could they, and we, miss the obvious? It certainly wasn't because either volume suffered from the selection of the wrong authors. As was the case in the 1950s, we have here a collection of some of the most thoughtful and influential thinkers in the world. The problem, of course, is that the future remains as unimaginable as ever.

One thing we *can* know is that the future is not a given—it depends on what we do. It does not just happen to us. We make it.

While that sometimes terrifies us, it also gives us hope.

The Future of Prediction

Gary Saul Morson and Morton Schapiro

Among all forms of mistake, prophecy is the most gratuitous.
—GEORGE ELIOT, *MIDDLEMARCH*

Everyone questions his memory, but no one questions his judgment.
—LA ROCHEFOUCAULD

The future just won't stay still. We imagine we can predict it, that we can diminish or erase its uncertainty, and that we can mitigate the power of the radically unknown. Almost always, events prove us wrong. Then we forget these mistakes and go on making predictions with undiminished confidence.

As Barry Glassner observes in the present volume, predictions of disaster seem to exercise special attraction, as if the more critical the problems we face, the more significant are our lives.[1] Today, the media report a wealth of catastrophes. Oil may run out, but no one predicts the end of terrifying predictions: new microorganisms, produced naturally or in some laboratory, and circulating accidentally or by design, threaten the human race; the more nations that have nuclear weapons, the more possible nuclear war becomes. Will the Cuban missile crisis look quaint some day? The older nuclear technology gets, the easier it will become to acquire it. The rise of powers more dangerous, because less given to self-preservation, than the former Soviet Union makes the old strategy of deterrence look less and less viable. So does the rise of terrorists without a state to deter. Or so we are told.

The technology that improves our lives also threatens to destroy them. The more dependent we become on GMOs (genetically modified organisms), the more destructive a disease affecting them might prove. Recent violations of civil and political liberties by the NSA and IRS, as well as corporate spying, suggest the possibility of a new totalitarianism. In *1984*, the ubiquitous "telescreens" destroyed privacy, but that image seemed like a paranoid fantasy on Orwell's part. The cameras everywhere in London, government tracing of emails, and the use of computers to do analysis that only recently required human beings may soon make privacy as outmoded as monks copying manuscripts.[2] And what if we are on the verge of reading people's minds by brain scans?

Many kinds of environmental disaster threaten. We read more and more predictions about the effects of climate change, which give us a spectrum of catastrophes. The very actions we take to forestall a disaster may make it more likely (an example given is the use of ethanol) or create new ones. Some predictors take it for granted that we will run out of natural resources, since the supply of anything is by definition limited.

Even when a problem seems to be advancing gradually, it is possible to draw a curve showing rapid acceleration to come. No one ever raised money to solve a problem that wasn't urgent. We may be at a "tipping point." How can we tell?

Indeed, the very popularity of new terms like "tipping point" and "inflection point" testify to our recent attitude to the future.[3] Even where things seem benign, they may be on the verge of horror. Right or wrong, many people still feel as if the present moment is especially urgent.

But might it not be that our view of the present is mistaken, the product of our temporal and temperamental egoism? Surely the 1930s and 1940s gave more reason for fearing the future than the present does. Is it possible to compare our attitude toward the future with that of earlier times? Every age has its "futuribles" (set of anticipated futures that could happen), so wouldn't some sort of comparative futurology give us perspective on our own obsessions about what is to come?[4]

In 1955, *Fortune* magazine marked its twenty-fifth anniversary by publishing *The Fabulous Future: America in 1980*, which brought together some of the smartest and most influential Americans to speculate on the world to come.[5] Contributors included John von Neumann, who not only made important contributions to mathematics and physics but also founded game theory and cybernetics; David Sarnoff, chairman of RCA, then synonymous with technological progress; Crawford Greenewalt, president of Du Pont; Adlai Stevenson, who was the Democratic candidate for president in 1952 and would be again in 1956; Chief Justice Earl Warren; AFL-CIO president George Meany; Treasury Secretary George Humphrey; Harvard president Nathan Pusey; and several others. Their contributions both reflected and shaped the wisdom of the times.

They weren't entirely mistaken. As they guessed, the pace of technological change sped up, polio was conquered, and "calculating machines" were invented. But in detail and in broad conception they were almost comically off the mark. Von Neumann foresaw a world in which "energy would be free—just like the unmetered air." Sarnoff deemed it indisputable that ships, aircraft, locomotives, and even automobiles would be atomic-powered. Houses and industrial plants would run on small atomic generators, and so coal, oil, and gas would be displaced as fuel. We would all commute in personal helicopters. Guided missiles would deliver intercontinental mail. We would have the capacity not only to predict the weather far in advance but also to change weather and climate. Naturally, we could foresee the effects of any such intervention.

Society would also improve. The workweek would continue to shorten. Soon we would be worrying not about how to create jobs but about how to spend all our leisure time. The economy would no longer be subject to serious recessions. Scientific discoveries would strengthen our faith in the Creator. War would cease to be an instrument of national policy, and as communication (especially television) improved, nations and individual people would understand one another better and grow less hostile. We would have a world police force.

Almost as remarkable is what was *not* foreseen. No one, not even von Neumann, who did so much to lay the groundwork for it, anticipated the information revolution. Neither did anyone imagine the biological revolution or nanotechnology. The future of science seemed to lie in the study of atomic power. Islamism was not mentioned, and authors still assumed that time was on the side of the Soviet Union.

Understandably enough, the writers tended to draw straight lines from the present. In their view, past predictions had proven wrong largely because they were insufficiently optimistic. When speaking of the future as surprising, they usually referred to the pace, not the nature, of change. The idea of radically contingent events altering the whole direction of change was underestimated. Progress, speed, continuation of present trends: these were the guiding assumptions.

As it happened, the volume was prophetic in another way. It exemplified a growing trend of failed predictions made with supreme confidence. To be sure, not all of these predictions were to be unreservedly optimistic. Perhaps the most widely read economist of his day, John Kenneth Galbraith predicted in 1967 that large corporations would be able to insulate themselves from competition and insure their dominance.[6] These supposedly invincible corporations have mostly been replaced by others, which—like Apple, Microsoft, and Walmart—did not exist or had just been founded in 1967.

Still more famously, Paul Ehrlich—in his 1968 best seller *The Population Bomb*, testimony before the U.S. Senate, commentary on television talk shows, and countless other appearances—predicted that overpopulation would cause a billion people to starve to death within a decade. He foresaw the rapid exhaustion of natural resources. Along with the Club of Rome, Zero Population Growth, and books such as *The Limits to Growth*,[7] he argued that humanity was exhausting limited resources and had already reached the point where catastrophe was unavoidable. *The New Republic* proclaimed that "world population has passed food supply. The famine has begun."[8]

In fact, the exact opposite was the case. Food supply per capita was growing, and starvation was soon to be a rare problem caused not by undersupply but by government mismanagement and by a lack of income needed to buy existing produce. All the same, the predictions seemed impervious to counter-evidence. "How often does a prophet have to be wrong before we no longer believe that he or she is a true prophet?" asked economist Julian Simon.[9]

Reasoning that if resources were to be exhausted, their price would rise, in 1980 Simon challenged Ehrlich in *Social Science Quarterly* to a thousand-dollar bet. Ehrlich could pick five metals he expected to grow increasingly scarce. If their price rose in ten years, Ehrlich would win the bet and Simon would pay Ehrlich the actual purchase price for those metals; if they fell, Ehrlich would pay Simon a thousand dollars. Ehrlich hurried to accept Simon's "astonishing offer before other greedy people jump in."[10] Because Ehrlich got to choose the metals, and because the most he could lose was the initial thousand-dollar stake while sufficient price rises made Simon's potential losses illimitable, the terms seemed to favor Ehrlich. By 1990, all five metals had declined in price, and Ehrlich wrote Simon a check. It would be hard to imagine a clearer test of a prediction, but Ehrlich still refused to admit he had been mistaken.

For his part, Simon had reasoned that Ehrlich's Malthusianism, based on a comparison of people to butterflies, overlooked the "ultimate resource" humans possess: ingenuity. Substitution effects, technological innovation, and efforts directed by a price mechanism could alter trends for people as they could not for butterflies. Resources tended to expand, not diminish, as new sources became technologically accessible and new productive methods could use different materials. But the rhetorical power of straight lines, especially if one has staked a great deal on predicting their continuation, is hard to overcome.[11]

It seems that neither the optimists nor the pessimists escape the trap of drawing straight lines and the temptations to see only what supports their views. One has only to program a computer to draw them in order to make one's projections seem "scientific."

* * *

Have we grown any smarter? It is easy enough to disparage the wisdom of 1955 (or any other year), just as we look down on earlier social views. Somehow history's most enlightened people are always ourselves at the present moment. The contributors to *The Fabulous Future* made fun of the wrongheadedness of past predictions, such as the 1844 declaration by the U.S. commissioner of patents that "the advancement of the arts from year to year taxes our credulity and seems to presage the arrival of that period when further improvements must end."[12] But they did not foresee how wrongheaded their own predictions would prove. If extrapolating from the past shows anything, it shows the hazard of extrapolating from the past. Perhaps the easiest thing to predict is the failure of widely accepted predictions. Astrology never dies, it only changes shape.

Surely it would be hard to assemble a group any smarter than these authors of sixty years ago. If they were wrong, it was not because of a lack of brain power. And so it is reasonably safe to assume that our best guesses will look as absurd half a century from now as theirs do today—or even more so, if the pace of change accelerates. After all, changes interact unpredictably with other changes in an ever-broadening spiral.

* * *

And yet, we cannot *not* predict. It is impossible to focus only on the present. We have to allocate our resources somehow, and if we are not to rely on pure chance, we must guess where they will be most needed or most productive. Every plan contains a prediction.

What's more, humanness itself entails anticipating a future. That is how we experience time. People live each moment as a step to moments to come. Every present contains multiple possible futures to which we orient ourselves; suspense is always with us. What's more, life would seem pointless otherwise, because unless the future is uncertain, unless it depends in part on what we do, human effort wouldn't matter. Action has meaning only if it can make a difference, and it can make a difference only if the future hangs in the balance.

For this reason, Dostoevsky argued that the real cruelty of capital punishment lies in its *certainty*. Its greatest horror resides in what happens to the condemned *before* the execution, at the sentencing. From the moment the prisoner hears he must die and no longer can entertain any hope, he surrenders the sense of a future in which effort matters. Before losing his life, he loses his humanness. Dostoevsky concluded that "murder by legal sentence" is far worse than murder by brigands, from which there is always hope to escape.[13]

We can learn a lot about people or cultures from their sense of possible futures. They are in part defined by the futures they entertain. Even ill-grounded predictions reveal the horizon of expectations of the people who make them. To understand their choices, one needs to know the dangers they deemed likely and the achievements they thought possible. The common wisdom in 1955, however mistaken, illuminates what life felt like then.

To live in 1955 meant presuming that atomic physics, if it did not lead to annihilation, would provide endless supplies of power. It entailed anticipating inequality to lessen; the workweek to shorten; and war, disease, and natural disasters to disappear, or all but disappear, in the face of human progress. Today we have an equivalent list of truisms about the future—call them "futurisms"—which do not seem naive precisely because they are ours.

If we are to understand the past, we must imagine past futures, those shadowy might-bes anticipated at earlier moments. Every past was an earlier present, and it looked out on apparently likely futures. The history of humanity includes all those futures that never were. Even in our personal lives, we can best recall our earlier selves by evoking that to which we once looked forward. Just as respect for human difference involves seeing the world as other cultures do, so it involves seeing it as earlier ages did.

If we neglect to do so, we are bound to smile complacently at those who did not foresee the world we experience today. How could they have been so stupid as not to have guessed what was so plainly bound to happen! We have a natural tendency to think that because the past did lead to us, it had to. We forget, or do not wish to consider, that what happened could easily not have happened, that the world could have been entirely different, and that current conditions are perhaps the result of successful efforts to avoid a much more likely outcome. It is unsettling to think that, but for all sorts of contingencies that easily could not have happened, we would not be here at all.

Wisdom begins when we surmount our own perspective and see what seems plausible to someone with experiences different from our own. Once we realize that history did not lead infallibly to ourselves, we are less likely to succumb to the hubris of the present moment, the sense that, unlike all those fools of the past, we have freed ourselves from prejudice and can see facts clearly.

* * *

How should predictions be assessed? And how can we learn from the failure of earlier predictions?

The fact is, most people make sure *not* to learn. No one likes to admit he or she was badly and publically mistaken, and so no matter what happens, people assure themselves that they were—or soon would be—proven correct. We have never seen a *New York Times* or *Wall Street Journal* editorial admitting that the people it criticized as "in denial" turned out to be right.

The English poet Sir John Harrington famously remarked in 1618:

> Treason doth never prosper. What's the reason?
> For if it prosper, none dare call it treason.[14]

In much the same spirit, we could add:

> No forecasts ever err. And why not some?
> For if they err, success is still to come.

If what we predicted didn't happen, we can always imagine it still might.

In his magnificent study *Expert Political Judgment: How Good Is It? How Can We Know?* Philip Tetlock catalogs a variety of excuses given by predictors in the face of evident failure.[15] Ehrlich famously compared Simon to "a guy who jumps off the Empire State Building and says how great things are going as he passed the tenth floor."[16] Thirty years after the bet, it is now abundantly evident that food production per capita has not collapsed but dramatically risen. Technological innovation has led to previously impossible extraction of oil and gas (as well as new sources of green power). Nevertheless, in a sequel to *The Population Bomb, The Population Explosion* (1990), Paul and Anne Ehrlich claimed complete vindication: "Then the fuse was burning; now the population bomb has detonated."[17] And in 2013 Ehrlich told an interviewer that *The Population Bomb* had proven "much too optimistic."[18]

In resisting disconfirming evidence, and in his repeated reference to opponents who cite such evidence as idiots and ignoramuses in denial, Ehrlich is far from alone. In their classic study of religious movements that forecast the imminent destruction of the world, *When Prophecy Fails*, Leon Festinger, Henry Riecken, and Stanley Schachter demonstrate that, often enough, the reaction to disconfirmation is to double down on the original beliefs. Indeed, the more thoroughly people have staked their reputations on a prediction, the less likely they are to reverse themselves no matter how incontrovertible the unwelcome facts turn out to be.

> Suppose an individual believes something with his whole heart;
> suppose further that he has a commitment to this belief—that

he has taken irrevocable actions because of it; finally, suppose that he is presented with evidence, unequivocal and undeniable evidence, that his belief is wrong; what will happen? The individual will frequently emerge, not only unshaken, but even more convinced of the truth of his beliefs than ever before. Indeed, he may even show a new fervor about convincing and converting other people to his view.[19]

Recalculation of the date is far from the only way to rescue a failure. Forecasters can always claim the predicted event *almost* happened. Sure, Canada didn't break up by 2000, but someone who assured us it would can protest that it came awfully close to doing so. Or that person can say that the prediction *would have* come true if not for the warning in the prediction itself—an excuse we might call "the self-defeating prophecy."

Often enough, people maintain that in spite of an outcome the exact opposite of what they forecast, the prediction was confirmed anyway. If an economic or social policy supposed to dramatically decrease crime, unemployment, or inflation is actually followed by no change or even by an increase, well, the problem would have been still worse without the policy! While in some instances they might actually have a case here, it is especially difficult to prove such a counterfactual. Alternatively, one can adjust the prediction by finding some *other* problem that *did* improve and claim credit for that. No one determined not to be wrong ever thinks he or she is.

In August 2000, the quantitative modelers of presidential elections at the American Political Science Association were unanimous that election campaigns did not matter and that in November Al Gore would certainly and decisively defeat George W. Bush.[20] Almost no one in the Slavic or Sovietology professions predicted the fall of the Soviet Union, but at conferences afterward speaker after speaker responded with outrage to the suggestion that perhaps professionals had left something out of their models or needed to rethink their methods.

There is no shortage of loopholes. Luck is a vastly more popular explanation when one has been proven wrong. It is also always possible to argue that one's opponents proved right for the wrong reason. One can apply laxer standards to one's own predictions than to those of others. And in a pinch, one can plead that the consequences of being wrong were minor compared to the disaster had they proven right. As Tetlock observes, "political belief systems are at continual risk of evolving into self-perpetuating worldviews, with their own self-serving criteria for judging judgment and keeping score, their own stock of favorite historical analogies, and their own pantheons of heroes and villains."[21]

Tetlock concedes that sometimes explanations of apparent disconfirmations might be persuasive. Sometimes one does fail by luck and some predictions turn out right for the wrong reason. But if we always argue that way, if we never seriously entertain counterevidence or admit our mistakes, we condemn ourselves to never learning from experience. And we commit a form of intellectual dishonesty.

If one is to avoid such dishonesty, it is important to practice what Tetlock calls "the art of self-overhearing."[22] One must train oneself to listen to one's rationalizations and ask how one would respond had one's opponents used one's preferred loophole. Specifying in advance what would prove one's prediction wrong also helps. It is hard to admit that one's judgment has failed, but it is even more difficult to learn unless one does.

Tetlock's study concludes that *how* one thinks makes more of a difference than *what* one thinks. It does not matter much whether someone is a liberal or conservative, doomster or boomster, realist or institutionalist. Neither does one's field of expertise. What turns out to make a difference is one's style of thought. To explain his point, Tetlock borrows Isaiah Berlin's famous distinction between "hedgehogs" and "foxes," terms drawn from the ancient Greek poet Archilochus: "The fox knows many things, the hedgehog one big thing."[23] Hedgehogs are the grand and bold systematizers, who identify a comprehensive explanation for everything, like Hegel, Spinoza, Marx, or Freud. Foxes, by contrast, tend to find contradictory forces, irreducible complexity, and the need for multiple perspectives. And, by and large, Tetlock argues, it is the foxes that prove more accurate and more capable of learning from experience.

* * *

In assessing predictions, it is important to distinguish three sorts of claims.

First, there is the prediction itself, the content of the forecast. Second, a prediction can allow for more or less uncertainty in the range of possible results. Third, and most often overlooked, it can be offered with different degrees of confidence.

Suppose we imagine that a social process resembles flipping a coin. It has two equally likely outcomes. We might predict that in a thousand flips, heads will come up "about 500 times." If we know probability theory, we might allow for a degree of uncertainty and assign a percentage likelihood that the outcome would be in a given range, say, between 400 and 600. Finally, we might be more or less confident of this prediction. How sure are we that the process really does resemble a coin flip? Could there be more than two outcomes, some not specifiable in advance? Is it possible that early results could constrain later ones? Could exogenous forces upset the entire system? To the extent that we answer these questions affirmatively, our degree of confidence should diminish.[24]

One ought to have supreme confidence regarding astronomers' predictions about the orbit of Saturn. To the extent one imagines social sciences to resemble astronomy, one will have similar confidence in its predictions. Conversely, to the extent that one thinks that too many factors, some not even imagined, could have concatenating and unpredictable effects, one's degree of confidence ought to be considerably less.

Overconfidence often results from not recognizing the possibility that a model adapted to fit some circumstances may have strayed into others. Ehrlich's certainty depended on his confidence in his field of expertise, ecology, but his prediction involved factors studied by economists, who were more likely to question his model. It is one thing to predict global climate change but quite another to maintain that a given treaty will be worth the cost of implementing it.

Degree of confidence makes a big difference. One bets the farm on an outcome that can't fail to happen. But one bets a lot less, and continually monitors results, when one expects the unexpected.

A prediction can be reasonable when overconfidence in it is not. It is obvious that one cannot devote 20 percent of one's resources to preventing each of a hundred predicted disasters, so one needs to know not only how likely a predicted disaster is, and how disastrous it would actually be if it happened, but also the degree of confidence we should have in our predictions.

Sometimes it is difficult to assess the prediction but easy to tell that nothing could justify the predictor's supreme confidence. He or she might be claiming knowledge no one has ever had. Or be extending the model far beyond its proper domain. Or be making predictions excessively precise, as if more decimal points signaled greater accuracy. Or, out of a sense of urgency, be exaggerating his or her confidence to inspire action.

One can state as a rule of thumb that the more a prediction accords with what one would be inclined to believe for other reasons, the more suspect it is. We do not trust polls undertaken by a political party or an organization allied with it. Groups that have a financial stake in widespread fear of a given disaster risk exaggerating their evidence. It is usually shepherds who cry wolf.

* * *

Some contributors to *The Fabulous Future* wrote as if no reasonable person could question their predictions. Sarnoff declared that "*it can be taken for granted* that before 1980 ships, aircraft, locomotives, and even automobiles will be atomically fueled."[25] He was doubly wrong, mistaken not only in his prediction but also in his assurance that he simply had to be right. Explaining how he had given his engineers orders for seemingly impossible inventions that they succeeded in creating, Sarnoff concludes that "*there is no longer margin for doubt* that whatever the mind of man visualizes, the genius of modern science can turn into functioning fact."[26] "Taken for granted," "no margin for doubt," "every educated person agrees": these are phrases to be used with caution and are almost never justified when applied to social or political affairs.

By contrast, von Neumann was much less confident. He was often wrong, but not doubly so, in the way Sarnoff was.[27] Experience, he warned, teaches that future technological and social changes "are not *a priori* predictable and that most contemporary 'first guesses' concerning them are wrong." It follows that "one should take neither present difficulties nor proposed reforms too seriously."[28] Crawford Greenewalt began his essay explaining that prediction is hazardous, in part because small changes may lead in many directions and interact in unforeseeable ways. What Greenewalt calls "bit-by-bit research . . . the day-to-day effort that produces results which over a short period seem inconsequential, but which over the long run are extraordinarily important," makes it impossible to see very far ahead.[29]

* * *

The present effort differs from *The Fabulous Future* in a number of ways. First, the contributors are for the most part less optimistic. The future may not be so fabulous. In 2040, Americans may very well envy previous generations. Second, the 1955 contributors speculated on any topic that struck them. They went far beyond their field of expertise. By contrast, we asked the authors to write about topics both specific and grounded in their specialized knowledge. Third, as the volume's changed subtitle suggests, our perspective is less U.S.-centric. In 1953 Charles E. Wilson, the president of General Motors, told Congress: "For years I thought that what was good for our country was good for General Motors and vice versa. The difference did not exist."[30] By the same token, it was taken for granted that what was good for the USA was good for the world. Today, the future importance of the United States is much more of an open question. Finally, the volume reflects a greater awareness of the limits of even the best-informed people's ability to predict. By and large, we are less sure of our prophetic abilities. We don't think we are any smarter than our predecessors and expect that, decades hence, when people look back on this volume, its predictions will seem as wrongheaded as those of its predecessor. But perhaps it will seem less brazenly confident. Humility, history suggests, is a great virtue when imagining the future.

Notes

1. For a more detailed treatment, see also Barry Glassner, *The Culture of Fear: Why Americans Are Afraid of the Wrong Things* (New York: Basic Books, 1999).

2. The 2006 German film *The Lives of Others* (*Das Leben der Anderen*) focused on a Stasi agent who, assigned to monitor a famous playwright, eventually becomes deeply involved in his life. New technologies imply that there no longer needs to be such a one-to-one ratio for a nation to keep tabs on its citizens.

3. The most popular statement on "tipping point" is Malcolm Gladwell's book *The Tipping Point: How Little Things Can Make a Big Difference* (Boston: Little, Brown, 2000). As we finalized revisions on this manuscript, MIT issued its *Final Report of the Institute-Wide Task Force on the Future of MIT Education* (July 28, 2014). Its introduction declares: "Higher education is at an inflection point."

4. The term "futuribles" belongs to Bertrand de Jouvenel. As he defines the term, it means "*possible futures*, with an emphasis on the plural; what is implied by

this denomination is our strong conviction that 'the present state of affairs' has different possible descendants, is not a *given* merely unknown but an outcome which may be this or that according to intervening actions." See Bertrand de Jouvenel, "Futuribles" (lecture, January 1965), 1, http://www.rand.org/content/dam/rand/pubs/papers/2008/P3045.pdf.

5. *The Fabulous Future: America in 1980* (New York: Dutton, 1955).

6. John Kenneth Galbraith, *The New Industrial State* (New York: Houghton Mifflin, 1967).

7. Donella H. Meadows, Dennis L. Meadows, Jørgen Randers, and William W. Behrens III, *The Limits to Growth: A Report for the Club of Rome's Project on the Predicament of Mankind* (New York: Macmillan, 1979).

8. As cited in Paul Sabin, *The Bet: Paul Ehrlich, Julian Simon, and Our Gamble Over the Earth's Future* (New Haven, Conn.: Yale University Press, 2013), 23.

9. Ibid., 134.

10. Ibid., 135.

11. On the danger of such extrapolation in international economics, see Ruchir Sharma, "The Ever-Emerging Markets: Why Economic Forecasts Fail," *Foreign Affairs* 93, no. 1 (January/February 2014): 52–56. Commenting on the failure of the BRICs (and the CIVERS and the MISTs) to live up to expectations, Sharma observes: "History shows that straight-line extrapolations are almost always wrong. Yet pundits cannot seem to resist them, lured on by wishful thinking and fear" (52). The reason is that "a would-be forecaster must track a shifting list of a dozen factors, from politics to credit and investment flows, to assess the growth prospects of each emerging nation over the next three to five years—the only useful time frame for political leaders, businesspeople, investors, or anyone else with a stake in current events" (56).

12. *Fabulous Future*, 5.

13. Fyodor Dostoevsky, *The Idiot*, trans. Constance Garnett (New York: Modern Library, 1962), 20.

14. Quoted in Fred R. Shapiro, ed., *The Yale Book of Quotations* (New Haven, Conn.: Yale University Press, 2006), 341.

15. Philip E. Tetlock, *Expert Political Judgment: How Good Is It? How Can We Know?* (Princeton, N.J.: Princeton University Press, 2005). For a recent extension of Tetlock's ideas, see Nate Silver, *The Signal and the Noise: Why So Many Predictions Fail—but Some Don't* (New York: Penguin, 2012).

16. Sabin, *Bet*, 184.

17. Ibid., 197.

18. "The Ehrlich Factor: A Brief History of the Fate of Humanity, with Dr. Paul R. Ehrlich," *Forbes*, January 15, 2013, http://www.forbes.com/sites/

michaeltobias/2013/01/16/the-ehrlich-factor-a-brief-history-of-the-fate-of-humanity-with-dr-paul-r-ehrlich/.

19. Leon Festinger, Henry W. Riecken, and Stanley Schachter, *When Prophecy Fails: A Social and Psychological Study of a Modern Group that Predicted the Destruction of the World* (New York: Harper, 1956), 3.

20. See Tetlock, *Expert Political Judgment*, 25, for this and similar errors. See also Silver, *Signal and Noise*, 11.

21. Tetlock, *Expert Political Judgment*, 4.

22. Tetlock borrows this phrase from Harold Bloom, *Shakespeare: The Invention of the Human* (New York: Riverhead, 1998).

23. See Isaiah Berlin, *The Hedgehog and the Fox: An Essay on Tolstoy's View of History*, ed. Henry Hardy (Princeton, N.J.: Princeton University Press, 2013), 1. The essay was originally published in 1951.

24. On the importance of acknowledging uncertainty, see Silver, *Signal and Noise*, 177–79 ("The Importance of Communicating Uncertainty"). Silver does not appear to distinguish between degree of uncertainty and degree of confidence.

25. *Fabulous Future*, 17, emphasis added.

26. Ibid., 16, emphasis added.

27. Silver cites von Neumann's cautions about prediction in a condition of uncertainty; Silver, *Signal and Noise,* 167.

28. *Fabulous Future*, 47.

29. Ibid., 101.

30. Quoted in Fred R. Shapiro, ed., *The Yale Book of Quotations* (New Haven, Conn.: Yale University Press, 2006), 828.

Organization of the Volume
and List of Contributors

Instead of selecting individual authors first, as was the case back in 1955, we began by selecting topics and then enlisted experts to reflect on them. It was no easy task limiting a discussion of the future to just a dozen areas. We made our selections after vigorous debate, and our choices undoubtedly reflect our own backgrounds and interests, as well as our experience coteaching an undergraduate course on modeling choice across the academic disciplines. Morson, a literary critic and an influential commentator on Russian literature and thought, is the Frances Hooper Professor of the Arts and Humanities at Northwestern University. He is the author of ten books, including the award-winning *Narrative and Freedom: The Shadows of Time*. Schapiro is professor of economics and president of Northwestern University, after serving in a similar capacity at Williams College. The author or coauthor of five books and the coeditor of two others, he is among the nation's leading authorities on the economics of higher education, with particular expertise on trends in educational costs and student aid. Morson and Schapiro are members of the American Academy of Arts and Sciences.

Part 1 of the volume deals with three of the basic aims of any society: wealth, health, and happiness. Economic scenarios are considered by Robert J. Gordon, Stanley G. Harris Professor of the Social Sciences at Northwestern University, a macroeconomist with a particular interest in unemployment, inflation, and both the long-run and cyclical aspects of labor productivity. His textbook in intermediate macroeconomics, now in its twelfth edition, has educated generations of economics students. He is a distinguished fellow of the American Economic Association, a fellow of the Econometric Society, and a member of the American

Academy of Arts and Sciences. For more than three decades, he has served on the National Bureau of Economic Research's Business Cycle Dating Committee, which determines the start and end dates for recessions in the United States. His recent work on America's declining economic prospects has provoked worldwide commentary.

Health prospects are discussed by Eileen M. Crimmins, AARP Professor of Gerontology at the University of Southern California, where she directs the USC/UCLA Center on Biodemography and Population Health, a Demography of Aging Center supported by the National Institute on Aging. Much of her work has focused on changes over time in health and mortality. She recently served as co-chair of a committee of the National Academy of Sciences on changes in life expectancy. She is a member of the Institute of Medicine of the National Academy of Sciences.

The section concludes with a chapter by Richard A. Easterlin, University Professor at the University of Southern California, who is widely recognized as one of the most influential and innovative economists of his generation. A distinguished fellow of the American Economic Association and a member of both the National Academy of Sciences and the American Academy of Arts and Sciences, he is past president of both the Population Association of America and the Economic History Association. He is perhaps best known for his work on the "Easterlin Paradox"—that is, that happiness at a national level does not in general increase with wealth. His topic is the course of individual satisfaction in the United States and abroad.

We turn in part 2 to politics, religion, and human rights. Discussing prospects for peace and war is Robert L. Gallucci, Distinguished Professor in the Practice of Diplomacy at Georgetown University. He previously served as president of the John D. and Catherine T. MacArthur Foundation and as dean of Georgetown University's Edmund A. Walsh School of Foreign Service. His governmental service includes positions as both ambassador at large and special envoy for the U.S. Department of State. He was chief negotiator with North Korea under President Clinton. He is the author or coauthor of a number of publications on political-military issues, including *Neither Peace Nor Honor: The Politics of American Military Policy in Vietnam* and the award-winning book *Going Critical: The First North Korean Nuclear Crisis.*

Writing about religion is Eboo Patel, founder and president of the Interfaith Youth Core and a key member of President Obama's Inaugural Advisory Council on Faith-Based Neighborhood Partnerships. A Muslim of Gujarati heritage and a former Rhodes Scholar, he has devoted his career to the cause of interfaith cooperation. His recent book is *Sacred Ground: Pluralism, Prejudice, and the Promise of America*.

The section concludes with a discussion of the future of civil liberties by Wendy Kaminer, a lawyer and social critic, who writes about law, liberty, feminism, religion, and popular culture. Her latest book is *Worst Instincts: Cowardice, Conformity, and the ACLU*. A former Guggenheim fellow and recipient of the Smith College Medal, she is the author of seven previous books, including *Free for All: Defending Liberty in America Today* and *A Fearful Freedom: Women's Flight from Equality*. She is an ardent civil libertarian.

Part 3 deals with science, technology, and the environment. It begins with an essay by Mark A. Ratner, one of the world's preeminent theoretical chemists, who serves as Lawrence B. Dumas Distinguished University Professor at Northwestern. With his son Daniel Ratner, he is the author of *Nanotechnology: A Gentle Introduction to the Next Big Idea* and *Nanotechnology and Homeland Security: New Weapons for New Wars*. A member of the National Academy of Sciences, he is the recipient of the Irving Langmuir Award in Chemical Physics for outstanding interdisciplinary research in chemistry and physics.

The future of technology is the topic for John Kelly III, senior vice president and head of IBM Research, where he oversees three thousand scientists and technical employees at twelve laboratories in ten countries around the world. His top priorities are to stimulate innovation in key areas of information technology, to bring those innovations into the marketplace, and to create the new businesses of IBM's future. He is a member of the National Academy of Engineering.

The section ends with a chapter by Mark R. Tercek and Jimmie Powell on the environmental future of the planet. Tercek is president and CEO of the Nature Conservancy, the world's largest conservation organization with more than one million members and over $5 billion in assets. A former partner and managing director of Goldman Sachs, he is the coauthor of the best seller *Nature's Fortune: How Business and Society Thrive by Investing in Nature*, which explores why responsible stewardship of nature is of the utmost importance to businesses, governments, and societies. Jimmie Powell is the team lead for Energy Strategies at the Nature Conservancy. Previously, he worked in several capacities during a twenty-year career with the United States Senate, concluding as the staff director of the Senate Committee on Environment and Public Works, where he worked for its chairman, Senator John Chafee. After leaving the Senate, he served for two years as the executive director of the Pew Oceans Commission and was also a member of the board of directors of the League of Conservation Voters.

Part 4, the final part of the book, addresses education, communication, and society. We have assigned ourselves the task of discussing the future of higher education in the United States and the world.

Our chapter is followed by that of Arianna Huffington, who considers the changing face of media. She is the chair, president, and editor-in-chief of the Huffington Post Media Group, a nationally syndicated columnist, and the author of fourteen books, including biographies of Maria Callas and Pablo Picasso. In 2005 she launched the Huffington Post, a news and blog site that quickly became one of the most widely read, linked to, and frequently cited media brands on the Internet. In 2012, the site won a Pulitzer Prize for national reporting.

Finally, Barry Glassner, professor of sociology and president of Lewis & Clark College, considers which of the usual societal worries are actually cause for alarm, which are not, and whether it is possible to tell the difference. He has written nine books on contemporary social issues, including the much-acclaimed best seller *The Culture of Fear*, in which he argues that many of Americans' concerns and fears are largely unfounded. His other books include *The Gospel of Food* and *Bodies*.

By design, the chapters are short and nontechnical enough that we see no reason as editors to provide extensive summaries. However, in the conclusion, we examine how the various predictions on widespread topics interrelate. How do they converge and diverge? And what do they say about the world of the future?

The Fabulous Future?

PART ONE

Wealth,

Health,

and

Happiness

CHAPTER 1

Wealth

The Future of Economic Growth: Slowing to a Crawl

Robert J. Gordon

Stanley G. Harris Professor of the Social Sciences,
Northwestern University

Fortune in 1955 forecast a fabulous future for the subsequent twenty-five years, and it was right. Real gross domestic product (GDP) per capita between 1955 and 1980 grew at 2.15 percent per year, enough for the standard of living to double in a mere thirty-two years. Americans have become used to a doubling of the standard of living every generation, but future growth will be much slower. Today's American youth will struggle to achieve the standard of living of their parents.

Future Growth in the Context of Three Industrial Revolutions

The gloomy forecast for the next twenty-five years—between 2015 and 2040—recognizes that there is no law of history that economic growth must continue at a constant rate. There was virtually no economic growth between the time of the Roman Empire and around 1750, when peasants tilled their land with tools and equipment little different from Roman times. Over the past two and a half centuries, life has been utterly transformed by three industrial revolutions, and to forecast out to the year 2040, we need to understand what these revolutions contributed and where we now stand in the arc of the history of technological progress.

Economists conventionally distinguish among three industrial revolutions. The first (IR1) began around 1780 and consisted of steam, cotton spinning, railroads, and steamships. The second (IR2) began in 1875 and included electricity, the internal combustion engine, running water and sewers, communication and entertainment, and the conquest of infant mortality. The third (IR3) began in 1960 and included the impact of computers, electronics, and digitalization, often abbreviated "ICT" for information and communications technology. The first two revolutions required at least one hundred years for the subsidiary inventions that were made possible by the initial discoveries to become pervasive. The jury is still out on how long the benefits of IR3 will persist, and this question is at the heart of debates about the future state of technology in 2040.

The nineteenth century began with travel limited to the speed of the "hoof and sail," whereas it ended with relatively rapid travel by train and steamships by 1900. More than a century after James Watt's workable steam engine, invented in 1781, the effects of IR1 were still benefitting humankind. For instance, 85 percent of American railway mileage was built between 1860 and 1910.

IR2 was the most transformative of the industrial revolutions. Within a few weeks in 1879 three of the most fundamental "general purpose technologies" were invented, later to spin off scores of world-changing inventions, including electric light and power, the internal combustion engine, and wireless transmission. Between 1890 and 1930 the American urban household became fully "networked," replacing its previous isolation by five types of connections—electricity, gas, telephone, running water, and sewer pipes. Running water and sewers in turn contributed not just to the first phase of female liberation but also to the conquest of infant mortality.

The third industrial revolution (IR3), involving everything about electronics, computers, and the digital age, has also been transformative, but along only one dimension compared to the multiple dimensions of IR2. The initial applications of the mainframe computer for bank statements, telephone bills, airline reservation systems, cash-dispensing automated teller machines (ATMs), and retail bar code scanning spanned the interval 1960 to 1990. Then came the invention of the personal computer, email, the Internet, and e-commerce during the period from 1980 to 2000. By 2000 the nature of office work had been transformed, and paper catalogs at libraries, mail order vendors, and automotive parts departments had disappeared, to be replaced by networked flat screens.

A simple piece of evidence demonstrates that IR2 was more important than IR3. Output per hour (labor productivity) grew at an annual rate of 2.3 percent between 1890 and 1972, but it registered a lower growth rate of 1.6 percent during the four decades since 1972. This is our starting point for a prediction that future growth will be slower than in the past.

Innovation and the Headwinds

Will the American standard of living in 2040 double from that of 2015, or will the ratio of future to present rise by 50, 30, or perhaps only 10 percent? The answer depends not only on the future pace of innovation but also on four "headwinds" that are currently in the process of slowing American economic growth—demography, education, inequality, and government debt.

The scope of this chapter is necessarily limited to the United States. Don't other countries matter? The future of U.S. growth matters for everyone else because the United States has been the technological leader since 1875—other nations, such as China, may grow faster as they catch up to the standard of living that Americans have already achieved, but any faltering of growth at the U.S. frontier would diminish opportunities available for the rest of the world. Subsequently, we discuss the worrying possibility that by 2040 other nations may have already moved ahead of the United States, ending its long-standing position at the frontier of technology.

Future Innovation as Viewed from 1955 and 2015

Some economic historians scoff at the notion that it is possible to predict future innovations, but they are wrong. There are many historical precedents of correct predictions made fifty or one hundred years in advance. Will these examples of accurate forecasting allow us a glimpse of economic life in 2040?

An early forecast of the future of technology is contained in Jules Verne's 1863 manuscript *Paris in the Twentieth Century*, in which Verne made bold predictions about the Paris of 1960.[1] In that early year, before Edison or Benz, Verne had already conceived of the basics of the twentieth century. He predicted rapid-transit cars running on overhead viaducts, motor cars with gas combustion engines, and streetlights connected by underground wires.

Much of IR2 was not a surprise. Looking ahead in the year 1875, inventors were feverishly working on turning the telegraph into the telephone, trying to harness electricity coming from batteries as the power source to create electric light, and trying to find a way of using the power of petroleum to create a lightweight and powerful internal combustion engine. The 1875 diaries of Edison, Bell, and Benz are full of such "we're almost there" speculation. Some of the most important sources of human progress over the 1890–1930 period were not new inventions at all, including running water and sewer pipes.

A remarkable forecast was published in November 1900 in an unlikely publication medium, the *Ladies' Home Journal*.[2] Some of the more interesting predictions in this 1900 article include the following:

- Hot and cold air will be turned on from spigots to regulate the temperature of the air just as we now turn on hot and cold water from spigots to regulate the temperature of the bath.
- Ready-cooked meals will be purchased from establishments much like our bakeries of today.
- Liquid-air refrigerators will keep large quantities of food fresh for long intervals.
- Photographs will be telegraphed from any distance. If there is a battle in China a century hence, photographs of the events will be published in newspapers an hour later.
- Automobiles will be cheaper than horses are today. Farmers will own automobile hay-wagons, automobile truck-wagons . . . automobiles will have been substituted for every horse-vehicle now known.
- Wireless telephone and telegraph circuits will span the world. We will be able to telephone to China just as readily as we can now talk from New York to Brooklyn.

The Jules Verne 1863 and the *Ladies' Home Journal* 1900 visions of future technological progress were true leaps of imagination. Somewhat less challenging were predictions of the future made at the 1939–40 New York World's Fair. By 1939–40, IR2 was almost complete in urban America, so it is no surprise that the exhibits at the fair could predict quite accurately the further complements to IR2 inventions, such as superhighways and air-conditioning, that came into fruition in the twenty-five-year period after 1940.

What was missing at the 1939–40 New York World's Fair was any vision of the computer revolution that created IR3. But Norbert Wiener, a visionary, in a 1949 essay that was ultimately rejected by the *New York Times*, got a lot of the future of IR3 right. Among his 1949 predictions:

> These new machines have a great capacity for upsetting the present basis of industry, and of reducing the economic value of the routine factory employee to a point at which he is not worth hiring at any price. . . . If we move in the direction of making machines which learn and whose behavior is modified by experience, we must face the fact that every degree of independence we give the machine is a degree of possible defiance of our wishes. The genie in the bottle will not willingly go back in the bottle, nor have we any reason to expect them to be well-disposed to us.[3]

Just as some future inventions have been a surprise, other anticipated inventions never came to pass. The cartoon Jetsons' vertical commuting car/plane never happened, and in fact high fuel costs caused many local helicopter short-haul aviation companies to shut down in the early 1970s. In the famous quip of Peter Theil, "we wanted flying cars, and they gave us 140 characters."[4]

Just as it was easy for visitors to the 1939 World's Fair to foresee the future, so it was to the contributors to the *Fortune* forecasts of 1955. By then the adoption of modern home appliances and air-conditioning was far along and could easily be predicted to become pervasive. Limited-access highways, such as the Pennsylvania Turnpike and Merritt Parkway, had been started before World War II, and so it was easy to forecast in 1955 that the interstate highway system was just over the horizon, making possible travel from coast to coast without encountering a traffic light. Transcontinental nonstop piston aircraft flights had been introduced in 1953 and the first (British) commercial jet airliner in 1954, and so the future of commercial air transport was easy to foresee. Network live television was already in most living rooms, and color TV had already been invented, as had antibiotics.

Important for our forecasting challenge is to reflect on those aspects of future growth that could not have been correctly predicted in 1955. One involves innovation—in the primitive early years of mainframe computers, it was difficult to foresee much if any of the computer revolution that would by 1980 bring us electronic terminals and personal computers.

Several other "misses" for 1955 forecasters involved concepts that comprise today's "headwinds." In that year the fertility rate was near its postwar peak of 3.7, and it was hard to foresee that soon the birth rate would plummet as women moved from housework to market work. That influx of women raised hours per capita and allowed real gross domestic product (GDP) per capita to rise faster than productivity. Also, 1955 marks the peak of income equality, with the income share of the top 1 percent of the population at its lowest point of the twentieth century. It was hard to foresee the inexorable rise of inequality that began in the late 1970s.

What Has Been Achieved in the Past Forty Years?

Thus far we have concluded that the electronic IR3 has been less important than IR2, as measured by productivity growth of 2.3 percent per year before 1972 and just 1.6 percent since 1972. Put another way, the *level* of productivity has increased by a factor of twelve since 1891, and of that a factor of nine had already been achieved by 1972.

While my basic growth forecast assumes that innovation will percolate along in the next twenty-five years as in the last forty, caution is warranted. It just might be that the most fruitful applications of ICT technology and digitalization have already occurred. In 1970 the electronic calculator had just been invented, but the computer terminal was still in the future. Starting from this world of 1970, by the year 2000 every office was equipped with a web-linked personal computer that could do word-processing and spreadsheet calculations and gather information from around the world. Today the equipment used in office work and the productivity of office employees closely resembles that of a decade ago, with little further improvement since then.

The scope of the electronic IR3 over the past forty years sets a hurdle for the next twenty-five years that is dauntingly high. The list of achievements extends outside the office as well and includes the following:

- Bar code scanning, ATM banking, cable and satellite TV
- Internet, email, web browsing, e-commerce
- Google, Amazon, Wikipedia, LinkedIn, Facebook
- Mobile phones, smartphones, iPads
- CDs, DVDs, iTunes, Netflix, movie streaming
- Airline reservation systems, supply-chain monitoring systems, electronic library catalogs

The Future of Innovation

The big question is: how important will innovations be over the next twenty-five years and how much will they impact future growth in productivity and the standard of living? Future advances that are widely anticipated can be grouped into four main categories—(1) medical and pharmaceutical advances, (2) small robots, artificial intelligence, and 3-D printing, (3) big data, and (4) driverless cars. It is worth examining the potential of each of these categories of future innovation.

Medical and Pharmaceutical Advances

Future advances in medicine related to the genome have already proved to be disappointing. The most important sources of higher life expectancy were achieved in the first half of the twentieth century, when infant mortality was conquered by the discovery of the germ theory of disease, the development of antitoxins for diphtheria, and the near elimination of air-and waterborne diseases through the construction of urban sanitation infrastructure.[5]

Many of the current basic tools of modern medicine were developed between 1940 and 1980, including antibiotics, heart procedures, chemotherapy, and radiation. The current status of science in medical treatment and pharmaceutical advance is well described by Jan Vijg.[6] Progress on physical disease and ailments is progressing faster than on mental disease, so that we can look forward by 2040 to an exponential rise in the burden of taking care of elderly Americans who are physically alive but in a state of mental dementia. Pharmaceutical research has reached a brick wall of rapidly increasing costs and declining benefits.

Small Robots, Artificial Intelligence, and 3-D Printing

The lack of multitasking ability is a current defect of robots. No current robot can drive the UPS truck, choose the correct package, and run up to your front porch, knowing exactly where to leave it. Surely multiple-function robots will be developed, but it will be a long and gradual process before robots outside of the manufacturing and wholesaling sectors become a significant factor in replacing human jobs.

Most jobs are not going to be replaced by robots anytime soon, or even in 2040. Supermarket shelves are still stocked by hand, and although self-checkout has been offered in some areas, it has not been widely embraced by consumers. There will be little replacement by robots of the vast majority of jobs in the service sector, including waiters, bartenders, cooks, cashiers, pedicurists, barbers, educators, nurses, doctors, dentists, janitors, TV anchors and producers, and many more.

3-D printing is another revolution described by the techno-optimists, but its potential impact is limited. Recent reports suggest that 3-D printing is best suited for one-off customized products. 3-D printing represents custom production rather than mass production, and thus it retreats from the economies of scale and efficiency of Henry Ford's 1913 assembly line. Doubtless it will raise productivity in design labs that create models of new products, but it has less potential to raise economy-wide productivity growth.

Big Data

Optimists about future progress often point to the exponential explosion of digital data. What is lost by the enthusiasts for big data is that most of it is a zero-sum game because the vast majority of big data is being analyzed within large corporations for marketing purposes. The *Economist* reported recently that corporate information technology (IT) expenditures for marketing purposes were increasing at three times the rate of other IT expenditures. The marketing wizards use big data to figure out what their customers buy, why they change their purchases from one category to another, and why they move from merchant to merchant.

The quantity of electronic data has been rising exponentially for decades. But diminishing returns have set in. The sharp slowdown in productivity growth in recent years has overlapped with the introduction of smartphones and iPads, which consume huge amounts of data. These sources of innovation have disappointed in what counts: their ability to boost output per hour in the American economy.

Driverless Cars

This category of future progress is demoted to last place because it offers benefits that are minor compared to the invention of the car itself, or the improvements in safety that have achieved a tenfold reduction in fatalities per vehicle-mile since 1950. The most important distinction is between cars and trucks. People are in cars to go from A to B, mainly for essential aspects of living such as commuting or shopping. Current drivers can already talk on the Bluetooth phone and listen to iPod music; only a minor increment in consumer surplus is provided by a driverless car that would allow passengers to surf the Web or watch movies. Driverless trucks and taxis are likely to become common by 2040 but will be handicapped by the difficulty that robot designers have faced in building multitasking ability into robots, since most truck drivers and taxi drivers don't just drive but also load and unload cargo and luggage.

The Headwinds Contribute to Slower Growth

The "headwinds" are an independent set of concerns about the future; they are like the biblical Four Horsemen of the Apocalypse, wrestling down the rate of growth no matter how inventive society may be in the future. Recall that growth in the standard of living equals growth in productivity plus the growth rate of hours worked per person. The first headwind concerns the inexorable downward pressure on hours per capita that will cause future growth in the standard of living to fall short of productivity growth.

Headwind 1: Demography

Forecasters have long recognized that the retirement of the baby boom generation will reduce hours per capita. Whenever a person retires, he or she remains in the population while making a transition from positive to zero hours of market work. But that is not all. Hours per employee have been pushed down in part by the dysfunctional traditional American medical care insurance system, which ties medical insurance to employment rather than providing it as a right of citizenship. Firms have forced employees into part-time status to avoid paying medical insurance costs.

A unique feature of the slow 2009–2014 economic recovery has been the fact that the unemployment rate has been steadily improving (from 10.0 percent in November 2009 to 5.7 percent in January 2015), while the participation rate has been declining as fast, so that there has been no improvement in the employment-to-population ratio. In fact, over the 4.5 years of recovery between April 2010 and January 2015, that ratio barely budged from 58.7 to 59.3 percent, compared to its prior peaks of 64.4 percent in 2000 and 63.0 percent in 2007.[7] Because jobs have been so scarce, many job seekers have given up and have dropped out of the labor force, making the official unemployment rate an increasingly misleading measure of labor market distress.

The decline in the participation rate involves more than just baby boomers' retirement. The devastating effect of manufacturing plant closures throughout the Midwest is captured by remarks of the newly appointed British consul general in Chicago, who toured the Midwest during the autumn of 2013 in the first three months of a four-year term. Asked for impressions of his travels, he said that "what surprised me most was the utter devastation and decay of the former one-factory small and middle-sized manufacturing towns."[8] Often people cannot move due to family ties or financial restrictions, and so they stay in the town with no jobs, and if they are lucky they will qualify for Social Security disability.

Headwind 2: Education

Since Edward Denison's first attempt in 1962, experts on economic growth have recognized the role of increasing educational attainment as a primary source of growth.[9] Goldin and Katz in 2008 estimated that educational attainment increased by 0.8 years per decade over the eight decades between 1890 and 1970.[10]

The increase of educational attainment has two parts, one referring to secondary education and the other relevant for higher education. The surge in high school graduation rates—from less than 10 percent of youth in 1900 to 80 percent by 1970—was a central driver of twentieth-century economic growth. But the percentage of eighteen-year-olds receiving bona fide high school diplomas had fallen to 74 percent by 2000, according to James Heckman.[11] The United States currently ranks eleventh among the developed nations in high school graduation rates and is the only country in which the graduation rates of those aged twenty-five through thirty-four is no higher than those aged fifty-five through sixty-four.[12] The role of education in holding back future economic growth is evident in the poor quality of educational outcomes at the secondary level. The international PISA tests of fifteen-year-olds in 2013 rated the United States as ranked seventeenth in reading, twentieth in science, and twenty-seventh in math.[13]

At the college level, long-standing problems of quality are joined with the newer issues of affordability and student debt. In most of the post–World War II period, a low-cost college education was within reach of a larger fraction of the population of the United States than in any other nation, thanks to free college education made possible by the GI Bill, and also minimal tuition for in-state students at state public universities and junior colleges. The United States led the world during most of the last century in the percentage of youth completing college. The percentage of twenty-five-year-olds who have earned a B.A. degree from a four-year college in the United States has inched up in the past fifteen years from 25 to 30 percent, but that percentage is now ranked twelfth among developed nations.[14]

Even when account is taken of the discounts from full tuition made possible by scholarships and fellowships, the current level of American college completion has been made possible only by a dramatic rise in student borrowing. Americans owe $1 trillion in college debt. While a four-year college degree still pays off in a much higher income and lower risk of unemployment than for high school graduates, still about one-quarter of college graduates will not obtain a college-level job in the first few years after graduation, leaving them to face their future as an indebted taxicab driver or barista.

To place the historic contribution of education to economic growth in perspective, Goldin and Katz have calculated that during most of the twentieth century, education's contribution to economic growth was around 0.35 percent per year. Estimates by Harvard's Dale Jorgenson suggest that education's growth contribution will decline by 0.27 percent in the future as compared to the past.[15]

Headwind 3: Inequality

What matters for most Americans is not average growth in real GDP per capita but the growth rate in the portion available to the bottom 99 percent of the income distribution. The Berkeley website of Emmanuel Saez reports that between 1993 and 2013, the average growth rate of real income for the bottom 99 percent of the income distribution was 0.35 percent slower than for the average of all real income.[16] Another indicator of the sharp divide between median and average real income growth is provided in the U.S. Census series on median real household income. Expressed in 2011 dollars, median real household income in 2012 was $52,100, below the 1998 level of $53,700.[17] Real income growth in middle America has already reached zero.

Will inequality continue to increase until 2040? Holding down wages is an explicit corporate strategy at retail firms like Walmart, which hires only temporary workers to fill job openings and forces many of its workers onto part-time shifts.[18] The Caterpillar corporation has become the poster child of rising inequality. It has broken strikes to enforce a two-tier wage system in which new hires are paid half of what existing workers make, even though both groups are members of the same labor union. In contrast, there was an 80 percent increase over two years in the compensation of Caterpillar's CEO, whose quoted mantra is "We can never make enough profit."[19]

Similarly, Boeing has threatened to move the manufacturing of its latest 777-X model from the unionized Seattle area to some other low-wage location. Only after facing an explicit threat that their jobs would be eliminated, members of Boeing's union in the Seattle area reluctantly agreed to a new contract that offers virtually no increases in real wages over the indefinite future as well as reductions in medical and pension benefit contributions.

The future of inequality is closely linked to the social breakdown in the bottom one-third of the income distribution, as family breakups deprive millions of children of the traditional support of a two-parent household. Charles Murray's *Coming Apart* (2011) carefully documents the decline of every relevant social indicator for the bottom third of the white U.S. population, which he calls "Fishtown."[20]

The Murray charts uniformly cover the five-decade interval from 1960 to 2010 and exhibit a consistent record of social breakdown and decay. The most devastating statistic of all is that in Fishtown for mothers age forty, the percentage of children living with both biological parents declined from 95 percent in 1960 to 34 percent in 2010. Children living in a single-parent family, usually with the mother as the head of household, are more likely to suffer from poverty and are more likely to drop out of high school.

The steady rise in the inequality of the American income distribution shows no sign of ending. Many of the new jobs created during the recent economic recovery have been low-paying jobs, often part-time. The push by employers to force employees into part-time jobs is accentuated by the increasing burden of medical insurance. Other countries avoid the destructive effect of rising medical care costs on insurance premiums and indirectly on job creation by making medical care coverage a right of citizenship paid for by a value-added tax that no one can avoid.

The rise of inequality shifts the forecasting task from a prediction of average income per capita in 2040 to the average income of the bottom 99 percent of the income distribution. Continuing trends of wealth accumulation at the top, a wage squeeze for the rest, and continuing pressure for shorter hours, lower benefits, and reduced pension plans all suggest that the rise of inequality will continue. Between 1993 and 2013 the growth of real income in the bottom 99 percent has been 0.35 percent per year slower than for the nationwide average. The growth of the "great divide" may even accelerate as the result of millions of fatherless children being unable to complete high school or make the transition to college.

Headwind 4: Repaying Debt

The future covered by these forecasts over the next twenty-five years includes the need to stop the rise of indebtedness of government at the federal, state, and local levels. The Congressional Budget Office (CBO) projects that trouble lies ahead beyond 2020. An inexorably rising debt-to-GDP ratio will be caused by the exploding costs of Medicare and Social Security. Many states also face large unfunded pension liabilities.

This is the fourth headwind, the near inevitability that over the next several decades taxes will rise faster and transfer payments rise more slowly than in the past. I estimate that the *disposable income* of the bottom 99 percent of the income distribution will decline by 0.2 percentage points per year relative to the before-taxes-transfers income of the same group.

Conclusion: Economic Life in 2040

When the post-1972 decline of innovation is combined with the four headwinds, the implication of this chapter is that future growth in the real disposable income of the bottom 99 percent of the income distribution between 2015 and 2040 will be about 0.2 percent per year, as compared to 2.0 percent in the 116 years before 2007. In 2040 the United States will be a more stratified society than today, with greater wealth among the top 1 percent and lower relative incomes and wealth for the bottom 99 percent. This implies that the standard of living of the bottom 99 percent will stagnate, rising by only 5 percent cumulatively over twenty-five years instead of the 64 percent cumulative increase that would have been made possible by a hypothetical future growth rate of 2.0 percent, the historical pre-2007 average.

There will be many new innovations, and the easiest to predict are a continuation of miniaturization made possible by advances in semiconductor technology. By 2040 our automobiles may contain hundreds of tiny computer devices instead of twenty to thirty on a current vehicle. There will be many sensors throughout our houses, and possibly robot-like vacuum cleaners. Home temperature and burglar alarm status will also be remotely viewable, including whether the dogs are sleeping or awake. Ever more sophisticated and inexpensive robots will replace human workers, especially in manufacturing and the wholesale sector, and robotic snowblowers may clear our driveways while we remain warm inside. Medical diagnosis equipment may become so much cheaper that doctors can administer computed tomography (CT) scans in their offices just as dentists can now create crowns on automatic computer-driven milling machines in their offices. Human-driven taxicabs may be partly replaced by driverless taxis summoned by smartphone.

Compared to the great leaps forward in the century before 1972, the standard of living is inching forward more slowly now. Looking back twenty-five years to 1990, our life is very similar with the exception of web- and smartphone-related inventions. Our houses have been networked since the 1920s, except for the recent additions of cable TV and Internet. There have been no important new kitchen inventions since the microwave. We drive to work and shop using the same local streets and expressways as we did twenty-five years ago, and it is unlikely that this aspect of daily life will differ much in 2040. Improvements have mainly taken the form of more variety—more organic produce, more TV channels, more sports and movies, the vast variety of facts and information available on the Internet, and the alternative of e-commerce to traditional brick-and-mortar stores or mail-order catalogs with items ordered by phone.

Our retrospective on the 1955 *Fortune* predictions highlights the fact that technology was easier to forecast back then than demography, education, or inequality. The same may be true on the road to 2040. By 2040 the baby boomers will all have retired, reducing downward pressure on hours per capita. Some of the decline of the labor force due to giving up and dropping out may turn around. But the blight of children growing up in fatherless homes will erode U.S. academic performance at both the high school and college level, and the dream of college attainment will become ever more elusive as the inexorable machine of college cost inflation and exploding student debt continues. A vicious spiral of downward mobility, due to the interaction of college debt, delayed household formation and childbirth, and declining population growth, could further the economic and social decline of the bottom 99 percent relative to other nations.

This leaves the last and most difficult questions about 2040. Will the United States by then have lost its position as the nation with the highest per capita real GDP?[21] By that year nations ranking high on international tests of student achievement and with more social equality, which allows all students to complete college instead of only a minority as in the United States, may well have caught up and surpassed the U.S. standard of living. Leading candidates are South Korea and the Nordic countries, and perhaps even Canada. The current socioeconomic decay of the United States would be hard to turn around even with a benevolent dictator carrying out the most effective policies that emerge from academic research. The current paralysis of the U.S. political system suggests that any such set of reforms may lie too far in the future to boost the U.S. standard of living by the year 2040.

Notes

1. Details about the posthumously published Verne book and its predictions come from Jan Vijg, *The American Technological Challenge: Stagnation and Decline in the 21st Century* (New York: Algora Press, 2011), 35–36.

2. John Elfreth Watkins Jr., "What May Happen in the Next Hundred Years," *Ladies' Home Journal*, November 1900, 8.

3. John Markoff, "In 1949, He Imagined an Age of Robots," *New York Times*, May 21, 2013, D8.

4. Peter Theil quoted in http://www.businessinsider.com/founders-fund-the-future-2011-7.

5. David M. Cutler and Grant Miller, "The Role of Public Health Improvements in Health Advances: The Twentieth Century United States," *Demography* 42, no. 1 (February 2005): 1–22.

6. Vijg, *American Technological Challenge*, 74–75.

7. Bureau of Labor Statistics, "The Employment Situation – October 2014," http://www.bls.gov/news.release/pdf/empsit.pdf.

8. This paragraph reports on a conversation at the author's dinner with the British consul general on November 20, 2013.

9. Edward F. Denison, *The Sources of Economic Growth and the Alternatives Before Us* (New York: Committee for Economic Development, 1962).

10. Claudia Goldin and Lawrence F. Katz, *The Race between Education and Technology* (Cambridge, Mass.: Belknap Press of Harvard University Press, 2008).

11. Heckman found that the economic outcomes of those who earned not a high school diploma but rather a General Education Development (GED) certificate performed no better economically than high school dropouts and that the decline in graduation rates could be explained, in part, by the rising share of youth who are in prison rather than in school.

12. John Cookson, "How U.S. Graduation Rates Compare with the Rest of the World," CNNWorld (blog), November 3, 2011, http://globalpublicsquare.blogs.cnn.com/2011/11/03/how-u-s-graduation-rates-compare-with-the-rest-of-the-world/.

13. http://www.oecd.org/unitedstates/PISA-2012-results-US.pdf.

14. http://www.ed.gov/college.

15. Jorgenson's estimate has become a consensus view, being adopted in the latest series of sources-of-growth projections by Bryne, Oliner, and Sichel (2013) and Gordon (2012). David M. Byrne, Stephen D. Oliner, and Daniel E. Sichel, "Is the Information Technology Revolution Over?" *International Productivity Monitor*, no. 25 (Spring 2013); Robert J. Gordon, "Is U.S. Economic Growth Over? Faltering Innovation Confronts the Six Headwinds" (NBER Working Paper 18315, August 2012).

16. http://topincomes.parisschoolofeconomics.eu/.

17. http://www.census.gov/hhes/www/income/data/historical/people/.

18. Facts in this and the next paragraph come from Steven Greenhouse, "Fighting Back against Wretched Wages," *New York Times*, July 28, 2013.

19. http://www.chicagobusiness.com/article/20130517/BLOGS08/130519807/caterpillar-ceo-we-can-never-make-enough-profit.

20. Charles Murray, *Coming Apart: The State of White America 1960–2010* (New York: Crown Forum, 2012).

21. We ignore the fact that certain nations with idiosyncratic advantages—for example, Luxembourg and Norway—currently have higher per capita real GDP than that of the United States.

CHAPTER 2

Health

Longer and Healthier Lives?

Eileen M. Crimmins

AARP Professor of Gerontology
at the University of Southern California

We can say with confidence that American health and life expectancy are likely to improve somewhat over the coming decades; but we can also be confident that there will be no tremendous breakthroughs leading to dramatically extended lives during this period or in the number of years people will live in good health. We can also safely predict that the United States is unlikely to regain the relative prominence it held at the middle of the twentieth century among the world leaders in life expectancy and other health indicators.

The twenty-five years between 2015 and 2040 are a period where we should focus on increasing the length of our *healthy* life; however, there are a number of disquieting trends in the United States that indicate accomplishing such a goal will require concerted effort. In fact, current trends suggest that changes in individual behavior and social policy will be needed to address the American "health problem." Otherwise, we are likely to have a difficult time maintaining even the current length of healthy life, as we continue to fall behind our peer nations in both life expectancy and health.

Life Expectancy Increase in Recent Decades

The increase in human life expectancy was probably the greatest accomplishment of the twentieth century—almost doubling in the United States, from around forty to seventy-eight years. This increase was accomplished by initially increasing the likelihood that children born would survive to old age and, only more recently, that people who survive to old age will survive to very old age.

Demographers routinely project life expectancy and disability seventy years ahead, so the twenty-five-year focus of this book is a relatively short demographic projection about which one can be relatively confident. We do not expect the coming decades to be like the mid-twentieth-century period when the earlier version of this book was written—a time of impressive increases in longevity and health. Instead, we can expect to add only a couple of additional years of life expectancy in the next few decades, but not more than that. While there are researchers who believe that life expectancy for those born now can reach one hundred (see Christensen et al., for example),[1] my view is that this is highly unlikely to occur even a century into the future. The only way this extreme life expectancy can be achieved is by almost entirely eliminating any deaths before age one hundred, which is unlikely for a number of reasons: at present only a small percentage of people live to become centenarians; the speed of decline in mortality that would be required to produce such increases in life expectancy at older ages has never been experienced; the trends in recent decades do not indicate that such a decline in mortality is currently happening; and there is no scientific advance on the immediate horizon that could result in such dramatic change in the next few decades. Therefore, I expect any increase in life expectancy to be modest in the years leading up to 2040.

U.S. Life Expectancy Trends in International Perspective

Trends over thirty years in life expectancy at birth—from 1980 to 2010—in the United States are shown in figure 2.1 for males and figure 2.2 for females. There have been relatively modest but continuous increases for men, but only very slow increases for women, including years of stagnation within this period. The relatively poor improvement for

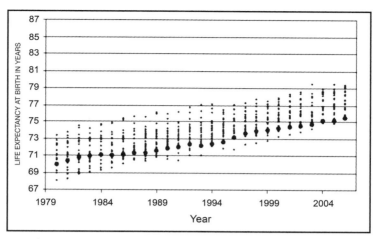

Figure 2.1. Life expectancy at birth, trends for U.S. males relative to 21 other OECD countries

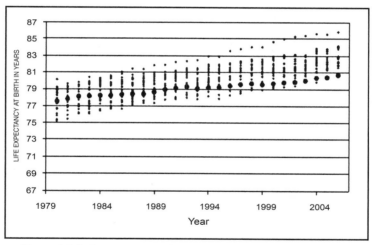

Figure 2.2. Life expectancy at birth, trends for U.S. females relative to 21 other OECD countries

Each dot represents life expectancy in one country among those in the Organization for Economic Cooperation and Development (OECD). The large circles represent the United States. The rest represent Australia, Austria, Belgium, Canada, Denmark, Finland, France, Iceland, Italy, Japan, Luxembourg, the Netherlands, New Zealand, Norway, Portugal, Spain, Sweden, Switzerland, the United Kingdom, and West Germany.

Source: E. M. Crimmins, S. H. Preston, and B. Cohen, eds., *Explaining Divergent Levels of Longevity in High-Income Countries* (Washington, D.C.: National Research Council, National Academies Press, 2011).

women relative to men is reason for some concern, but it is the trends in the United States relative to other countries that raise the most serious issues among Americans about both our current health situation and the outlook for the future. As indicated in the two figures, the relative rank of U.S. life expectancy has dropped markedly. The United States has fallen well behind leaders such as Japan, Australia, France, and Italy, and today the United States has levels of life expectancy similar to the eastern European countries. These differences between the United States and other countries were first clarified in a National Research Council report that focused on the population age fifty years old and older.[2] Additional work focusing on the relative health of those younger than age fifty found that the United States fared even more poorly at younger ages.[3] In a comparison of the ranking of mortality at each age among seventeen peer countries, the United States ranks worst or second to worst at every age up to seventy-five. As indicated in figure 2.3, only at the oldest ages do Americans compare relatively well.

This poor performance in life expectancy for the United States is due to a set of wide-ranging causes. Some of these causes are clearly rooted in social or political values. For example, it is not surprising that violent deaths—particularly those involving firearms—are a significant cause of international differences at younger ages. But deaths from transportation accidents are also an important cause of international differences. The reasons behind high levels of transportation-related mortality are not immediately obvious. More miles are driven in the United States than in most peer countries, particularly by teenagers; affluence may be the reason teenagers drive more, but the relative lack of availability of public transportation may also be a factor. In turn, the availability of public transportation may be linked to the particular geography of the country. Deaths from automobile accidents may also be related to the level of drinking alcoholic beverages, particularly among the young, and the level of enforcement of laws against drinking and driving. Then there are additional deaths from drug usage, infant mortality, and maternal mortality. All of these factors differ across countries. In sum, the causes of lower life expectancy and higher mortality in the United States before old age are wide ranging.

Higher levels of chronic disease, particularly heart disease and diabe-

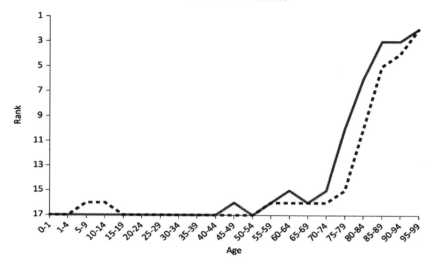

Figure 2.3. Ranking of U.S. mortality rates at each age among
17 peer countries, 2006–2008

Rank of mortality rate of the United States compared to 16 other countries; 17 indicates
the highest mortality rate at a given age and 1 the lowest mortality rate. Countries include
the United States, Australia, Austria, Canada, Denmark, Finland, France, Germany, Italy,
Japan, the Netherlands, Norway, Portugal, Spain, Sweden, Switzerland, and the United
Kingdom.

Source: S. H. Woolf and L. Aron, eds., *U.S. Health in International Perspective: Shorter Lives, Poorer
Health* (Washington, D.C.: National Research Council, National Academies Press, 2013).

tes, account for most of the difference in life expectancy beyond middle
age between Americans and people in other countries. Americans have
smoked more in the past on average than people in other countries; they
are more likely to be obese than people in most countries; and they may
be more likely to be sedentary than people in other countries. Americans
reach old age with more risk factors for cardiovascular disease than people in Europe and elsewhere, and they have higher mortality.

The United States is the only one of the peer countries examined in
these studies without universal health insurance, so Americans, particularly those younger than age sixty-five, are more likely to be without
a regular source of health care than people in other countries. Recent

changes in the availability of health insurance may reduce the role of this factor in causing differences between the United States and other countries, but the reasons underlying these health differences are only partly related to differences in health care.

Differentials within the United States

It is useful to consider differences within the United States as well as differences between the United States and other countries. The United States has long had differentials by socioeconomic status in average length of life and in most health indicators. People who are wealthier or who have more education live longer on average, and that difference has been growing over time as increases in life expectancy are increasingly concentrated among those with the highest education. Between 1990 and 2008 life expectancy among women with less than a high school education actually declined by about five years.[4] It is also true that a large number of U.S. counties, primarily in the South, experienced declining life expectancy among women over the twenty-five-year period from 1985 to 2010.[5]

Declines in life expectancy are certainly not something that we ever expected to observe. So while our overall progress has been modest, our disparities have been growing. Relative to Europe, socioeconomic differences in health appear to be wider in the United States. However, it is important to note that these differences are not the reason Americans are less healthy than Europeans: even nonminority Americans with relatively high education do poorly relative to their European counterparts.[6]

Diseases and Conditions Causing Health Problems

One of the reasons that we can be fairly confident about only modest life extension in the relative short term is that the United States and other high-income countries are now places where people die of chronic diseases, the course of which are many decades long. Many of these diseases have their roots in earlier life circumstances and lifestyles. In the 1955 edition of *The Fabulous Future*, likely cures for polio and tuberculosis were predicted. The source of these optimistic projections was the science underlying cures or prevention and virtual elimination of deaths from infectious diseases that took place after World War II. These successes gave us great confidence that we could do the same for other diseases and conditions. After we developed the antibiotics to virtually eliminate deaths from infection, deaths became most likely the result of heart disease or cancer. Assuming our ability to cure diseases would continue, we began "wars" on heart disease and cancer in the 1960s. As with other wars undertaken during this time period, these have neither been won nor totally lost. They have been long, drawn-out campaigns with some successes obtained at great cost.

Reducing mortality from heart disease has been our greatest success story of the last half of the twentieth century. Heart disease death rates have tumbled; they are now only about 50 percent of what they were in 1950. We did not accomplish this reduction in mortality the way we expected, by understanding the causes of heart disease and eliminating it from our population, as we had with most infectious diseases. Rather, our success has been due to some combination of improved behaviors, such as a reduction in smoking and fat consumption, and better medical and pharmaceutical interventions. We have also probably received a largely unrecognized benefit from the long-term development of healthier and stronger bodies, reflecting the long-term decline in infectious illnesses and better nutrition over the human life cycle. These two factors have resulted in people reaching older age with less organ damage.

We have been successful in preventing the progression of heart disease to disability and death among people who have it, but we have done little to prevent the onset of heart disease. In fact, the number of people with heart disease has been increasing over time. If we look at the numbers of people with risk factors for heart disease—diagnosed hypertension, high cholesterol, overweight—we also see increases in recent decades. However, we have had some successes, particularly after people have been diagnosed with hypertension and cholesterol risks, as they have experienced impressive increases over time in treatment and control. The use of prescription drugs has markedly reduced the number of people who have uncontrolled hypertension and high cholesterol. It is likely that the use of these drugs has also resulted in a reduction in the mortality risks associated with obesity.

While we began a war on cancer at the same time we began our attempt to put a man on the moon, it was more than twenty years after men walked on the moon in 1969 that we began to see some decline in overall cancer death rates. However, we had some interim successes, particularly in childhood cancers. In the twenty-first century we have seen some reduction in cancer death rates, which has resulted from the earlier diagnosis occurring with increased screening and the development of multiple new approaches to treatment. Such success is based on scientific foundations that are likely to continue and be the source of some improvement in life expectancy. Changes in behavior can also lead to reductions in cancer onset. Lung cancer rates are closely related to smoking behavior, and they have declined with decreases in smoking. Reductions in the use of hormone replacement therapy have also resulted in some decrease in breast cancer incidence. It is hard to predict changes in cancer onset due to other environmental exposure, since causation is still not well understood.

Type II diabetes is a disease with worrisome trends; rates have been increasing for decades along with the increase in obesity. While survival rates for those with diabetes have risen, the increase in onset, especially at younger ages, has resulted from increases in obesity among young people. Obesity trends appear to have leveled off in the last few years, but we have never before had generations of people living with obesity for so many years before reaching the older ages. Mitigating this effect will be one of our major health challenges going forward.

What Do We Predict from the Joint Trends in Life Expectancy and Health?

In recent decades the concept of healthy life expectancy (expected years in good health) has joined that of life expectancy (total expected length of life) in evaluating health changes and policy. It is the combination of rates of onset and recovery from disease and disability, along with mortality among the sick and disabled and those free of such conditions, that determines the average length of healthy life. Empirical evidence indicates that since 1980 we have managed to increase the length of life without severe disability enough that it has exceeded the increase in overall life expectancy.[7] That is extremely good news. However, the bad news is that the length of life with disease has also increased, so that a greater proportion of life is now spent grappling with major chronic diseases.

Conclusion

The outlook presented here is unfortunately rather negative. But given the current situation and recent trends, it seems realistic. We will be fortunate to continue to add even modestly to our current levels of life expectancy. It is a lot harder to increase life expectancy when, as is currently the case in the United States (and in many other developed countries), most people die in their eighties. Life expectancy was more easily increased in the twentieth century, when death rates for babies and children could be reduced.

It will be difficult to increase the relative length of healthy life expectancy without some major changes in the incidence of chronic health problems. While survival among those with health problems is likely to improve somewhat as we learn to treat our current conditions better, the relatively poor status of younger persons makes it hard to project great improvements in health. The key toward increasing the length of healthy life is to improve health by delaying to older ages the onset of health problems, and this will require major behavioral changes as well as scientific advances.

Improving health and life expectancy does not rest simply on increasing expenditures. If it did, there would be a plausible solution to increasing years of healthy living. Presently, Americans spend about twice as much on health care as do people in peer countries that rank above the United States in life expectancy. It would be possible, perhaps, to improve health through a redistribution of some of this spending. Funds could improve health more if reallocated toward preventative care, mental health, and greater access to care for those who do not have it. While the United States ranks first among nations in expenditures on health care, rankings on social service expenditures lag far behind. Some reallocation of funds from health care to social services might improve U.S. health by improving people's well-being and levels of stress. Behavioral changes are also required for Americans to see improved health. Individuals choose to eat more than they should, be less physically active, drink alcohol and then drive, possess firearms, and use illicit drugs and misuse prescription drugs. While people certainly have the right to do some of these things, there are social costs to having these rights. Understanding how to incentivize behavior to improve health may prove to be an even more important source of progress over the next twenty-five years than either scientific discoveries or improving access to health care.

Notes

1. K. Christensen et al., "Ageing Populations: The Challenges Ahead," *Lancet* 374, no. 9696 (2009): 1196–208.

2. E. M. Crimmins, S. H. Preston, and B. Cohen, eds., *Explaining Divergent Levels of Longevity in High-Income Countries* (Washington, D.C.: National Research Council: National Academies Press, 2011).

3. S. H. Woolf and L. Aron, eds., *U.S. Health in International Perspective: Shorter Lives, Poorer Health* (Washington, D.C.: National Research Council and Institute of Medicine, National Academies Press, 2013).

4. S. J. Olshansky et al., "Differences in Life Expectancy Due to Race and Educational Differences Are Widening, and May Not Catch Up," *Health Affairs* 31, no. 8 (2012): 1803–13.

5. H. Wang et al., "Left Behind: Widening Disparities for Males and Females in US County Life Expectancy, 1985–2010." *Population Health Metrics* 11, no. 8 (2013); doi: 10.1186/1478-7954-11-8.

6. Crimmins, Preston, and Cohen, *Explaining Divergent Levels*.

7. E. M. Crimmins et al., "Changes in Disability-Free Life Expectancy for Americans 70 Years old and Older," *Demography* 46, no. 3 (2009): 627–46.

CHAPTER 3

Happiness

A Happier World?

Richard A. Easterlin
University Professor, University of Southern California

In 2003 at a conference in Milan, Italy, I sat around a table with a half dozen leading scholars in the "economics of happiness." The question came up: Does "happiness" have a future in economics? In the world? Of those assembled, I was the most pessimistic. Indeed, virtually everyone else thought happiness was going to blossom. That was only about ten years ago, and I have already been proven wrong. So here I am now writing about the outlook for happiness twenty-five years down the road, in 2040. As far as my predictions go, I think you know what to expect.

In what way was I wrong? Well, in economics, happiness is now a recognized subject of study with its own category included in the American Economic Association's *Journal of Economic Literature* classification system. And while there are few courses on happiness included in economics curricula, publications on the subject by economists in the last few years numbered several hundred. On the world front, international agencies such as the United Nations and the Organization for Economic Cooperation and Development (OECD) are now promoting the collec-

I am grateful to Robson Morgan for help in the preparation of this manuscript and to the University of Southern California for financial support.

tion of happiness data. The governments of the United Kingdom, France, the Netherlands, Italy, Poland, New Zealand, Australia, and Canada are considering or have started collecting official statistics on happiness. Even the United States has dipped a toe in the water. There is currently a National Research Council panel charged with determining whether research has advanced to a point that warrants the federal government initiating the collection of statistics on a subset of happiness data relating to momentary emotions. In *The Fabulous Future* of 1955, the subject of happiness is not even mentioned. And now it warrants a full chapter.

So here are the predictions for twenty-five years hence of a somewhat more positively minded student of the subject:

1. People will, on average, be happier than at present.

2. The reason for the increase in happiness will not be economic growth (though this almost certainly will continue); rather, it will be that many governments have recognized that full employment policies and a universal social safety net significantly increase people's feelings of well-being.

My reasoning and some of the evidence on which it is based follow. But first, a few words about the concept of happiness.

Concept

"Happiness" as used here and in the social science literature more generally is the response to survey questions of the following type asked in the World Values Survey:

> Taking all things together, would you say you are:
>
> 1 = Very happy; 2 = Quite happy; 3 = Not very happy;
> 4 = Not at all happy

A closely related measure is "life satisfaction":

> All things considered, how satisfied are you with your life as a whole these days? Please use this card to help with your answer.
>
> Dissatisfied 1 2 3 4 5 6 7 8 9 10 Satisfied

The distribution of responses on life satisfaction is similar to that on happiness. The two measures are highly correlated and are commonly used interchangeably by analysts as indicative of "subjective well-being" (the rubric under which such measures fall).

Clearly in this survey approach, each individual responds based on his or her own notion of happiness, and these notions could conceivably differ widely among individuals. If one puts together the answers of a nationally representative sample of the American population and computes an "average" value of happiness, is the result meaningful?

There are two ways of answering this question. The first is by appeal to authority. In 2008 then-president Sarkozy of France appointed a twenty-five-member Commission on the Measurement of Economic Performance and Social Progress to propose more meaningful measures of well-being than the traditional indicator, gross domestic product (GDP) per capita. The commission members were almost entirely economists, and their ranks included five Nobel Prize winners. The commission's judgment, based on a review of the literature that had accumulated on measures of subjective well-being, was as follows:

> Research has shown that it is possible to collect meaningful and reliable data on *subjective* as well as *objective* well-being. . . . The types of questions that have proved their value within small-scale and unofficial surveys should be included in larger scale surveys undertaken by official statistical offices.[1] [*emphasis added*]

This judgment is not a casual one. The commission members were from an economics cohort trained in the view that measures of one's observable external circumstances, especially income, are sufficient to assess well-being and that self-reports of feelings such as happiness should be summarily dismissed. The commission's judgment in 2008 that personal statements about one's feelings of well-being were meaningful represents a revolutionary change in the attitude of the economics discipline—a willingness to pay attention to what people say, not just observe what they do.

A second way to assess the meaningfulness of happiness responses is by considering what people report when asked what makes them happy.

Although conceivably the sources of happiness might be quite different among individuals, it turns out that the happiness of most people everywhere—in rich and poor countries, communist and noncommunist—depends mainly on the same set of concerns, such as material living conditions, family life, health, and work. When one thinks about it, this worldwide similarity in responses makes sense. The time of most people everywhere is spent chiefly on these concerns, and people tend to think they have some control over them; that is, that they can do something about their income, health, family circumstances, and job. It is this similarity among people in the underlying determinants of happiness that makes it meaningful to average the individual responses and to compare the changes in happiness over time and the differences among countries. This is not to say that individuals' happiness can be compared on a person-to-person basis, but comparisons of groups are meaningful.

It is important to note that happiness as measured here is a statement about "what is"; that is, how happy people say they are. It is not a statement about "what should be." Until a half century ago, the subject of happiness was the province of philosophers who sought by deductive reasoning to identify what *should* make people happy, the "good life." This approach resulted in numerous plausible but different concepts of happiness. The social science approach followed here relies not on such a priori judgments—what should be—but simply on what people personally report about their feelings of well-being—what is. Thus, the social science approach is *describing* what people say about their happiness, not *prescribing* what they should do to be happy. Nor is the social science approach saying that people should pursue happiness. It is simply trying to find out how happy people are and what is responsible for these feelings. But if individuals or governments want to measure and pursue happiness, the findings of social science research should provide a useful guide.

Economic Growth and Happiness

Economic growth has been spreading throughout the world, particularly since around 1950, when marked increases in the growth rate of GDP per capita became common in many developing countries.[2] At the start of this chapter I suggested that economic growth does not in itself raise happiness. The evidence for this comes from comparing growth rates of GDP per capita, the common index of economic growth, with growth rates of happiness. If economic growth has a positive impact on happiness, then one would expect that countries with a higher growth rate of GDP per capita would also typically have a greater improvement in happiness.

In fact, the evidence is that there is no statistically significant association between the growth rates of GDP per capita and happiness. My colleagues at the University of Southern California and I have assembled data for thirty-seven countries worldwide.[3] For each country the happiness data are for the longest periods we could find, a minimum of twelve years but in most cases more—the average is twenty-two years. We compared growth rates of GDP per capita and happiness, first for a group of seventeen developed countries, then for eleven countries of eastern Europe transitioning from socialism to capitalism, and finally for nine developing countries scattered across Asia, Latin America, and Africa. The pattern was the same in each of the three groups—countries with high rates of economic growth had, on average, no greater improvement in happiness than countries with low rates of economic growth. When we analyzed all thirty-seven countries together, there was still no association between economic growth and happiness. In short, for richer, poorer, and transition countries, whether pooled or analyzed separately, there is no time-series evidence that a higher rate of economic growth leads to a higher rate of improvement in happiness.

I have noted that we sought to analyze as long a time series as possible—at least twelve years but preferably more. The reason for this is that in the short run, as the economy goes up and down with recession and recovery, so too does happiness. The long- and short-run association between economic growth and happiness is illustrated schematically in figure 3.1. In the figure, the short-term ups and downs in GDP per capita are accompanied by corresponding movements in happiness—this is illustrated by the solid lines. But the long-term trend of GDP per capita is upward while that of happiness is flat—compare the broken lines. Analysts who study time series spanning periods of only a few years observe the positive short-term association but often misread it as the long-term association.[4]

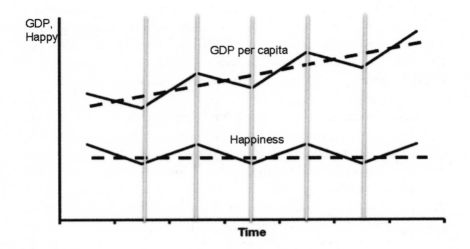

Figure 3.1. Schematic Illustration of Short-Term Fluctuations and
Long-Term Trends in Happiness and Gross Domestic Product Per Capita

Reasonably comparable time-series data on subjective well-being
(SWB) in less-developed countries are in short supply. In Easterlin et
al. (2010), the World Values Survey (WVS) was the principal source,
and only nine less-developed countries were available with reasonably
long time series data that were comparable across the years.[5] Fortunately, the annual Latinobarometer surveys, covering seventeen Latin
American countries since 1994, provide a new and additional body of
data on the experience of lower-income nations. The life satisfaction
question in the Latinobarometer surveys changes too frequently to be
used, but the question on one's current economic situation is the same
from 1994 to 2006: "How would you define, in general, the current
economic situation of yourself and your family? Would you say that
it is . . .

1 = Very bad; 2 = Bad; 3 = Regular; 4 = Good; 5 = Very good"

One would expect that the responses to this question would be even
more closely linked to economic growth than life satisfaction, because
the central feature of growth is a rapid increase of real incomes, and such

an increase would presumably lead directly to greater satisfaction with one's economic situation. Hence, one might expect that countries with higher growth rates of GDP per capita would have greater increments in people's satisfaction with their economic situation.

In fact, there is no evidence that a greater increase in satisfaction with one's economic situation accompanies more rapid economic growth. As in the earlier analysis of WVS data, there is a nil relationship. The results from the Latinobarometer buttress those from the World Values Survey.

If there is any less-developed country where one would expect a positive impact of economic growth on SWB, it is China, whose growth since 1990 from an initially very low value has been at the highest rate ever recorded, a fourfold multiplication of real GDP per capita in two decades.[6] Household appliances such as refrigerators and washing machines—quite rare in 1990—are now commonplace in urban areas. Color television sets currently average over one per household. By 2008, almost one in ten urban households owned a car and China had become the world's leading automobile producer.

Yet, the combined evidence from six happiness surveys is that life satisfaction in China has not improved and, if anything, may have declined somewhat.[7] Life satisfaction appears to have followed a U-shaped trajectory, bottoming out in the first part of this millennium and then recovering by 2010 to a value somewhat short of its initial level. The result for China is similar to the previous findings for developed, developing, and transition countries—economic growth does not result in greater happiness.

Happiness, Employment, and a Social Safety Net

If economic growth does not increase happiness, what does? The answer suggested by the evidence is a high level of employment and a substantial social safety net. The evidence for this is of three types—first, previous findings reported in the literature; second, a comparison of European welfare states; and third, the experience of countries transitioning from socialism to capitalism.

There is extensive evidence in the happiness literature that unemployment has a significant and sizable negative impact on SWB.[8] This negative effect of unemployment is felt by employed as well as unemployed persons, presumably because of increased anxiety as coworkers are laid off, as reported by DiTella, MacCulloch, and Oswald (2001).[9] The policy implication is straightforward—full employment policies increase happiness.

The positive effect of safety net policies on happiness is suggested in another study by DiTella, MacCulloch, and Oswald (2003).[10] In a multivariate analysis they find that among workers who are laid off those with greater unemployment insurance benefits are significantly happier. The political science literature on SWB also provides statistical support for the positive impact of safety net policies on SWB. Among developed countries, those with a more comprehensive social safety net are happier.[11]

In what follows, I present additional evidence on the positive relation between happiness, on the one hand, and full employment and safety net policies, on the other, based on recent collaborative research (reported in Easterlin 2013).[12] First, I compare two sets of European countries with the same GDP per capita but different socioeconomic policies to see whether there is any difference in happiness. Second, I examine the course of happiness in China and a European transition country (the former German Democratic Republic, or East Germany) in the period when employment and safety net policies were effectively abandoned.

European Welfare States

For simplicity, Denmark, Sweden, and Finland are grouped together here as "ultra welfare states" and France, Germany, Austria, and the United Kingdom as "semi welfare states." In 2007, macroeconomic conditions—GDP per capita and rates of inflation and unemployment—in the two groups were virtually identical. Public policies in the ultra welfare states, however, were more generous and comprehensive than in the semi welfare states. Although wide-ranging summary measures of such policies do not exist, there is a close approximation in the "benefit generosity indexes" created by political scientist Lyle Scruggs (2004), who, in turn, built on the earlier work of Gøsta Esping-Andersen (1990).[13] Scruggs's indexes take account of income replacement rates and the scope and duration of benefit coverage in three policy areas—unemployment, sickness, and pensions.

Scruggs's estimates indicate that the ultra welfare states are considerably more generous than the semi welfare states in each of the three policy areas examined. This difference in public policies between the two sets of countries is reflected in people's satisfaction with their lives. When asked about their satisfaction with various aspects of their lives, such as work, health, and family, respondents in the ultra welfare states said they were, on average, more satisfied in all three domains than those in the semi welfare states, and they also reported greater satisfaction with life in general.

The correspondence between the satisfaction and public policy differences for the two sets of countries is consistent with the findings in the SWB literature that there is a causal connection running from full employment and safety net policies to happiness. But, as a check, we investigated whether people give any evidence that they are aware of and responsive to these policy differences. One indication is provided by respondents' ratings of public services. On average, those in ultra welfare states gave consistently higher ratings of a wide range of public services: health, education, care of children and the elderly, and public pensions. They also consistently expressed greater trust in the political system. These survey results suggest that, in general, people are aware of and responsive to more generous economic and social policies and, because of these policies, are more satisfied with their lives. Although the ultra and semi welfare states have similar macroeconomic conditions, happiness is higher in the set of countries where socioeconomic policies are more generous and comprehensive.

Transition Countries

The second piece of new evidence that happiness is positively related to full employment and safety net policies comes from the experience of the transition countries. In countries moving from socialism to capitalism, there has been a substantial retreat from these policies. Hence one would expect an adverse impact on happiness, which is in fact what the evidence suggests.

Prior to the transition, the typical situation in these countries was one of full employment and a comprehensive social safety net. Here is a description of workers' pretransition conditions in three transition countries:

China

> Job rights have until very recently been firmly entrenched in urban China. . . . State-owned enterprises have . . . supplied extensive welfare benefits, including housing, medical services, pensions, childcare, and jobs for [grown] children. . . . Almost all state employees, and many in the larger collectives, have thus enjoyed an "iron rice bowl" . . . lifetime tenure of their job and a relatively high wage in the enterprise representing a "mini welfare state."[14]

East Germany

> Over the 40 years of its existence, the DDR [Deutsche Demokratische Republic (East Germany)] had developed as a completely different state from the BDR [Bundesrepublik Deutschland (West Germany)]. There was no unemployment, no (open) inflation, low work intensity, free medical services, [and] low prices for housing and public transport.[15]

Soviet Union

> Before 1989, Russians lived in a country that provided economic security: unemployment was virtually unknown, pensions were guaranteed and provided a standard of living perceived to be adequate, and macroeconomic instability did not much effect the average citizen.[16]

The similarity among these descriptions in three separate studies is striking—clearly full employment and a comprehensive safety net were the norm in these countries prior to the transition.

The movement from socialism to capitalism brought an end to full employment and the social safety net. Unemployment rates rose from near zero to two-digit levels. Safety net benefits, which were typically provided through state-owned enterprises, disappeared as workers lost jobs and/or shifted to private firms. The severity in China of the effects of this "restructuring" of the economy are suggested by the following quotations from a World Bank document:

> By all measures, S.O.E. [state-owned enterprise] restructuring had a profound effect on the functioning of the labor market

and the welfare of millions of urban workers. Most urban centers experienced a sharp rise in unemployment and a large reduction in labor force participation as many older and discouraged workers left the labor force.[17]

S.O.E. restructuring . . . mark[ed] the end of the "iron rice bowl" of guaranteed lifetime employment and benefits for urban workers.[18]

As has been seen, life satisfaction in China over the last two decades remained constant or perhaps even declined, despite a more than fourfold multiplication of output and incomes. It seems reasonable to infer that with the emergence and rise of unemployment and breakdown of the social safety net, new concerns arose among workers about such things as jobs and income security, the availability of health care and pensions, and provision for care of children and the elderly. Rapid economic growth may have partially alleviated these concerns by providing employment opportunities, but the net effect was no gain in happiness.

The survey data for East Germany, the former German Democratic Republic (GDR), provide specific evidence of the emergence of job and safety net concerns. The East German surveys ask about satisfaction not only with life in general but also about satisfaction with various aspects or domains of life, data not available for China.

Between June 1990 (just prior to the transition) and 2004, East Germans' satisfaction increased with a number of material aspects of life (as shown in the following table, Positive Changes section). Particularly noteworthy is the marked increase in satisfaction with the environment and availability of goods. These are two features of life in the GDR that were often spoken of disparagingly by contemporary observers. All of the other material dimensions of life in the table also show at least modest improvement.

Counterbalancing these improvements, however, are sizable decreases in satisfaction with health, work, and childcare (Negative Changes section of the table). Prior to the transition, people were assured of jobs and substantial social support. With the retreat from full employment and a social safety net, concerns regarding these important aspects of life mounted, and satisfaction correspondingly declined. The outcome, as in the case of China, was a negative impact on happiness, and there was no improvement in overall life satisfaction.

Satisfaction with various life domains,
East Germany, 1990 and 2004 (scale 0–10)

Domain	1990	2004	Change 1990 to 2004
Positive Changes			
Environment	3.11	6.47	+3.36
Goods availability	3.16	6.20	+3.04
Dwelling	6.93	7.36	+0.43
Standard of living	6.34	6.63	+0.29
Household income	5.52	5.61	+0.09
Negative Changes			
Health	6.62	6.20	-0.42
Work	7.23	6.48	-0.75
Childcare	7.54	6.48	-1.06
Overall life satisfaction	6.57	6.55	-0.02

Source: J. P. Haisken-DeNew and J. R. Frick, *Desktop Companion to the German Socieo-Economic Panel (SOEP), Version 8.0 DIW* (Berlin: German Institute for Economic Research, 2005).

The general conclusion is that full employment and safety net policies increase happiness. This is suggested, first, by prior studies in the happiness literature. It is seen here in the comparison of two sets of European welfare states, where, controlling for GDP per capita, people in countries with more generous and comprehensive socioeconomic policies reported greater happiness, and give subjective evidence that it is such policies that are responsible for their happiness. Finally, it is evidenced in the experience of two transition countries examined here, China and the former GDR. Despite a marked difference in their output trajectories, the two countries exhibit a similar life satisfaction pattern of no long-term improvement, resulting from a common retreat from full employment and a comprehensive safety net.

Conclusion

Since the 1990s there has been a retreat from "welfare state" policies of the sort shown here to increase happiness. Why, then, would one predict a "happier world" twenty-five years hence?

The answer is premised on the growing interest in measures of happiness among the general public and their governments and a faith that in the long run, advances in knowledge result in better government policies. As data on subjective well-being continue to accumulate, increasingly under official auspices, awareness will grow of the findings already emerging in the scholarly literature on the relation between public policy and the improvement of happiness. In the leading welfare states these policies already have widespread public support,[19] and the mounting demonstration of their value is almost certain to increasingly capture the attention of policy makers throughout the world. And, as governments respond to their constituents with appropriate public policies, there should emerge, in the course of time, a happier world.

And if this doesn't come to pass? Well, I warned you of my record for prediction.

Notes

1. J. E. Stiglitz, A. Sen, and J .P. Fitoussi, "Report of the Commission on the Measurement of Economic Performance and Social Progress," 2008, accessed November 15, 2014, http://www.stiglitz-sen-fitoussi.fr/documents/rapport_anglais.pdf.

2. R. A. Easterlin, *Growth Triumphant: The Twenty-first Century in Historical Perspective* (Ann Arbor: University of Michigan Press, 1996).

3. R. A. Easterlin et al., "The Happiness-Income Paradox Revisited," *Proceedings of the National Academy of Sciences* 107, no. 52 (2010): 22463–68.

4. Compare, for example, A. Deaton, "The Financial Crisis and Well-Being of Americans" (working paper 19128, National Bureau of Economic Research, 2011); E. Diener, L. Tay, and S. Oishi, "Rising Income and the Subjective Well-Being of Nations," *Journal of Personality and Social Psychology*, 104, no. 2 (2013): 267–76; D. W. Sacks, B. Stevenson, and J. Wolfers, "Subjective Well-Being, Income, Economic Development, and Growth," in . . . *and the Pursuit of Happi-*

ness: Well-Being and the Role of Government, ed. P. Booth (London: Institute of Economic Affairs, 2012).

5. Easterlin et al., "Happiness-Income Paradox Revisited."

6. A. Heston, R. Summers, and B. Aten, *Penn World Table Version 7.0*, Center for International Comparisons of Production, Income and Prices at the University of Pennsylvania, May 2011.

7. R. A. Easterlin et al., "China's Life Satisfaction, 1990–2010," *Proceedings of the National Academy of Sciences* 109, no. 25 (2012): 9775–80.

8. See S. C. Kassenboehmer and J. P. Haisken-DeNew, "You're Fired! The Causal Negative Effect of Entry Unemployment on Life Satisfaction," *Economic Journal* 119 (2009): 448–62, and references therein.

9. R. DiTella, R. J. MacCulloch, and A. J. Oswald, "Preferences over Inflation and Unemployment: Evidence from Surveys of Happiness," *American Economic Review* 91, no. 1 (2001): 335–41.

10. R. DiTella, R. J. MacCulloch, and A. J. Oswald, "The Macro-Economics of Happiness," *Review of Economics and Statistics* 85, no. 4 (2003): 809–27.

11. See, for example, P. Flavin, A. C. Pacek, and B. Radcliff, "State Intervention and Subjective Well-Being in Advanced Industrial Democracies," *Politics and Policy* 39, no. 2 (2011): 251–69, and references therein.

12. R. A. Easterlin, "Happiness, Growth and Public Policy," *Economic Enquiry* 51, no. 1 (2013): 1–15.

13. L. Scruggs, "Welfare State Entitlement Data Set: A Comparative Institutional Analysis of 18 Welfare States, Version 1.1" (June 1, 2005), 2004; G. Esping-Andersen, *The Three Worlds of Welfare Capitalism* (Princeton, N.J.: Princeton University Press, 1990).

14. J. Knight and L. Song, *Towards a Labour Market in China* (New York: Oxford University Press, 2005), 16–17.

15. R. Lumley, "Labour Markets and Employment Relations in Transition in Countries of Central and Eastern Europe," *Employee Relations* 17 (1995): 24–37, at 29.

16. E. Brainerd and D. M. Cutler, "Autopsy on an Empire: Understanding Mortality in Russia and the Former Soviet Union," *Journal of Economic Perspectives* 19, no. 1 (2005): 107–30, at 125.

17. World Bank, *China's Modernizing Labor Market: Trends and Emerging Challenges* (Washington, D.C.: World Bank, 2007), 19.

18. Ibid., 17.

19. G. Esping-Andersen, *Welfare States in Transition: National Adaptations in Global Economies* (London: Sage, 1996); S. Haggard and R. R. Kaufman, *Development, Democracy, and Welfare States: Latin America, East Asia, and Eastern Europe* (Princeton, N.J.: Princeton University Press, 2008).

Part Two

Politics,

Religion,

and

Human

Rights

CHAPTER 4

Politics

The World in 2040

Robert L. Gallucci

Distinguished Professor in the Practice of Diplomacy,
Georgetown University

The purpose of this brief chapter is to offer thoughts about what the world of international affairs will look like in twenty-five years. This has been tried before with mixed results, at best. Predictions about what's in store for us seem to fail most often in one of two ways: they project current trends as continuing apace, producing, after a quarter century of evolution, an entirely new landscape which, in fact, never emerges; or they predict little change, based upon the apparent weight of current conditions, a welcome or regrettable stability to the international scene, which proves to be unimaginative in the wake of surprising, singular developments of major importance. Recognizing that philosophers have spent a good bit of time contemplating the implications of free will and determinism, it still seems as though we should be better at predicting the future, if we truly understood the present and how we got here.

Aside from being humbled by the task, then, what does this observation suggest about what would be most *useful* to include in this chapter, to speculate about, recognizing how inaccurate a picture is likely to emerge? Perhaps the best that can be done is to first identify qualities of the current landscape that we expect to continue essentially unchanged, then trends that we expect to continue, and to so change the scene in important, predictable ways, and finally those "black swans" that we know are out there and would have a hugely disruptive impact on the picture in the next twenty-five years, if they were actually to cross our path.

While we are at it, though, we should also be mindful of what sorts of developments it would pay us to know of in advance. Bad things, for example, we might want to try to prevent or mitigate, or, considering the consequences, figure out ways to adapt to, if they are in fact inevitable. Knowing some of the characteristics of our situation in 2040 now could also create opportunities to take advantage of developments, not just guard against negative ones. So the plan is to note what is likely to stay the same in international politics, what we should expect to change slowly, what might really surprise us, and finally where our country is likely to fit into the picture that emerges. Clearly we may be humbled by the task, but we are not discouraged.

The System

The most fundamental, defining feature of the international system is that it is ungoverned. In twenty-five years, it will still be so. Called by some theorists a "self-help system" and by others a "state of nature," a large number of mostly sovereign states will make up the international system in 2040, and they will have to look after their own security to ensure their survival.[1] Virtually all states will continue to acquire weapons to defend themselves and their interests from other states, and they will declare that they do so for self-defense. Since the first duty of the state will always be to provide for the security of its citizens, all this armament, increasingly sophisticated and lethal in so many hands, will continue to "make sense." This, again, as long as there is no world government with an armed police force to provide security, which there will not be during the first half of the twenty-first century.

One may ask, if the use of force is going to continue to be one option states will be free to elect to achieve their goals, should we expect efforts at arms control, disarmament, and peaceful resolution of conflicts to inevitably fail? The answer is, of course, no. But the availability of the option to resort to military force will remain the key conditioning factor in any effort aimed at the resolution of disputes through negotiation or at achieving agreed limits on the development, deployment, or use of the weapons of warfare.

This realist, or even structural realist, view of the world will be seen by many as atavistic and not at all sensitive to trends in globalization, democratization, and the increasingly important role of nonstate actors, multinational corporations, and international institutions. Add here the emerging class of superwealthy global plutocrats—influential, even powerful in political and commercial areas but patriots of no nation in particular. Critics are more likely to see the international system in 2040 defined by these relatively recent trends and not the actions of governments driven by the classic security dilemma. The middle ground between these divergent views of what will matter in the future is reached by recognizing that, in general, only in matters of vital interest to governments should resort to military force be expected, and therefore it should not be a common occurrence.

Indeed, many of the interactions between people around the world will not involve governments at all, and when they do, government's role may be limited to regulating and facilitating. And when the state's interests are involved, the most salient measure of a government's ability to achieve its objectives may be in what has been called its "soft power" assets.[2] But that said, when the stakes are critical for a government, and the dispute sharp, it will be hard power, not soft, that antagonists will be measuring.

Warfare

Figuring out exactly how technology will impact the conduct of military operations when war does occur is no less challenging and arguably a lot more important than predictions in other areas of human endeavor. Anyone who has participated in war games with the American military lately will have been struck by at least two phenomena that will plausibly persist for decades to come.

The first is the continuing importance of traditional elements of military strategy, such as logistics; mobility; lethality of weaponry; achieving air superiority; control of the seas; stabile deterrence at the strategic level; flexibility and resilience in command, control, and communication; maintaining awareness of events at the tactical and operational levels of engagement; and the availability of intelligence from a variety of sources on the political and military activity of an adversary, usefully analyzed to support decision making. This has been true for centuries of modern warfare and will certainly remain so for the foreseeable future.

The second phenomenon is the way new technology, at critical moments, may create unexpected opportunities and vulnerabilities, particularly for adversaries who lack all the traditional assets that are desirable in large, protracted engagements. Think particularly about cyber and space warfare. Indeed, we have been thinking about both for decades, but we have not truly integrated that thinking into our planning, partly for bureaucratic reasons and partly because they present moving targets, hard to take account of. What is most disturbing about these technologies, as compared to other innovations, such as stealth and perhaps drones, for example, which create marginal and often temporary advantages, is that so much else in traditional military strategy depends on space and cyber assets performing as expected. And if governments decide to protect these assets by deterrence rather than genuine defense, as they appear to be doing by default, they then risk "hardwiring" dramatic escalation into their planning, particularly against an adversary whose own planning is asymmetrically focused on attacking those assets. Another way to capture this situation is to appreciate, first, the relative weakness of an adversary who, in the midst of a conflict, has no choice but to attack America's connective tissue; and second, the unwise decision on our part to promise crippling retaliation if so attacked, rather than to mount a defense. In other words, we are planning for disastrous escalation. This is not good.

Turning briefly to the causes of war, we should expect that the traditional sources of conflict between nations—that is, territorial acquisition, religious and cultural differences sharpened by historical antagonisms, and desire for regional dominance, among other causes—will still provoke armed conflict. We should add, however, that a new, intensified competition for resources may lead to war as population growth adds to demand and the effects of climate change reduce supply. Freshwater is often identified as a likely resource over which people may fight in the future, but others, from food to minerals to energy, may push nations into conflicts as well.

Finally, if we were to live through the next twenty-five years without a war between India and Pakistan, we would be fortunate indeed. There are other regions where "war is always possible," such as the Middle East, Northeast Asia, or even between China and the United States, but South Asia is different. In political and military terms, there is greater risk because of unique conditions. The history of Hindu–Muslim hostility, the circumstances of the creation of Pakistan, multiple wars, territorial loss, intermittent military engagements, significant terrorist incidents, and the simmering status of Kashmir set an unstable scene. With the Pakistani view of India as presenting a mortal threat to its existence, and an asymmetrical conventional force imbalance favoring India, Pakistan's growing nuclear weapons capability makes not just war but nuclear war plausible. For many who witnessed the evolution of NATO nuclear strategy in the 1950s, intended to counter the Warsaw Pact's perceived conventional advantage by the first use of "tactical nuclear weapons," Pakistan's declaratory policy today is eerily familiar and scary. The way out of this frame is through a change in the Pakistani view of India from its greatest threat to its best chance for economic development. But as long as the Pakistani military remain the dominant political force in that country, there will be little incentive to change the national narrative. This is a space to watch.

Power and Condition

We are inevitably attracted to two kinds of generalizations about the distribution of power in the international system: those that predict the decline of the United States and those that describe the latest rising power. In the past, these predictions have been more wrong than right. By most measures, the United States is still the greatest world power, and neither Japan nor Iran has risen as many expected some decades ago. That said, the United States is, in fact, declining, relative to a clearly rising China. If one were interested in the distribution of power in the future, beyond the question of who occupies the number one position, a simple characterization might be that Asia—from India to the Republic of Korea, to include China and Japan—will come to have more of the world's wealth and productive capacity than Europe and North America combined. That will be a change. Sub-Saharan Africa, portions of South Asia, and Latin America will continue to claim the world's poorest citizens, though their absolute level of poverty should not be as bad in the future as it has been in the past. Decades of effort in private sector investment as well as development assistance from governments, international organizations, and regional development banks aimed at improving infrastructure, health, and educational outcomes will continue to make a difference.

How exactly the shift to Asia is experienced in the West, and how dramatic it is, is yet to be determined. If India and China can sustain both solid, if not phenomenal, growth rates and a high degree of political stability—the second depending a great deal on the first—the picture is bright. The situation in the West is different, where innovation and growth need to be spurred and economies energized. Government effectiveness rather than stability is the issue, but no obvious solutions appear on the horizon.

However power is distributed in 2040, three trends likely to be important to the quality of life for large numbers of citizens in coming decades are urbanization, aging populations, and advances in information technology. By 2040, per the United Nations Population Division, 86 percent of the American population and 60 percent of the world's population will live in cities. That's about six billion people, or twice today's urban population. The magnitude of the implications that are expected to follow from such concentration is understood to be significant, but there is quite a difference in view over the "sign"; that is, whether the implications will be positive or negative for the earth's inhabitants. Virtually every aspect of life will be impacted—our security, privacy, access to food, health care, jobs, transportation, energy, environment, and recreation. Indeed, they will all be "driven" by the phenomena of urbanization. That said, the integrated study of the process has only just begun.

And if the first thing one notices about the world in twenty-five years is that its citizens live in the cities, the second thing is likely to be that so many people will be old. We are already aware of the impact on economies and questions of intergenerational equity arising from demographic change in developed countries, but the greatest stress will be felt in the less-developed world, where the population will grow old before it becomes well off and the burden of supporting the old will be felt by the young in disproportionate ways. As one study of aging put it, we will be seeing more walkers than strollers.[3] Those societies whose governments fail to plan for the consequences in their tax, welfare, and health systems, for starters, will have only painful options from which to choose in dealing with the consequences.

A third piece of the picture we will see emerge in a couple of decades will follow from continued technological advance in the collection, transmission, and analysis of information. There will be dramatic change in the global availability of what we now consider "news," in commercially useful data and communication, in access to personal interactions of all kinds, and in that which facilitates governance. Much of this we will appreciate because it will make life easier and more entertaining and make business and government more efficient and potentially more responsive. The international and the domestic context will continue to merge, and we will have the opportunity to appreciate developments anywhere in the world as local to us. But privacy in our actions and communication, as we had come to know it until the beginning of the twenty-first century, will be gone. This is a trend to watch and to manage.

Finally, with somewhat less enthusiasm than we might have expected to accompany this prediction only a few years ago, it seems entirely likely that the "wave of democracy" will continue to wash over the shores of more and more countries in the coming years. The level of enthusiasm one has for the growing numbers of democracies in the world, following the fall of the Soviet Union and the end of so many command economies run by authoritarian governments, depends greatly on one's expectations. If having relatively "free" elections is considered the essential indicator of democracy, without as much concern for freedom of expression, rule of law, and respect for individual rights, then the trend is entirely positive. If, on the other hand, the expectation is that liberal democracy is spreading as a durable phenomenon, along with responsive, effective governance in the best interest of citizens, and that some version of a "democratic peace" will follow, to mean conflict resolution without resort to force, then one might be quite disappointed. The current situation in Russia, the recent experience with the Arab Spring, and the uneven course of events in Latin America and Africa come to mind. In short, a cautious view would have us acknowledge the positive aspects of the disappearance of communism as a coherent, political-economic model competing with a democratic, market-oriented system of government. But, it would also have us not be so quick to exclude backsliding and shortfalls in the outcomes for citizens internally, and nations externally, of the democratic trends. The landscape in these terms in 2040 will probably not look dramatically different from the way it looks today.

Black Swans

To refer to black swan events at all rigorously is to identify a truly surprising event, with major impact, that may seem easily explained only after its occurrence. The impact or consequences may be bad or good, as long as they are in some sense significant. Almost by definition, then, making a list of genuine black swan events that have not yet occurred should not be possible. Undeterred, I offer here three such events that could occur over the next twenty-five years.

First, China may disintegrate as a national state rather than rise to become the world's preeminent power. The centrifugal forces that would pull China apart would be driven by a dramatic drop in the rate of growth of its economy. In the absence of any ideological or religious bonds or an external threat to provoke an impulse to binding nationalism, together with the burden of a dramatically aging population, the willingness of the people to accept centralized, authoritarian government may evaporate. This would leave a decentralized political entity that would be a good deal less than the sum of its parts. The basic assumption here is that China as a nation is substantially more fragile than most analysts believe. Of course, the Chinese government could be expected to respond with economic and political moves to mitigate the impact of any destabilizing activity before irresistible momentum could build. Interestingly, such action could include manufacturing an incident or set of incidents with the United States or Japan to create a threat intended to stimulate a nationalism that would otherwise have remained dormant. War might be chosen over internal instability. More likely, of course, China will remain whole and continue its rise, with the key question becoming whether the United States and China can accommodate each other's interests in the Asia-Pacific region, embracing competition while avoiding conflict.

A second black swan event would be the simultaneous detonation of ten-kiloton nuclear explosions in, say, four American cities—notionally New York, Washington, Chicago, and Houston. While nuclear terrorism has been called the number one external threat to the nation's security by presidents and candidates for that office since 2001, many obvious steps that could be taken to reduce the risk of a terrorist attack have not been taken. This is because such an attack is generally regarded as having a very low probability of occurrence, as well as catastrophic consequences. The argument here, however, is that large amounts of plutonium are maintained both in weapons stockpiles and in active energy programs, and that highly enriched uranium continues to be produced. Moreover, the prospects for secret transfer of such fissile material by a rogue state, or leakage from a state with an advanced but not perfectly secured energy sector, are real. Over decades, then, such transfer or leakage could easily provide a terrorist group with the necessary fissile material to overcome the single greatest obstacle to making an improvised nuclear explosive device.

Perhaps even more interesting, though, is the proposition that the probability that four American cities will be destroyed one morning is not much less than that only one city would be struck. If this were to happen, roughly a million Americans would die relatively promptly from blast, fire, and radiation following the detonations. And attacking multiple cities is something terrorists like to do to terrorize a nation. It becomes a plausible scenario because the quantity of fissile material needed to produce a yield a bit less than Hiroshima-size is so small as compared to the amount that may be accessible to terrorists. In other words, the number of cities attacked may not be sensitive to the amount of fissile material required for each weapon. If this most horrendous of events should occur in the coming decades, it would appear, after the fact, as having been "overdetermined," with hardly anyone being surprised, except possibly by the number of targets and the fact that it had not happened sooner: a true black swan event.

It is worth noting here that in the world of catastrophic events of low probability but high consequence, certain biological events could dwarf even the multiple nuclear terrorist attacks in terms of casualties. A repeat of the flulike pandemic that occurred one hundred years ago comes to mind, as does the release of an engineered, highly communicable, and lethal virus for which no vaccine was available. But more thought has gone into planning for, mitigating, and preventing such events so that they seem less like true black swans than does the nuclear terrorist scenario.

The third event that could surprise us would be the resolution of the Palestinian–Israeli conflict. This would not be the same as the outbreak of peace in the Middle East. It would be an acceptance by most Palestinian factions of the resolution of the three principal issues—the status of Jerusalem, the right of return of refugees, and a territorial settlement on the West Bank—that have for so long been claimed to be the basis for the hostility of Arabs to the state of Israel and the rejection of its right to exist.

There have been moments when this outcome seemed to be at hand, perhaps most notably in September 2000, when failure was snatched from the jaws of success. It is plausible that so long as efforts continue, those representing Palestinians in Gaza and on the West Bank will come together with an Israeli leader who has the essential domestic support to reach a durable agreement. Many observers would see such a historic breakthrough in the seemingly never-ending "peace process" as fundamentally changing the face of Middle Eastern politics forever. It would not. The unwillingness of the fabled Arab "street" to reverse its view of Israel's legitimacy should not be underestimated, nor should the continuation of division among the Arab states of the Gulf and the Levant, between Arabs and Persians, between Sunni and Shia Muslims. Peace between major factions of the Palestinians and Israel would be a surprising and welcome development, but it would fall far short of "changing everything" in the Middle East.

The United States in the World of 2040

It is now commonplace for experts in American foreign policy to characterize the threats from within our country as having a greater likelihood of damaging the nation's security than threats from abroad. This reflects a recognition, broadly shared, that the American political system is dysfunctional, lacking the basic capacity for compromise that is essential for effective governance, and that the nation's competitive position in economic and political terms has suffered and will continue to decline unless remedies can be found. First references are usually to budget and fiscal issues, which have become chronic problems in the absence of the necessary political consensus for resolution. Just below the surface of these policy disputes lie fundamental differences in the country over the proper role of government and how best to protect the individual while advancing the common good. Then the hyperconcentration of wealth and income, together with loss of economic and social mobility across generations, has undercut the presumption of fairness and equality of opportunity, historically so important to the American narrative. And finally, the intensity and anger manifest in political debate have been magnified by media that thrive on the polarization and rhetorical extremes of their daily product.

The electorate has been driven to new levels of cynicism, compounded by ignorance, creating little opportunity to persuade through evidence but an irresistible audience for "bumper sticker" arguments. At the same time, there is ample reason for cynics to thrive in light of the role that money has come to play in elections and the policies made by those who prevailed at the polls thanks to our primary system and gerrymandered districts, as well as to the largesse of the most wealthy few in American society.

In short, the first observation to make about the place of the United States in the world of 2040 is that, absent a serious adjustment in important elements of our political system that somehow provides new incentives for government at all levels to act in the best interests of the Republic, the country will increasingly become far less desirable in terms of social justice and quality of life in the eyes of its own citizens and not much of an example for the rest of the world.

That said, if we were to consider the power of the United States, judged primarily in military terms, twenty-five years hence, we would find our country still uniquely capable of projecting force with great lethality and impressive precision virtually anyplace on earth. This will be the result of the continued enthusiasm of the U.S. Congress to fund the development and deployment of the most technologically advanced weapon systems in the world and, by and large, the popularity of such systems with the American people. In short, we may fall way behind many countries in social and economic opportunity, quality of public education, basic infrastructure, competiveness, and productivity but, ironically, maintain our position as the world's number one military power.

This leads to the inevitable next question of just what the American people will be prepared to do with that power in twenty-five years. Following more than a decade of war, will the U.S. enthusiasm wane for finding vital interests far from our shores, or humanitarian interests anywhere as being any of "our business," if intervention involves significant cost in lives or treasure?

There is a connection, certainly, between perceived economic capacity for intervention and the political will to intervene, but too much should not be made of the nation's economy as limiting its capacity to act, as the determining factor in any embrace of isolation. Much more important will be the psychological impact of the economy; the nation's perceived economic health; and the openness of its people to rhetoric from political leaders that resonates with Americans' values, sense of responsibility for others, and place in the world, as well as their fundamental optimism that what we do can make a difference. Belief in American exceptionalism can motivate truly regrettable policies, but it can also be the base from which the United States can prudently intervene, ideally in coalition with others, to discourage aggression and stop atrocities.

All in all, we have painted a picture with significant risk along with some opportunities to mitigate harmful developments and promote positive outcomes. We can influence that picture by the policies we adopt or fail to embrace. Realism about the choices ahead will help us toward better outcomes; cynicism will not. Credible leadership will be in demand at home and abroad, but particularly at home. More than anything else, the United States needs an interested and informed citizenry, responsive and effective governance, and a sophisticated and subtle appreciation in its leadership of the risks and opportunities open to the nation.

Notes

1. The phrase "state of nature" has deep roots and differing meanings in the writings of several seventeenth- and eighteenth-century political philosophers, but here we mean what Hobbes meant in applying it to the character of relations between independent nation-states, where only the laws of nature apply. "Self-help," in this context, is a term used as a defining characteristic of the international political system, and a tenet of twentieth-century international relations theory, which leaves each nation-state on its own to find the means to survive. The relevance is that, according to some classical and modern political theory, the essential anarchy of the international system guarantees the permanent possibility of armed conflict between nation-states. The best discussion of this point is still found in Kenneth N. Waltz's enduring work, *Man, the State, and War* (New York: Columbia University Press, 2001), first published in 1959.

2. The term "soft power" has come to mean a way of influencing the behavior of nations that depends upon co-opting and attracting them to a desired

position, rather than moving them to it by coercion or inducement. See Joseph S. Nye Jr., *Soft Power: The Means to Success in World Politics* (New York: Public Affairs, 2004).

3. The MacArthur Foundation's "Research Network on an Aging Society" asks us "to imagine a society with many more seniors with walkers than youngsters in strollers."

CHAPTER 5

Religion

The Future of American Religion

Eboo Patel
Founder and President, Interfaith Youth Core

For my money, the most penetrating insight into the future of religion in twenty-first-century America came from a Canadian scholar writing about South Asia in the 1940s. Wilfred Cantwell Smith was teaching at a Christian missionary college in Lahore (then a part of an undivided India under British rule, now located in Pakistan) and one day woke up to a realization both remarkable and obvious: most of his faculty colleagues were Hindus, Sikhs, and Muslims, as were the majority of his students. For Cantwell Smith, both a committed Presbyterian and a budding scholar of comparative religions, it was an observation that set off a series of questions. How might frequent and intense interaction between people of various faiths impact everything from the religious identities of individuals to the theologies of religious traditions to the self-understanding and social cohesion of increasingly religiously diverse societies?

Such questions were underscored by the larger context in which Cantwell Smith lived. After all, it was not just the microenvironment of that missionary college in Lahore that was religiously diverse; the entire subcontinent was roiling with religious energies. Gandhi's Hindu-based satyagraha movement was poised to liberate India. Jinnah's push for a separate state for Muslims was gaining steam. Chapters of inspiring interreligious cooperation alternated regularly with spasms of religiously motivated slaughter. The worst of the violence took place at the time of partition, when a million people murdered one another in hand-to-hand combat, most of them Hindus, Sikhs, and Muslims, members of the very same communities teaching and studying together in Cantwell Smith's college.

One of the most interesting parts of Cantwell Smith's essay is the section he includes on the cities of North America. From his perch amid the diversity of 1940s Lahore, he couldn't help but see Louisville and Los Angeles as an "oversimplified religious society . . . partial and unrepresentative."[1] He cautioned that they would not remain so for long. The seemingly exceptional diversity he was experiencing in the subcontinent would soon become the norm around the world. "The religious life of humankind from now on, if it is to be lived at all," he wrote, "will be lived in a context of religious pluralism."[2]

I thought of Cantwell Smith as I stood on the National Mall on a cold January day in 2009, listening to President Barack Obama declare in his first inaugural address:

> For we know that our patchwork heritage is a strength, not a weakness. We are a nation of Christians and Muslims, Jews and Hindus, and non-believers. We are shaped by every language and culture, drawn from every end of this Earth . . . we cannot help but believe that the old hatreds shall someday pass; that the lines of tribe shall soon dissolve; that as the world grows smaller, our common humanity shall reveal itself; and that America must play its role in ushering in a new era of peace.[3]

The first African American president of the United States, staring out at the Lincoln Memorial as he addressed the nation and the world, chose to highlight the religious dimensions of the country's diversity. He could have added to the list of American faith communities Sikhs, Jains, Buddhists, and practitioners of indigenous traditions. The United States has sizable communities of all of the above, and many more religious groups as well. In the words of Harvard scholar Diana Eck, the United States has gone from a Christian country to the most religiously diverse nation in human history. Much of this change has occurred in the past fifty years and went largely unnoticed until the events of September 11, 2001.

Like Cantwell Smith's Christian missionary college in Lahore, the United States is a relatively peaceful island in a world of clashing religious energies. Most certainly, faith-fueled violence has impacted these shores—9/11, Fort Hood, the Boston Marathon, the murderous rampage at the Oak Creek Gurudwara—but it is a far cry from the regular violence that marks daily life in countries like Iraq, Egypt, Afghanistan, Syria, and even Northern Ireland and India. Yet diaspora groups from all sides of those conflicts live here in the United States, and American foreign policy has a hand (and in some cases an army) involved in each of the countries above. Our religious diversity can become barriers of division, bubbles of isolation, bombs of destruction, or bridges of cooperation. This chapter explores what that broad religious diversity and intense interaction mean for the future of the United States. But before hazarding guesses about the quarter century ahead, I want to take a quick look back. The recent past presents the themes we ought to be exploring and the trend lines we should be watching. Good stuff, in other words, to argue about.

The 1950s and 1960s

One hallmark of the 1950s and 1960s was greater acceptance for Catholics and Jews in American life. The notion of America as a "Judeo-Christian" nation was a creation of this period. In 1948, 20 percent of Americans told pollsters they would not want a Jew for a neighbor. By 1959, that number had fallen to 2 percent. In 1960, the nation elected its first Catholic president in John F. Kennedy, and fears of the pope taking up residence in the White House did not come to pass. A central theme in Will Herberg's 1955 book *Protestant-Catholic-Jew*, perhaps the era's most influential work in the sociology of religion, was that the United States had become a nation of three religions, each viewed as equally American. It was a message reinforced by statements from President Eisenhower—"Whatever our individual church, whatever our personal creed, our common faith in God is a common bond among us"—and in national campaigns such as Brotherhood Week.[4]

It was not just the nation adapting to diversity: the church was changing as well. The early 1960s saw the most important theological shifts in Catholicism in centuries. In the Second Vatican Council conferences that took place from 1962 to 1965, the Roman Catholic Church (influenced in no small part by the American Jesuit theologian John Courtney Murray) articulated clear support for religious freedom and highlighted its commonalities with other religious traditions. Georgetown scholar John W. O'Malley says that one of the main themes of Vatican II was reconciliation with other faiths: "For the first time, Catholics were encouraged to foster friendly relations with Orthodox and Protestant Christians, as well as Jews and Muslims, and even to pray with them. The council condemned all forms of anti-Semitism and insisted on respect for Judaism and Islam as Abrahamic faiths, like Christianity."[5]

Just as the United States was growing comfortable with understanding itself as a Judeo-Christian society, a whole new set of people were landing on these shores. The Immigration Act of 1965 opened America's doors to immigrants from Asia, Africa, and Latin America. À la Cantwell Smith, Lahore was literally coming to Los Angeles and Louisville. The people who arrived brought with them not only their advanced degrees in medicine and engineering (the law had strong preferences for people trained in the applied sciences) but also such Eastern religions as Islam, Hinduism, and Buddhism. It's interesting to note that significant Catholic and Jewish immigration to the United States occurred largely in the mid-to-late nineteenth and early twentieth centuries. It took American society approximately eighty years to fully adapt its national identity from a Protestant country to a Judeo-Christian nation. We are now at about the fifty-year mark from the beginning of large-scale immigration of Muslims and communities outside of the Abrahamic traditions to the United States.

Religion played a prominent role in the era's politics in its influence in the civil rights movement. African American churches were central organizing hubs for demonstrators, and African American preachers were the movement's most important leaders. Reverend Dr. Martin Luther King Jr. once said: "I am many things to many people, but in the quiet recesses of my heart, I am fundamentally a clergyman, a Baptist preacher. This is my being and my heritage . . ."[6]

The 1970s and 1980s

The 1950s was a high point for religiosity in the United States. Between 1950 and 1957, for example, weekly church attendance skyrocketed from 31 to 51 percent for young adults (in their twenties). Also in 1957, 69 percent of Americans told pollsters that "religion is increasing its influence on American life" and presumably saw it as a good thing.[7] The crash came quickly. In 1962, the percentage of Americans who saw religion's influence growing fell 24 percentage points from its high in 1957 to 45 percent. In 1965, it was 33 percent; in 1968 it was 18 percent; in 1969 and 1970 it was 14 percent.[8] No doubt such statistical trends encouraged a set of scholars to advance secularization theory (the idea that as societies modernize, they necessarily become less religious) and justified *Time* magazine's famous "Is God Dead?" cover in 1966.[9]

American religiosity defied the predictions and made a comeback in the 1970s. The percentage of Americans who told pollsters that religion's influence was growing jumped from the low of 14 percent in 1970 to 44 percent in 1976.[10] That same year the United States elected its first avowedly "born-again" Christian president, Jimmy Carter.

Two forms of evangelical Christian religiosity grew prominent in the 1970s and 1980s. The first was the rise of "megachurches," defined by sociologists as churches with more than two thousand members in average weekend attendance. The archetypal institutions of this movement include Willow Creek (founded in the suburbs of Chicago in 1975) and Saddleback (founded in the sprawl of Southern California in 1980). The second form that defined the religiosity comeback of the 1970s and 1980s was the rise of the religious right. The archetypal figures here are Jerry Falwell and Pat Robertson. They also ran huge and highly effective organizations, but were both more overtly political and gleefully polarizing than their megachurch brethren. The religious right's biggest victory was helping to bring Ronald Reagan to power in the 1980s. Jimmy Carter, though born-again, was not sharply enough to the right for them.

Megachurch Christians smiled and hugged while religious right Christians scowled and scolded, but both leaned the same way on key social and political issues, especially issues that revolved around the politics and practice of sex. In fact, as social scientists Robert Putnam and David Campbell convincingly show in *American Grace*, views on the practice and politics of sexuality have been the key dividing line in American religion for the past half century.[11] To put it somewhat crassly, a critical mass of young people rejected the traditional religious strictures around premarital sex in the 1960s and chose sleeping in each other's beds on Saturday nights over sitting in the pews on Sunday morning. In the 1970s, the pews fought back, reasserting their views around traditional sexual practice in the broader culture. They were especially galvanized by the 1973 *Roe v. Wade* ruling that legalized abortion, essentially angered into political action by their view that the Supreme Court was siding with the sexual libertines.

The prominence of sexual politics was the reason behind one of the most remarkable shifts in the socioreligious landscape in American history: the alignment of Catholics with evangelical Protestants. Evangelicals had long been the loudest anti-Catholic voices in the United States. In the election of 1960, even such mainstream evangelical preachers as Billy Graham overtly organized against Kennedy. Starting in the 1970s, evangelicals and Catholics (the largest two religious communities in the country) decided to put aside their differences and past prejudices and made common cause on everything from abortion to homosexuality to the "coarsening" (read: too much sex) of Hollywood movies and rock music. It is a fascinating example of how shifting politics can catalyze interesting new alignments.

As religion's influence in American politics grew in this period, so did its role in world affairs more generally. Pope John Paul II galvanized the Solidarity movement in Poland. Archbishop Desmond Tutu played a key role in the struggle against apartheid in South Africa. The Mujahideen (with U.S. backing) ejected the Soviets from Afghanistan. And, most remarkably, a movement of religious zealots overthrew the Western-backed dictatorship of the Shah in Iran and installed their version of a Shia Muslim theocracy under Ayatollah Khomeini.

One of the hottest theories about religion in the 1980s is that it had become "privatized," meaning essentially that faith might stay alive in people's hearts and homes but would no longer play a role in politics or the public square. Like the secularization theories of the 1960s, the facts on the ground simply spoke louder than the books of the scholars. The bottom line was that religion refused to be quarantined. Instead, in various ways, it demanded to be heard, frequently with the sound of an explosion.

The 1990s to Now

Religion continued to play a powerful role in world affairs in the late twentieth and early twenty-first centuries, most prominently in the form of violence and conflict. The Taliban, a totalitarian Muslim group, emerged from the post-Soviet civil war in Afghanistan to rule that nation, oppressing women and other Muslim groups along the way. One of their policies was to give shelter to the leadership of a global Muslim extremist movement called Al Qaeda, which, one year, nine months, and eleven days into the new century, changed the world in the most violent and vicious fashion. The attacks of 9/11 set in motion the American-led wars in Iraq and Afghanistan. They also made a clear statement about the continuing influence of religion in world affairs.

The international headlines of the past quarter century seem to be one long commercial for Samuel Huntington's clash-of-civilizations theory (first advanced in a 1993 *Foreign Affairs* article), which posited that violence rooted in religious identity would play a key role in the post–Cold War world order.[12] Slobodan Milošević's Serbian army, holding up three fingers (meant to signify the Trinity), ran roughshod over Muslim-majority areas in Bosnia in the early 1990s. In 1998, India elected the Hindu-nationalist BJP, which tested a nuclear device and named it "the Hindu bomb." Pakistan responded with its own nuclear test, dubbed "the Muslim bomb." Homegrown Christian terrorists have murdered people in dramatic fashion in the United States, most prominently at the Atlanta Olympics. The hope of the Oslo Accords for peace between Israelis and Palestinians dissolved in the assassination of Yitzhak Rabin and the disappointment at Camp David.

Some observers wondered whether there could be a clash of civilizations in the United States. Given the prevalence of Arabic prayer as the soundtrack to so much of the violence on the international news, the spotlight turned to Muslims in the United States. Was Islam—which Huntington famously said "had bloody borders"—a fifth column within the country? It was a question that many people were not too shy to ask. Conservative talk show host Glenn Beck's opening line to his guest Keith Ellison, the first Muslim ever elected to the U.S. Congress, was, "Sir, prove to me that you are not working with our enemies."[13]

The concern around Muslims in the United States came to the fore when a prominent Sufi imam named Feisal Abdul Rauf tried to start a Muslim community center near New York City's Ground Zero in 2010. Imam Rauf initially called the project Cordoba House, a name meant to evoke a Muslim civilization in medieval Andalusia marked by cooperation between different religions. He described it as a sort of Muslim YMCA with programs that would benefit the whole neighborhood. The growing U.S. anti-Muslim movement saw a ripe target. Imam Rauf and his supporters (of which I was one) found themselves under constant attack by claims that Cordoba House was intended as a victory mosque to honor the extremists of 9/11 and would be used as a terrorist command center. The "Ground Zero Mosque" story dominated the news that summer and became a prominent theme in many of the political races in 2010. Truth be told, the opposition won the battle. The grand designs for Cordoba House had to be shelved; its operations and programs went forward but are far more modest than originally hoped.

Partly as a result of controversies like the one surrounding Cordoba House and the rising prejudice against Muslims and other religious minorities in the United States (Sikhs have experienced vicious attacks, with the turbans observant Sikh men wear often mistaken as a symbol of Islam), mainstream civic and political institutions have started engaging religious diversity in the United States. One part of this engagement is examining the sources of prejudice. The Center for American Progress issued a report entitled *Fear Inc.*, which revealed that the anti–Cordoba House movement was not so much spontaneous citizen activism as a network of well-funded organizations waiting for a ripe opportunity to marginalize Muslims. Another part is promoting religious pluralism as a central American value. As think tanks such as the Aspen Institute issued reports calling the religious diversity of the United States an important national resource, scholarly research on religious diversity grew, as did the number of interfaith nonprofit organizations, and the White House got involved by launching the President's Interfaith and Community Service Campus Challenge, which engaged five hundred college campuses in interfaith action.

The other big theme of the last quarter century was the sexual abuse crisis in the Roman Catholic Church. Not only was priest after priest in country after country found to have molested children, but bishops the world over were involved in covering up the scandal, reassigning accused priests to other parishes rather than referring them to the civil authorities. As might have been expected, the clerical abuse and cover-up crisis caused a drove of Catholics to leave the church. As people examined the exodus, they discovered that Catholics leaving the church was not just a recent trend, it was a consistent process that had been taking place since the 1960s. Since that time, *60 percent* of white Catholics have either switched to another faith or lapsed. This means that roughly 10 percent of all Americans are *former* Catholics. Many of the pews abandoned by white Catholics have been filled by Latino Catholics, but even there the story is not all good for the church as an increasing number of Latinos convert to charismatic Protestant communities or become "religious nones."[14]

Catholics are not the only ones affected by decline. Roughly 60 percent of mainline Protestants have switched or lapsed since the 1960s.[15] Unlike with Catholics, no new immigrant group is replacing the people who have left those Protestant churches. Jewish decline appears equally steep. While only 7 percent of "greatest generation" Jews (born between 1914 and 1927) call themselves "Jews of no religion," 32 percent of millennial Jews (born after 1980) say that's the case.[16]

This growth in the category of "religious nones" is one of the most important religion stories of recent times. The number has risen in dramatic fashion in a brief period, from about 7 percent of the total American population in 1990 to about 20 percent today. Most alarming, one out of three eighteen- to twenty-nine-year-olds checks the "none" box on surveys of religion.[17]

There is a tendency to conflate the increase in religious nones with the growth of "aggressive atheist" voices in public life, but the data do not bear out such a connection. For all the attention that writers such as Christopher Hitchens and Sam Harris have gotten in the past few years, their views represent a fairly small percentage of Americans as a whole, including the "nones." In the United States, it turns out that two-thirds of our self-described nonreligious people believe in God and about one-fifth report praying on a daily basis. Some even go to church on occasion.[18]

If a principled absence of religious belief does not explain the rise in the nones over the past quarter century, what does? Putnam and

Campbell again point to sex. As culturally conservative religion flexed its muscles in public life in the 1970s and 1980s, a whole new generation of young people responded by leaving the pews. If religion meant condemning homosexuality and refraining from premarital sex, they decided it was not for them.

The Future

If religion were a stock and you were the betting type in 1957, you would have probably bought. All signs pointed up. Ten years later, the last thing you would have wanted in your portfolio was religion. And so it goes in the volatile world of predicting religion. Sometimes the line goes straight and sometimes it zigzags. Before hazarding my guesses about the future, let me say that I'm a moderately progressive American Muslim who has a doctorate in the sociology of religion and runs an interfaith organization that works largely in higher education. I'm also an optimist. No doubt my predictions are colored by those various lenses.

As I said at the beginning of this chapter, I think the most important theme in American religion is wider religious diversity and more frequent interaction between people who orient around religion differently, including the nones. That diversity can take four major forms: bubbles of isolation, barriers of division, bombs of destruction, or bridges of cooperation.

I believe that in 2040 American religious diversity will be defined largely by bridges of cooperation. I also believe this will be fairly unique in the world. The reason for this is that the most organized groups in the large number of new democracies across the world (which includes not only majority-Muslim countries such as Egypt, Iraq, Libya, and Afghanistan but also countries such as Myanmar, where the Muslim minority faces violence from an extremist Buddhist movement) are organized along ethno-religious fault lines (Sunni/Shia/Kurd in Iraq, secular versus Muslim Brotherhood in Egypt). The battle for the levers of government in these countries is unlikely to be entirely peaceful for a long, long time. Whether another Osama bin Laden will emerge and build an Al Qaeda–like global network that tilts the axis of world affairs is not beyond the scope of possibility, but the fact that governments are now on the lookout for such a group makes it somewhat less likely.

Religious Diversity in the United States

I believe that by 2040 the United States will proudly view itself as an interfaith country, much the way we take pride in our multiculturalism today. History is a useful guide here. A century ago, the United States was both profoundly antisemitic and anti-Catholic. Today, Catholics and Jews are among the most favorably viewed religious communities in the country.

I think the same forces that propelled Catholics and Jews into the American mainstream are at work with newer religious minorities such as Muslims. The first is a growing interfaith movement in civil society. In the early twentieth century, organizations such as the National Conference on Christians and Jews (NCCJ) ran programs and campaigns that helped create both the civic fabric and the public consciousness of the United States as a "Judeo-Christian" nation. The NCCJ emerged in large part to fight the anti-Catholic forces that came to the fore against Al Smith in the 1928 presidential campaign. As religious prejudice has grown in recent years, a twenty-first-century version of this movement is doing the same for the nation's wider religious diversity. The general pattern in American history is that the forces of prejudice strike first and win a few battles, and then the forces of pluralism go into action and win the war. We are already seeing this pattern emerge once again.

Since the events of September 11, there has been a dramatic growth in interfaith activities and organizations. Generally speaking, there is little quality control or sense of focus regarding these activities. That will change in the next twenty-five years. Civic sectors focused on education, public health, and poverty alleviation have been transformed by the scientific use of data and the application of management techniques. As interfaith becomes a thriving sector, it will have to employ the same approaches—naming what it hopes to achieve and showing progress toward specific goals.

The second force at work propelling Muslims into the American mainstream is the national narrative about integrating newcomers into the American fabric, welcoming their contributions and appreciating their differences. We take pride in the motto *E Pluribus Unum*—out of many, one. This narrative is deeply woven into the American psyche and has practical consequences. Think of the way Barack Obama ran his first presidential campaign. Ralph Ellison aptly captured this arc in the following way: "The irrepressible movement of American culture towards integration of its most diverse elements continues, confounding the circumlocutions of its staunchest opponents."[19]

The final force at work is the Americanization of religious minority groups. I mean this entirely positively, and I see it happening with Muslims in the United States in real time. When Muslims from South Asia and the Middle East started immigrating in the 1960s and 1970s, they largely balkanized along different ethnic, national, and theological lines (different mosques for different groups) and sought to bubble themselves off from American culture, just as recently immigrated Jews and Catholics did in their day.

And similar to the second and third generations of those communities, American Muslims are going from an attitude of balkanization to a "big tent" mentality and from trying to bubble themselves off from the culture to building bridges to the broader society. There might still be separate mosques for the first generation, but the children of Shias from Iran and Sunnis from Egypt pray together in the same campus Muslim student associations and, generally speaking, have two words for each other: fellow Muslims. Moreover, even as they were raised with stories (hugely mythologized) of their parents' homelands, they cannot help but view the United States as the country where they will raise families and make careers, and so they begin to set about not only wholeheartedly building their lives here but also shaping their nation. We see this process at work with the impressive growth in an American Muslim civil sector, with organizations such as the Inner City Muslim Action Network in Chicago proudly declaring its Muslim inspiration to serve all. This process is accelerated by the fact that the most important scholars in American Islam are emphatic that it is a Muslim duty to enrich the society in which you live rather than focusing only on what is happening "back home."

Religion, Sex, and Politics

The headlines of the day suggest the continued intersection of sexual politics and religion, especially with respect to gay marriage and contraception. This intersection has been hugely divisive and is the primary reason for the exodus of young people from religious communities over the past twenty-five years. This is one key reason that I don't believe sexual issues will dominate religion's role in politics in the next quarter century. Many of the older people who oppose gay marriage now simply will not be around. Those who are will find that they have a gay grandson or granddaughter whose wedding they would like to attend. My guess is they will go, party like rock stars, and change their minds about homosexuality.

I believe that in 2040 the big issues on which religious communities will carve out a major role will be climate change and poverty alleviation. I think there are several reasons for this. The first is that climate change and poverty alleviation touch on deep-rooted values across religious traditions (stewardship and justice, to name two), and in a quarter century they will be genuine social crises on which religious communities will have a powerful opportunity to cooperate and unique standing on which to speak.

The best recent example of this involvement is Pope Francis. The approach he's carved out early in his papacy is the road that most American religious communities will be taking in a quarter century. In his own words, "it is not necessary to talk of these things [abortion, contraception] all the time."[20] He famously likened the church to a field hospital and said that when a doctor treats someone on the battlefield, it's not the patient's cholesterol level that is the doctor's primary concern. Right now, religious communities are the walking wounded, and if they hope to thrive in the next quarter century, they will choose to emphasize matters of cosmic significance (as climate change and inequality are) without being flagrantly divisive, either between generations or between religions.

I think there is a larger lesson to the positive attention Pope Francis has received: religious figures still have remarkable power. If an ordinary person is asked how he or she feels about gay people and responds by saying, "Who am I to judge?" it is entirely forgettable. When a major religious leader says the same thing, it makes headlines for months. When a home health care aide washes the feet of his or her patients and the aide and the patient happen to be of different religions, it's just a part of the job. When a pope washes people's feet and two of those people happen to be Muslim, it changes the atmosphere between huge communities. There is a deep hunger, in the United States especially, for religious figures who lift people up.

The Religious Nones

Will Pope Francis or anyone else shift what is probably the single largest religious phenomenon in the United States—namely, the blasé attitude toward faith communities? Religious innovators in the form of megachurch pastors such as Bill Hybels of Willow Creek and Rick Warren of Saddleback emerged in the 1970s to recapture some of the religious nones of their era. I'm confident that the tradition of American religious innovation will continue, and new leaders and institutions will emerge to bring some of the nones back into various religious folds. However excellent these leaders may be, they will be battling the broader cultural wind. The growth of individualism, the continual erosion of confidence in institutional structures, the delaying of adulthood markers (such as marriage) associated with churchgoing, the ease with which one can sit in bed and get what one wants with the touch of a button (and soon, when Google Glass becomes standard, with the twitch of an eye) makes any kind of community that asks things of its members hard to form and maintain. My own guess is that, like today, there will be a lot of churn—switching between religious communities, leaving for a while and then going back, and so on. The upshot is that the number of nones will remain largely the same twenty-five years from now—20 percent of Americans as a whole, 33 percent of younger people.

Frankly, this keeps me up at night, not out of concern for the souls of the nones (I believe God's mercy and welcome are wider than we can ever imagine) or the moral character of the nation (I've met enough religious jerks to know that belief in God does not necessarily make a good person) but for the future of American social capital. In *American Grace*, Putnam and Campbell find that people involved in faith communities give money and volunteer time more frequently, to more places and in larger quantities, than their secular counterparts do. And they don't just direct their energies toward their own faith communities but also to secular causes that benefit a broad range of people. In fact, at least half of American social capital—our volunteerism, our philanthropy, our civic institutions from hospitals to social service agencies—is related to religious communities. We take for granted the crucial role they play in our nation. As religious communities lose members and vitality, there seems no way of avoiding an adverse impact on civil society.

Notes

1. Wilfred C. Smith, *Patterns of Faith around the World*, 3rd edition (Boston: Oneworld Publications, 1998), 22.

2. Ibid.

3. Barack Obama, "Inaugural Address," Jan. 21, 2009, http://www.whitehouse.gov/.

4. Interfraternity Conference Minutes, Sessions 39–40 (1947–48), 39th Annual Session, Nov. 28–29, 1947, 122–26, cited in Kevin M. Schultz, *Tri-Faith America* (New York, Oxford University Press, 2011), 75.

5. John W. O'Malley, "Opening the Church to the World," *New York Times*, http://www.nytimes.com/2012/10/11/opinion/vatican-ii-opened-the-church-to-the-world.html.

6. Charles Marsh, *The Beloved Community* (New York: Basic Books, 2005), 6.

7. Robert D. Putnam and David E. Campbell, *American Grace: How Religion Divides and Unites Us* (New York: Simon and Schuster, 2010), 90.

8. Ibid., chapter 3.

9. Ibid., 95.

10. Ibid., 100.

11. Ibid., chapter 4.

12. Samuel Huntington, "The Clash of Civilizations?" *Foreign Affiars* 72, no. 3 (Summer 2013), http://www.foreignaffairs.com/articles/48950/samuel-p-huntington/the-clash-of-civilizations.

13. Glenn Beck quoted in CNN Transcripts, November 14, 2006, http://transcripts.cnn.com/TRANSCRIPTS/0611/14/gb.01.html.

14. Putnam and Campbell, chapter 5.

15. Ibid., 141.

16. Pew, "Survey of Jewish Americans," 2013, http://www.pewforum.org/2013/12/03/infographic-survey-of-jewish-americans/#spotlight-on-jews-of-no-religion-and-on-intermarriage.

17. Pew, "'Nones' on the Rise," 2012, http://www.pewforum.org/2012/10/09/nones-on-the-rise/.

18. Ibid.

19. Jeffrey Stout, *Democracy and Tradition* (Princeton, N.J.: Princeton University Press, 2004), 47.

20. Pope Francis, quoted in Antonio Spadaro, "A Big Heart Open to God," *America: The National Catholic Review*, September 30, 2013.

CHAPTER 6

Human Rights

Freedom's Future

Wendy Kaminer
Lawyer and Social Critic

"I reckon I got to light out for the territory," Huck Finn famously concludes, considering the alternative: adoption by Tom's Aunt Sally and submission to the restraints of "sivilized" society. Huck's capture by custom and culture would have been metaphoric. Jim had been in chains. From his perspective, Huck had always been free. But Huck won't settle (and we wouldn't have him settle) for not being enslaved. Freedom is relative. For Jim it means, "I owns myself." For Huck it requires escape from respectability—the religious and social norms of "sivilization." He disconnects, lighting out for the West, alone.

Put community first, and you might see him lighting out for anarchy and anomie. Put freedom first, and you see him heading toward autonomy, recognizing in the relatively anarchic territories the prospect of self-invention. Put freedom first, and you might envy him his opportunities.

It's not the loss of virgin territories that imprisons us today. The frontier was settled long ago. It's the loss of privacy and the anonymity that privacy enables. Huck can escape his past and the roles it thrust upon him. Forging a new identity, he can fashion an unencumbered future. We can't.

Try to imagine shedding your old identity and inventing a new one in an age of ubiquitous surveillance. To travel incognito, or communicate with anyone privately, without revealing your location, you'd need the resources and skills of Jason Bourne, who is, after all, a fictional character. Yet armed with multiple passports, fluent in multiple languages, even he couldn't evade every surveillance camera on earth. How would you? Let's say you undergo extensive facial reconstruction to fool facial recognition software. You'd still need a magic wand to erase the virtual profile of you compiled by government and corporate snoops. Even if you've never established a Twitter or Facebook account or engaged in any social media, you have an invisible but indelible digital shadow. You deepen it every day.

Freedom's death may be greatly exaggerated, but its decline is indisputable and its future is in doubt. It will be expanded, restricted, or redefined by rapidly evolving technologies that make speculating about the next forty years like speculating about the next four hundred. It's contingent as well on states of war, peace, and scarcity. Looking ahead, perhaps all you can say with relative certainty is that people who hold unchecked power will abuse it. Governments will seek to spy on their citizens, sometimes with "good" intentions, and always with the aid of new technologies. Looking ahead, we might look back to the warning Supreme Court Justice Louis Brandeis issued nearly one hundred years ago: in a famous dissent, he urged application of Fourth Amendment protections to telephones and other new communication technologies that arm governments with "subtler and more far-reaching means of invading privacy. . . . The progress of science in furnishing the Government with means of espionage is not likely to stop with wiretapping."[1]

As science progresses, the intrusive impulses of government officials will stay the same, Brandeis suggested. Plus ça change, you might say (unless you expect technology to alter human nature). Predictions seem infelicitous. Having failed to preserve our freedom, we first need to account for what's been lost, to prepare for the possibility and formidable challenge of restoring it.

The Bill of Rights is not yet dead letter, but it does sometimes seem in danger of becoming a Bill of Right—the Second Amendment right to bear arms. First Amendment freedoms of speech and association, Fourth Amendment rights against unwarranted search and seizure, and Fifth and Sixth Amendment due process and fair trial rights are all under assault and greatly diminished. Surveillance is a primary weapon in the war on rights, which means that regaining some measure of privacy is essential to any hope of defeating it.

Freedom, as many of us knew it, resided partly in a private sphere of thoughts and actions, not the business of the state. That sphere has been shrinking for years, as legal and regulatory regimes have grown, limiting speech as well as conduct; dramatic expansions of the federal criminal code have been especially corrosive. The war on drugs began the evisceration of Fourth Amendment rights that the war on terror seems intent on completing. 9/11 intensified an ongoing government assault on freedom, widening and deepening official intrusions into what were once our private lives.

Many of us have participated willingly, even enthusiastically, in the destruction of boundaries between private and public, trading privacy for the promise and pleasures of social media or embracing the exhibitionism of celebrity culture and, in the process, acclimating ourselves to surveillance. Many have participated inadvertently as communication, business, and social relations have moved online. All of us have lost control, unwittingly. Even people who intentionally trade privacy for publicity probably don't intend to trade control over what they reveal and conceal. Whether we welcomed or accepted life online, we were not necessarily welcoming or accepting the loss of agency and possibility of a personal life.

Still a majority of Americans did acquiesce in the creation of a security/surveillance state, not because we were tempted by technology but because we were terrified. Fear has always been the enemy of freedom. The public's fear of street crime helped enable a repressive, counterproductive war on drugs, characterized by increasingly violent, militarized police forces[2] and a harsh mandatory sentencing regime that made the United States a leader in imprisoning its own citizens. The public's fear of terror rationalized summary, indefinite detentions, the demonization of political movements, and crackdowns on political protests.[3] Fear combined with twenty-first-century technologies enabled unprecedented surveillance.

It's an indirect, invisible, but hardly ineffective means of silencing political dissent and deterring political change. Surveillance inevitably (and perhaps intentionally) chills free speech. People are a lot less likely to voice opinions, disseminate information, or engage in conversations that would anger or merely displease a watchful, distrustful, and punitive government. A 2013 survey by PEN America found that "American writers are not only overwhelmingly worried about government surveillance, but are engaging in self-censorship as a result."[4]

Political speech doesn't require much courage or sacrifice in a genuine democracy. But silence is a rational, risk-averse response to an intrusive, authoritarian state, which instills, fuels, and feeds off fear, including fear of change wrought by social and political protests. It's a familiar dynamic that enabled less comprehensive twentieth-century surveillance. The National Security Agency, created in 1952, began spying on Americans during the Cold War. Later, the FBI and CIA targeted civil rights activists and antiwar protesters. In the wake of Nixon Administration scandals, the Church Committee, led by Idaho Senator Frank Church, investigated, exposed, and limited these abuses, temporarily.[5]

Prospects for comparable congressional action in our post-9/11 world can best be described as uncertain, but not entirely utopian. Even modest reforms, however, depend on relative calm and an increased public sense of security, or a new willingness to tolerate risk. And if we don't suffer another large-scale attack, members of Congress or the judiciary, inclined to restrict surveillance and contract the security state, would still face greater challenges in the twenty-first century than their twentieth-century counterparts might have imagined. The disregard for liberty of federal security agencies and the treacherous tendency of high-ranking officials to trust themselves with unaccountable power are unchanged, but technology is not, to say the least; and it will not easily be limited by law. J. Edgar Hoover launched his career in the 1920s armed with index cards targeting political dissidents. Law enforcement and national security tsars today exploit digital surveillance tools that covertly see, hear, record, and store detailed information about virtually everyone. They have violated laws in the past and will violate them again in the future. If enacting substantive curbs on surveillance is hard, enforcing them is even harder. If Hoover were born again today, he'd think he'd died and gone to heaven.

While the future of freedom is in doubt, continued surveillance is assured. It will only "get worse," Edward Snowden has warned:

The storage capability of these systems increases every year consistently by orders of magnitude to where it's getting to the point—you don't have to have done anything wrong. You simply have to eventually fall under suspicion from somebody, even by a wrong call. And then they can use this system to go back in time and scrutinize every decision you've ever made, every friend you've ever discussed something with. And attack you on that basis to sort of derive suspicion from an innocent life and paint anyone in the context of a wrongdoer.... it's gonna get worse with the next generation and the next generation who extend the capabilities of this sort of architecture of oppression.[6]

We are slouching toward totalism. It's safe to say that Snowden understands this "architecture of oppression" much more than members of Congress who defend it. His warning that surveillance capacities will only expand, increasing the risk of persecution for innocent people in the future, should not be dismissed as alarmism—not when we're under the paranoid eye of the surveillance state in the present.

Civil liberties groups chronicled and challenged war on terror excesses for years. Snowden and a few intrepid journalists exposed the depth and scope of domestic spying. The gratuitous abuses of counterterror initiatives, like torture and indefinite detention, have been regularly documented. (You could look them up.) For now, consider as an example just one, simple, relatively small and primitive branch of the surveillance state not dependent on a renegade National Security Agency (NSA)—state and local, post-9/11 "fusion centers," intended to collect reports of suspicious activity, in the interests of deterring terrorism. In 2010 a Senate subcommittee found that these centers were wasteful intelligence failures: they "often produced irrelevant, useless or inappropriate intelligence reporting to (the Department of Homeland Security), and many produced no intelligence reporting whatsoever."[7] They did succeed, however, in curtailing civil liberty.

"Around the country, peaceful political organizations have been monitored and labeled as 'terrorist' groups," the ACLU of Massachusetts observed. "In Virginia, it was historically black colleges and universities. In Maryland, it was Amnesty International and an ardent death penalty coalition. In Missouri, it was Libertarian Party supporters. In California, environmental and labor union activism ended up in terrorism related databases."[8]

But you didn't have to attend a political rally (or a historically black college) to end up in a terrorist database. You might simply have innocently photographed a new building or bridge. In 2008, the Los Angeles Police Department issued policy guidelines on reporting legal activity that "could indicate" terrorism related activity. Allegedly suspicious behaviors included taking measurements or notes, or taking pictures or video footage "with no apparent esthetic value."[9] As these guidelines suggest, and a subsequent Brennan Center investigation of police intelligence gathering found, "police are operating without adequate standards and oversight mechanisms, routinely amassing mountains of data—including personal information about law-abiding Americans—with little or no counterterrorism value."[10]

Multiply the dangers of fusion centers and other local surveillance operations by a gazillion and you might approximate the reach of the post-9/11 surveillance state, which may defy dismantling. It comprises a vast, shadowy, virtually unknowable network of government agents and private contractors, involving state and local as well as federal officials and including police forces, for whom wholesale, warrantless data collection has also become a routine crime-fighting tool. The surveillance state is "a hidden world, growing beyond control," the *Washington Post* reported back in 2010 (before the Snowden revelations).

> Some 1,271 government organizations and 1,931 private companies work on programs related to counterterrorism, homeland security and intelligence in about 10,000 locations across the United States . . . The top-secret world the government created in response to the terrorist attacks of Sept. 11, 2001, has become so large, so unwieldy and so secretive that no one knows how much money it costs, how many people it employs, how many programs exist within it or exactly how many agencies do the same work.[11]

As our lives have become increasingly transparent, the government has become increasingly opaque. Privacy and the freedom it enables depend partly on reversing this trend. So, perhaps, does security. Secrecy shields incompetence as well as abuse, and "top secret America" is a highly inefficient and insecure security bureaucracy, as Snowden demonstrated. In some ways, everyone and no one, including the president, is in charge. You might find some cold comfort in this: a fragmented surveillance regime may, at the moment, be one of our best defenses against an omniscient, totalistic regime. But it is not a good defense against terrorism, much less a source of hope for freedom. If you're always watched, you're never free.

So I find it hard to be hopeful about the future of freedom while writing about it under surveillance, having surrendered the privacy of a typewriter for the convenience of computing long ago. You're reading this under surveillance, if you're reading a digital version or hard copy purchased with a credit card or other digital currency.

Do you care? Are you wary of being watched? Do you miss writing, reading, traveling, attending political rallies or social events in relative privacy, at least? Do you value privacy and imagine resurrecting it? Or are you resigned to its permanent loss and indifferent to the creation of a virtual panopticon? We can't quantify the effect of cultural exhibitionism, pop therapeutic "sharing," or the professional necessities of a social media presence, but we can safely assume that for many Americans anonymity is more unwelcome than publicity.

Consider our early twenty-first-century mantra: "If you have nothing to hide you have nothing to fear." Don't believe it. You have more to hide than you know. You expose more information about yourself than you intend. We're all suspects or potential suspects when we're all under surveillance. When you're under watch, you're under guard. "Even if you're not doing anything wrong you're being watched and recorded," as Edward Snowden stressed.

Everyone has something to hide, whether or not they're engaged in wrongful, righteous, or morally neutral conduct. Privacy is not simply a shield for bad behavior, as surveillance hawks suggest. People seek it when they're engaged in good works (such as donating to charities anonymously) as well as bad. And those who don't value privacy for its own sake might consider its practical uses.

Everyone has something to hide, partly because words and actions that are or seem legal today may be criminalized tomorrow. A voluminous, vague, and elastic federal criminal code has enabled overzealous, vindictive, and generally unaccountable federal prosecutors to indict almost anyone they choose to target. This too is an old story (predating 9/11), but it's essential to any understanding of the freedoms we need to regain. As veteran defense attorney Harvey Silverglate demonstrated in *Three Felonies a Day: How the Feds Target the Innocent*, virtually "every citizen is vulnerable to prosecution and prison . . . it is only a slight exaggeration to say that the average busy professional in this country wakes up in the morning, goes to work, comes home, takes care of personal and family obligations, and then goes to sleep, unaware that he or she likely committed several felonies that day."[12]

The danger of being indicted for unwitting, questionable, technical "crimes" is practically impossible to measure. If a majority of us will not be prosecuted, virtually all of us remain at risk, because prosecutorial power may be exercised arbitrarily. Instead of choosing their cases, prosecutors sometimes choose their defendants. As a result "normal daily activities expose us to potential prosecution at the whim of a government official."[13]

Don't rest assured that presumptions of innocence will protect you from wrongful conviction of a relatively weak or even fanciful charge. The vast majority of cases are plea-bargained, in no small part because harsh mandatory sentencing laws effectively empower prosecutors to extort pleas: they "structure plea bargains in ways that make it nearly impossible for normal, rational, self-interest calculating people to risk going to trial."[14]

The systematic abuse of plea bargaining has been a defining characteristic of federal drug cases, in which defendants are routinely threatened with decades-long, mandatory sentences for nonviolent crimes if they dare exercise the right to a trial. Not surprisingly, 97% of defendants charged with federal drug offenses plead guilty,[15] although many of these pleas are not exactly voluntary:

"To coerce guilty pleas, and sometimes to coerce cooperation as well, prosecutors routinely threaten ultra-harsh, enhanced mandatory sentences that no one—not even the prosecutors themselves—thinks are appropriate," Federal District Court Judge John Gleeson stressed in 2013, in *U.S.A. v Kupa*.[16] "And to demonstrate to defendants generally that those threats are sincere, prosecutors insist on the imposition of the unjust punishments when the threatened defendants refuse to plead guilty."

Defendant Lulzim Kupa reluctantly agreed to a plea carrying an eleven-year sentence, Judge Gleeson stressed. He was initially offered a plea carrying about a nine-year sentence (not including credits for "good time"), a plea he was given only one day to consider. Because he failed to accept it immediately, prosecutors increased the sentence they offered in a second, one-day-only deal. They increased it again a third time, when he failed to accept the second offer quickly. Not surprisingly, Kupa gave in and accepted the third plea deal carrying an additional two years over the first offer because, he told Judge Gleeson, he didn't want to risk life imprisonment and he "wanted to plead guilty, before things get worse."

This looks less like a justice system than a protection racket. Kupa was a drug dealer, but he seems less of a threat than his thuggish prosecutors, who wielded formidable official power, unmitigated by fairness or a sense of proportion. Their abuses were normalized by the war on drugs and accentuated by gross racial disparities in drug war enforcement.[17]

Then came the war on terror. It brought us torture; a lawless, secret surveillance state; the summary, indefinite detention of people rightly or wrongly suspected of terrorism; increased racial profiling; blacklists of questionable accuracy that keep harmless people off airplanes or covertly deny them credit and employment;[18] and criminal prohibitions on pure political speech reminiscent of early twentieth-century red scares.[19] The war on drugs dramatically eroded civil liberty. The war on terror could deliver the coup de grace.

Can liberty be restored without a coup d'état? Perhaps, with a combination of technological defenses to surveillance[20] and legal reforms, including demilitarizing local police forces, curtailing prosecutorial power, and reinstating defendants' rights. Reforms will depend on strengthening the nascent, left/right coalition of security/surveillance state critics and mobilizing a voting public that's a lot less susceptible to fearmongering and a lot more alert to incursions on liberty. Civil libertarians can cite some reason to hope: the drug war has fallen out of favor, at last. It is a widely acknowledged, costly, counterproductive failure, and an unprecedented majority of Americans now favor legalizing marijuana.[21] The Snowden revelations sparked awareness of surveillance that could eventually result in a few reforms.

But to date (October 2014) increased concern about privacy and militarized policing hasn't inspired significant opposition to security state abuses or inefficiencies. Instead, renewed fear of terrorism, following the broadcast beheadings of journalists and aid workers, have increased support for surveillance and decreased support for reform, predictably. Public opinion on the balance between liberty and security is labile, shaped by the news of the day and the fear it inspires.

A year before ISIS dominated the news, the public desire for privacy seemed strong enough to challenge the need to feel safe and protected by government spies. A November 2013 *Washington Post* poll found that a majority of Americans (60 percent) believed that Edward Snowden "damaged national security," at the same time that a slightly stronger majority (68 percent) believed that the NSA intrudes on some privacy rights. "Dueling concerns about privacy and national security are fueling a division over the NSA's efforts," the *Post* quite reasonably concluded.[22] A January 2014 Pew Research poll found the public evenly divided over whether Snowden's actions served or harmed the public interest.[23]

Nine months later, however, the Pew Research Center found "a shifting balance between concerns about civil liberties and protection from terrorism. In a reversal from last year after Edward Snowden's NSA leaks, 50% today say they are more concerned that government anti-terrorism policies have not gone far enough to protect the country, while 35% are more concerned that the policies have gone too far in restricting civil liberties."[24]

Compare public support for government surveillance when fear predominates, or relative passivity in the face of surveillance in calmer times, with skepticism about big government and right-wing elegies for freedom. The cognitive dissonance wrought by attacks on Big Brother and demands for his protection is practically deafening. But it's not hard to understand.

Electronic surveillance is a particularly insidious threat to liberty because it's invisible and immaterial. We can't see or feel it. If police officers broke into all our homes and riffled through our papers and personal effects, we'd be outraged. (If they were searching for illegal guns, the NRA would call for revolution.) But empower a huge, unwieldy, unaccountable government bureaucracy to covertly compile digital profiles of our personal and professional lives? Many of us shrug and accept the loss of privacy as the price of feeling safe.

Still, the surveillance state doesn't simply rely on our fear or indifference. Its operation is a mystery to millions of people with relatively limited technological sophistication. The systems described in documents released by Snowden are complicated and arcane, and, I suspect, beyond the ken of most of us. Barton Gellman, who covered national security issues for the *Washington Post*, stressed the difficulties of analyzing documents obtained from Snowden. "On first reading, I understood maybe half of any given memo or slide deck in the materials," he told the *New Yorker*. "These are internal documents, dense with jargon and acronyms and references to things that are common knowledge at Fort Meade (NSA headquarters)."[25]

Gellman and others, notably Glenn Greenwald, broke the materials down for us. Still, the number of people who have followed their stories closely probably constitutes a small percentage of the population. The number who have followed their stories and accurately recall the details must be even smaller. Even if majorities are generally aware that the government is tracking us, only a relatively small minority of people seem likely to comprehend what that tracking entails. I doubt that many of our elected representatives are among them.

Do aging federal court judges understand the surveillance state? The Supreme Court is still grappling with email, according to Justice Elena Kagan. "The justices are not necessarily the most technologically sophisticated people," she acknowledged.[26] In the short term at least, this does not bode well for liberty. These unsophisticated people are powerful arbiters (sometimes the final arbiters) of freedom in the digital age. Judges struggling to master email are probably flummoxed by an iPhone. How can they determine if complex systems that they don't understand intrude gratuitously and unconstitutionally infringe on fundamental freedoms?

We can look forward, perhaps, to the technological sophistication of older judges increasing over time. We know that a younger generation more at ease with technology will eventually dominate the federal bench, and we can hope that a critical mass of them will be solicitous of liberty. Is there reason for at least cautious optimism?

Younger Americans do tend to be more critical of the surveillance state, perhaps because they're more sophisticated technologically (and more likely to live online). A majority of Americans age sixty-four and older condemn Edward Snowden as a traitor, according to a 2013 *Reason Magazine* poll, while a plurality of Americans between the ages of eighteen and thirty-four regard him as a patriot.[27]

Libertarians claim their movement is growing and attracting the young, and perhaps they're right. Twenty-two percent of Americans harbor libertarian sympathies, according to a 2013 poll by the Public Religion Research Institute.[28] Seven percent are "consistent libertarians" and 15 percent of Americans "lean libertarian." Almost all are white, more than two-thirds are male, and nearly two-thirds are under age fifty. The CATO Institute, a libertarian think tank, has identified 14 percent of voters as libertarian and notes, "other surveys find a larger number of people who hold views . . . best described as libertarian. A 2009 Gallup poll found that 23 percent held libertarian views." Acknowledging that young Americans "defy easy ideological categorization," CATO found that "there is a large bloc of young people who can fairly be described as libertarian," meaning they're socially liberal and fiscally conservative.[29] According to a Pew Research Center survey on political rhetoric, "the word libertarian receives a very positive reaction from younger Americans, older people tend to view it negatively."[30]

Will a "rising tide" of young libertarians save us? We're accustomed to pinning hopes for the future on the young. (What choice do we have?) Our hopes that they'll succeed where their elders have failed in curbing surveillance with legal reforms, or thwarting it with new technologies (such as secure communications systems or privacy wear for you and your phone), may not be misplaced. But we shouldn't assume a generational commitment to liberty. CATO is probably right that a "large bloc" of young people skew libertarian, but I suspect that an equally large bloc are antilibertarian, considering attitudes toward free speech (and due process for students accused of sexual misconduct) that prevail on U.S. campuses and among many young, self-identified feminists.

It is conventional wisdom on college and university campuses (and off campus among many self-proclaimed progressives) that "free speech doesn't include hate speech or a right to offend." This is dangerous nonsense. The purpose of free speech is the protection of speech deemed hateful or offensive by people who'd like to silence it. But this is popular nonsense too, reflected in campus speech and harassment codes that give administrators broad discretion to punish "bad" speech typically described by such vague, subjective terms as annoying, insulting, hateful, unwelcome, or inappropriate.[31]

Students who identify as progressive tend to support and exploit these codes to protect an imagined civil right not to take offense, at the obvious expense of a right to give it. A "large bloc" of young people have internalized the notion that speech they deem "bullying," insulting, or demeaning—including speech that insults or demeans on the basis of race, sex, sexual orientation, religion, ethnicity, or vaguely defined personal and political characteristics, such as appearance, attire, and beliefs—is not speech but an actionable form of discrimination.

Colleges and universities are training generations of educated Americans (tomorrow's leaders) to devalue our first, foundational freedom of speech, whether it protects insults, epithets, or unpopular religious ideals and political opinions. The belief that unwelcome speech is the equivalent of unwelcome action, properly subject to equivalent regulation, is entrenched on American campuses and will not soon be dislodged. From this perspective, the First Amendment is a civility code designed to discourage or punish harsh criticisms and strenuous arguments that offend or upset people with diminished power. From this perspective, free speech is nice or, at worst, indifferent speech that supports social norms and the status quo instead of challenging them.

This is a therapeutic approach to democracy that's fundamentally hostile to civil liberty. It effectively condemns freedom, especially freedom of speech, as the victimization of presumptively vulnerable people and a bar to equality. An approach conceived by the left, decades ago, it's now mirrored on the right by religious conservatives who condemn the freedom for minority beliefs secured by separation of church and state as the victimization of Christians—the annual casualties of an imaginary war on Christmas.

Right and left, these therapeutic perspectives tend to confuse assertions of power with demands for freedom. Pro-censorship progressives frame the power to suppress "verbal assaults" or harassment, vaguely defined, as the exercise of their right to be free from speech presumed to retard equality. Religious conservatives frame the power to impose officially sanctioned sectarian prayer on participants in public events or students in public schools as exercises of their own religious freedom. In this view, freedom is a zero-sum game in which my freedom to speak offensively violates your freedom not to be offended, and my freedom to abstain from prayer violates your freedom to engage in it.

Whether it's disingenuous or simply delusional, this characterization of power as an exercise or guarantor of freedom dangerously complements and supports the paternalistic post-9/11 surveillance state. It too markets power (like the power to spy on us, trampling freedoms of association and speech) as an essential safeguard of freedom from terrorism.

"Freedom is about authority," former New York City Mayor Rudy Giuliani explained. "Freedom is about the willingness of every single human being to cede to lawful authority a great deal of discretion about what you do."[32] NSA officials and others who exercise immense authority, or crave it, probably agree. The disdain of people in power for individual liberty is familiar and perhaps inevitable. Liberty is a leash on power, requiring a firm, fearless grip and a refusal to identify with "lawful authorities" in the mistaken belief that their interests reliably coincide with your own. "Experience should teach us to be most on our guard to protect liberty when the Government's purposes are beneficent," Justice Brandeis observed.[33] In a relatively democratic society, liberty is most at risk when the subjects of power agree to unleash it for their own imagined good.

If a majority or influential minority of Americans adopts the authoritarian definition of freedom as voluntary obeisance, then freedom's future as a rhetorical device is secure. This sad future, in which freedom is merely a word, is too easily imagined, considering the electronic "architecture of oppression" created since 9/11. Can we envision and establish an alternative, a country in which freedom is a state of being and we're at liberty to choose relative autonomy, privacy, and self-expression over immersion in "sivilization" and submission to a government unbound? Is this a vision that many Americans embrace? It requires sacrificing the sense of security offered by an omniscient security/surveillance state and the comfort of belonging to an orderly collective. Liberty doesn't just require eternal vigilance: It relies on individualism. It demands resilience and acceptance of risks that cannot be controlled.

For freedom to prevail, it must be fervently desired. How much, at what cost, do we want to be free? John Stuart Mill wondered, lamenting the "despotism of custom . . . a social tyranny more formidable than many kinds of political oppression."[34] Easy for him to say, you might respond; Mill never experienced political oppression. But we are obviously shaped and inhibited by custom, which, these days reflects the despotism of fear. Freedom's fate depends on our escape. The future is our only untamed territory.

Notes

1. *Olmstead et al. v United States*, 277 U.S. 438, 1928.

2. Radley Balko, *Rise of the Warrior Cop: The Militarization of America's Police Forces* (New York: PublicAffairs, 2013).

3. The Animal Enterprise Terrorism Act, for example, passed in 2006, includes in its definition of terrorism nonviolent animal rights protests. See, http://ccrjustice.org/learn-more/faqs/factsheet%3A-animal-enterprise-terrorism-act-%28aeta%29.

4. The FDR Group, "Chilling Effects: NSA Surveillance Drives U.S. Writers to Self-Censor," Pen.org, November 12, 2013, http://www.pen.org/sites/default/files/2014-08-01_Full%20Report_Chilling%20Effects%20w%20Color%20cover-UPDATED.pdf.

5. Church Committee investigations led to creation of the Foreign Intelligence Surveillance Court, which was intended to check domestic spying but eventually began to defer to it. For a brief account of the Church Committee, see Report and Recommendations of The President's Review Group on Intelligence and Communications Technologies, "Liberty and Security in a Changing World," December 12, 2013, 57–65.

6. Alan Rusbridger, "The Snowden Leaks and the Public," *The New York Review of Books* online, November 21, 2013, http://www.nybooks.com/articles/archives/2013/nov/21/snowden-leaks-and-public/.

7. "Investigative Report Criticizes Counterterrorism Reporting, Waste at State & Local Intelligence Fusion Centers," Permanent Subcommittee on Investigations, U.S. Senate Department on Homeland Security and Government Affairs, October 3, 2012, http://www.hsgac.senate.gov/subcommittees/investigations/media/investigative-report-criticizes-counterterrorism-reporting-waste-at-state-and-local-intelligence-fusion-centers.

8. "Massachusetts Privacy and Data Protection Bill—Fact Sheet," DocStoc.com, last modified March 11, 2013, http://www.docstoc.com/docs/148297455/Massachusetts-Privacy-and-Data-Protection-Bill----Fact-Sheet.

9. Mike German and Jay Stanley, "Fusion Center Update," American Civil Liberties Union, July 2008, https://www.aclu.org/files/pdfs/privacy/fusion_update_20080729.pdf.

10. "New Report: Police Intelligence Gathering Lacks Standards, Threatens

National Security and Civil Liberties," Brennan Center for Justice, December 10, 2013, http://www.brennancenter.org/press-release/new-report-police-intelligence-gathering-lacks-effective-standards-threatening.

11. Dana Priest and William M. Arkin, "Top Secret America," *Washington Post* video, last modified September 2010, http://projects.washingtonpost.com/top-secret-america/.

12. Harvey Silverglate, *Three Felonies a Day: How the Feds Target the Innocent* (New York: Encounter, 2009), xxx.

13. Ibid., xxxi.

14. Ibid., xxxviii.

15. Jamie Fellner, "An Offer You Can't Refuse: How U.S. Federal Prosecutors Force Drug Defendants to Plead Guilty," Human Rights Watch, December 5, 2013, http://www.hrw.org/reports/2013/12/05/offer-you-can-t-refuse.

16. "U.S. District Judge Gleeson Assails DOJ Use of MM Sentencing Threats to Force Pleas," *Sentencing Law and Policy* (blog), October 10, 2013, http://sentencing.typepad.com/sentencing_law_and_policy/.

17. Michelle Alexander, *The New Jim Crow: Mass Incarceration in the Age of Colorblindness* (New York: The New Press, 2010).

18. Shirin Sinnar, "The OFAC List: How a Treasury Department Terrorist Watchlist Ensnares Everyday Consumers," Lawyers' Committee for Civil Rights of the San Francisco Bay Area report, March 1, 2007, citation from Stanford Law School website, http://www.law.stanford.edu/publications/the-ofac-list-how-a-treasury-department-terrorist-watchlist-ensnares-everyday-consumers.

19. Wendy Kaminer, "'Material Support' Bans and the Criminalization of Political Advocacy," June 21, 2010, *The Atlantic* online, http://theatlantic.com/national/archive/2010/06/material-support-bans-and-the-criminalization-of-political-advocacy/58469/.

20. Craig Timberg, "Apple Will No Longer Unlock Most iPhones, iPads for Police, Even with Search Warrants," *The Washington Post* online, September 18, 2014, http://washingtonpost.com/business/technology/apple-will-no-longer-unlock-most-iphones-ipads-for-police-even-with-search-warrants/2014/09/17/2612af58-3ed2-11e4-b03f-de718edeb92f_story.html.

21. Tony Newman, "Breakthrough Pew Poll: Marijuana Legalization Wins Majority Support Nationwide," Drug Policy Alliance, April 4, 2013, http://www.drugpolicy.org/news/2013/04/breakthrough-pew-poll-marijuana-legalization-wins-majority-support-nationwide.

22. Scott Clement, "Poll: Most Americans Say Snowden Leaks Harmed National Security," *The Washington Post* online, November 20, 2013, http://www.washingtonpost.com/politics/poll-most-americans-say-snowden-

leaks-harmed-national-security/2013/11/20/13cc20b8-5229-11e3-9e2c-e1d01116fd98_story.html.

23. Seth Motel, "NSA Coverage Wins Pulitzer, but Americans Remain Divided on Snowden Leaks," Pew Research Center, April 15, 2014, http://www.pewresearch.org/fact-tank/2014/04/15/nsa-coverage-wins-pulitzer-but-americans-remain-divided-on-snowden-leaks/.

24. "Growing Concern about Rise of Islamic Extremism at Home and Abroad," Pew Research Center for the People and the Press, September 10, 2014, http://www.people-press.org/2014/09/10/growing-concern-about-rise-of-islamic-extremism-at-home-and-abroad/.

25. Ken Auletta, "Freedom of Information," *New Yorker* online, October 7, 2013, http://newyorker.com/magazine/2013/10/07/freedom-of-information.

26. "Elana Kagan: SCOTUS Hasn't 'Gotten To' Email," Politico.com, August 20, 2013, http://www.politico.com/story/2013/08/kagan-supreme-court-email-95724.html.

27. Emily Ekins, "Poll Finds Public Split on Whether Edward Snowden Is a Hero or Traitor," Reason Rupe Poll, Reason.com, September 19, 2013, http://reason.com/poll/2013/09/19/poll-finds-public-split-on-whether-edwa2.

28. "2013 American Values Survey: In Search of Libertarians in America," Public Religion Research Institute, October 29, 2013, http://publicreligion.org/research/2013/10/2013/-american-values-survey/.

29. David Kirby and David Boaz, "The Libertarian Vote in the Age of Obama," Cato Institute, January 21, 2010, http://www.cato.org/publications/policy analysis/libertarian-vote-age-obama.

30. "Little Change in Public's Response to 'Capitalism,' 'Socialism,'" Pew Research Center for the People and the Press, December 28, 2011, http://www.people-press.org/2011/12/28/little-change-in-publics-response-to-capitalism-socialism/.

31. For reports on campus speech codes, see thefire.org.

32. "'Freedom Is about Authority': Excerpts from Giuliani Speech on Crime," *New York Times* online, March 20, 1994, http://www.nytimes.com/1994/03/20/nyregion/freedom-is-about-authority-excerpts-from-guiliani-speech-on-crime.html.

33. *Olmstead et al. v Unites States*, 277 U.S 438, 1928.

34. John Stuart Mill, *On Liberty* (Harmondsworth, UK: Penguin, 1985), 63, 136.

PART
THREE

Science,

Technology,

and

the

Environment

CHAPTER 7

Science

Especially about the Future

Mark A. Ratner

Lawrence B. Dumas Distinguished University Professor,
Northwestern University

The great Danish physicist and philosopher Niels Bohr is credited with saying, "Prediction is very difficult, especially about the future." In Denmark, this remark is usually attributed to Storm P, a creative newspaper cartoonist of the early twentieth century. When thinking about predicting or even imagining the scientific advances by the year 2040, it is wise to remember that these remarks came both from a physicist/philosopher and from a newsman/cartoonist. While the word "science" has its roots in the Greek word meaning "knowledge," much of science comes from the collaboration/conflict of knowledge and imagination. And it's almost certainly true that in 2015 our imagination of where science will be twenty-five years out is going to be incorrect, unimaginative, and wide of the mark. It is a challenge, and an opportunity to have fun—what *will* science be like in 2040?

Looking Backward

One way to analyze looking forward is to take the Edward Bellamy approach and look backward first—if we go back, for example, some forty years to 1975, we see some things that are highly familiar, and we mark the absence of great discoveries and advances that have occurred in the four decades between then and now. In 1975 there were no scanning tunneling microscopes, no analyses of the genome of any animal or plant, no observations of single molecule behavior, and no "big data." There were no genetic synthesis methodologies (short strands of DNA could be made; sequencing the DNA of any species was thought about but certainly not yet possible). The Higgs boson was a concept, not a reality.

More strikingly, there were some now-accepted sciences that simply didn't exist—or existed in a very jejune and halting way—including materials science, computer science, chemical biology, and nanoscience.

In 1975, wonderful science was being done outside of universities, academies, and not-for-profit laboratories. Great labs existed—Bell Laboratories, Xerox, Kodak, Exxon, Amoco, and a number of big pharma firms—and nearly every science was pursued by industries large and small.

In 1973–74, Nobel Prizes in Physics were awarded for work in tunneling phenomena in semiconductors and superconductors, for radio astrophysics, and for the discovery of pulsars. In chemistry, they were awarded for fundamental achievements in the physical chemistry of macromolecules and for organometallic sandwich compounds. In physiology and medicine, they were awarded for the organization of individual and social behavior patterns and for the structural and functional organization of the cell. These topics are still of substantial importance—the continuity of science, as it goes from focus in one area to focus in another but does not forget the first, suggests that we can indeed say something not too silly about what will happen in the next four decades.

There is another view. For example, the English physicist Paul Dirac wrote, "The fundamental laws necessary for the mathematical treatment of a large part of physics and the whole of chemistry are thus completely known, and the difficulty lies only in the fact that application of these laws leads to equations that are too complex to be solved."[1] The exponential growth of computational capability over the last four decades has permitted use of the quantum mechanics (that Dirac helped invent) to predict, clarify, and understand all sorts of chemistry, from the color of dyes to the production of better magnets to the chemical properties of DNA. But this does not cause the end of chemistry—rather, it deepens the chemical discipline by insights based on physics, and permits easier bridging of the chemical sciences to physics, materials science, biology, medicine, climatology, engineering science, and earth science.

John Horgan, a science writer and journalist, wrote a book in 1996 called *The End of Science*. In his earlier article, entitled "The Death of Proof," that appeared in the October 1993 number of *Scientific American* (Horgan apparently liked deaths and ends), he claimed that the traditional concepts of mathematical proof were being undermined by new complexity and by the application of computation. David Hoffmann said that this article had generated "torrents of howls and complaints from mathematicians."[2] *The End of Science* essentially claimed that we both knew too much and were (as a society) too timid. The book was actually brought on by the cancellation of the superconducting super-collider, and a general feeling that support for scientific research in the United States was failing.

Horgan felt that such great advances as Darwin's theory of evolution, the Watson-Crick structure of DNA's double helix, and the major advances in physics, from relativity and quantum mechanics on, were great strides and were being replaced by strides that didn't seem so great.

The response to Horgan's book was pretty striking. Most scientists didn't like it, and some highly articulate scientists responded quite negatively. Philip Anderson, a distinguished solid state physicist and Nobel Prize winner, said, "The reason that Horgan's pessimism is so wrong lies in the nature of science itself. Whenever a question receives an answer, science moves on and asks a new kind of question, of which there seem to be an endless supply."[3] Horgan and his book are important, because that endless supply isn't always clear. Indeed, seeing that endless supply requires vision—vision that will often be rewarded by huge advances in experiment, in modeling, in understanding, and in imagination (and even by a home in Silicon Valley).

Questions, Answers, and More Questions

Science is in the business of asking these questions. I. I. Rabi (another thoughtful Nobel Prize winner in physics) relates the story that when he returned home from school, his mother didn't ask him what he had learned today but rather "did you ask a good question today?"[4] Asking the right good questions, and answering them as best we can, is the hallmark of true science. And as humans we do question, and when we stop questioning, we stop learning. So it seems that the nature of the human being is going to result in vibrant, ongoing science four decades out, and far beyond.

Another way of seeing is technology. When I polled my undergraduate students on what science is going to be like twenty-five years out, they wrote quite persuasively about the disappearance of computer screens, the omnipresence of communications, the biomedical devices that will make our lives far richer, self-driving and self-parking cars, and all the other advances that will certainly happen and will probably be dwarfed by other accomplishments of technology. But predicting technology twenty-five years out is even more fraught than doing that for science. Science depends on imagination, on experiment, and on the building of understanding. Technology is the powerful, lusty, productive, ungoverned love child of science and business. Advances in technology travel many roads, from the Edisonian approach of trying many things (which has now become, in slicked-up form, one of the ways of doing both molecular and materials discovery) to the computational data discovery and data mining that are one of the flavors of today. So our discussion here will exclude technology, because unlike science, it's not so much about asking questions as about anticipating, answering, and creating demands and interacting with the requirements and desires of people.

Why, How, and Looking Forward

The drivers of scientific inquiry have varied over the years. The alchemists were driven by desire both for riches and for ways to interfere with the mortality tables. Despite this, they contributed tremendously to the growth of modern chemistry. For roughly the last 150 years, the major drivers for science were a combination of military (Rumford, Heisenberg, Haber, and others), curiosity (Faraday, Hilbert, Einstein, etc.), and nutrition (Borlaug, Haber, Carver, et al.). A great deal of science came from simple need for filthy lucre: while it didn't pay very well in most cases, scientific endeavor was rewarded by the society, and some outstanding scientists could attain unimagined status—excellent scientists such as Lavoisier, Rutherford, Gibbs, Crick, Langmuir, and many others lived very well indeed.

The foregoing list is entirely male and entirely white. This homogeneity has begun to change, with huge advantages both for the creativity of science and for the ability of science to explain the universe. The scientific workforce of 2015 is more diverse in every area than it has ever been before—gender, race, age, residence, and social standing are less determinative of scientific success. In 2040, the scientific workforce will be driven by curiosity, by the wish for reward, and by human needs. Human needs–driven science is already important (National Institutes of Health!), but it will be more so twenty-five years out, when (provided diplomacy keeps up with science) the world will, for the first time, no longer have hunger as a cause of death. Human needs involving health, creativity, leisure, longevity, and the opportunity to create, to enjoy, and to savor the best parts of life will be principal drivers for scientific exploration.

In 2040 the interest in, and domination of, life sciences will be even greater than it is now. We will continue to seek understanding of biological processes, both synthetic and natural. One huge challenge in life science has to do with the enormous diversity that living creatures represent. This has generated a set of life sciences that are breathtaking in their breadth, depth, and importance. They are also balkanized in their rules and understandings.

Mathematics has crucially important theorems and methodologies, going back to Newton and Leibnitz and proceeding through Gauss, Hilbert, and many others. Physics has Newton's laws and Einstein's extension of them; it has the laws of thermodynamics (which it shares with chemistry) and the laws of quantum mechanics (which it shares with all the other sciences). Earth science has all of chemistry and physics to support it, in addition to the understandings of Wegener concerning continental drift that has dominated much of the evolution of and on the earth for the past few million years. Chemistry is the most syncretic and broad of all the sciences. It requires for its understanding all of the above, plus ideas and methods such as Faraday's laws for electrochemistry, the quantum and statistical mechanics of physics, polymer science, and many other themes gathered from the knowledge that humanity has developed since the Greeks.

But biology is different. Published in 2015, the wonderful compendium entitled *Molecular Biology of the Cell* (by Alberts et al.) contains twenty-five chapters.[5] Written by some of the true leaders in the life sciences, it describes issues ranging from antibodies to zooplankton. But overall integrating concepts and quantitative relationships are nearly lacking. Moreover, life science is more essentially compartmentalized than earth science, physics, chemistry, and others. The science required to understand the nervous system and the science required to understand photosynthesis are intrinsically different. DNA replication has little to do with kidney function; brain science and bone science rely on different interpretations of structure and behavior.

In 2040, the quest for more general organizing principles in the biological sciences will have advanced substantially. In 2015, the wonderful ability to maintain understandings by a series of well-defined equations (the cornerstone of physics) fails to describe biological structure and dynamics. Even twenty-five years out, it is not clear that those understandings will have been completed in life science.

In 2015, we are aware of the existence of millions of exoplanets (planets circling stars that are not our sun), and it is probable that there are at least a million times (or a hundred million or a billion or . . .) that many. Certainly some of these planets have water on them, and the combination of the water and the sunlight, plus a nitrogenous atmosphere from historical times, strongly suggests that some sort of life might well have evolved on those planets. At some time in the future (unless the human inhabitants of Earth destroy it), there will be communication between Earth and one of these planets. That will be the most awesome (a word popular among young people in 2015) event in the history of humankind. Proof that we are not alone, that elsewhere in the universe there is life—and life that in some sense is akin to our own—would be the greatest news story ever, and it would arise from astrophysics. This will eventually happen. With advances in radio astronomy and detection, as well as our knowledge of the existence of exoplanets, it could well happen by 2040. Carl Sagan, using the Drake equation and some reasonable assumptions, deduced in the twentieth century that there are thriving civilizations in our galactic neighborhood. Making their acquaintance would be stupendous!

Some Actual Predictions

The late Irving Klotz, an articulate and distinguished faculty member in the Northwestern University Chemistry Department, was fond of saying of many scientists that they were "frequently in error, but never in doubt." Being in error—in an intelligent, creative, falsifiable, and combinative way—is a great accomplishment in science, and these predictions certainly demonstrate that.

Technology will continue, both unstopped and unstoppable. We will have universal connectivity among individuals worldwide, and we will have driverless cars. We may have fully renewable energy sources. We'll have instant daily diagnosis of diseases, life expectancy will exceed one hundred years, and we will probably have many more artificial components to our bodies than we do now. But these engineering accomplishments, though they will certainly change our lives (and probably mostly for the better) are not disruptive at the level of the great inventions of the past. Those included tonal music, evolution, the classification of animals and plants, calculus, relativity, thermodynamics, evolution, flight, the printing press, radio, the steam engine, fire, splitting atoms, anesthesia, and quantum mechanics. But asking the right question is frequently the most important thing in science. New questions will be asked, and new conceptual breakthroughs—perhaps in a class with music, flight, and fire—will be born.

The growth of science is remarkable. It is estimated that more than 50 percent of all the scientists who ever lived were born after 1900. Indeed, the word "scientist" is relatively new—it was coined by William Whewell in 1833. In 2015, there are more scientists alive than there ever have been previously, and they are better supported by government, by individuals, by companies, and by philanthropy. This could not possibly have been imagined when Michael Faraday was supposed to have said to Gladstone (who had asked what good would come from electricity), "Why, sir, there is every probability that you will soon be able to tax it."[6]

The philosopher of science Karl Popper claimed that a true scientific fact had to be falsifiable—that is, such statements as "this is a happy onion" or "that rock is really distressed" are not scientific statements because they can't be disproven. Accordingly, it has become a norm in experimental science over the last century to publish results in open journals so that they can be reproduced or not. Quoting the *Economist* (October 13, 2013), "The idea that the same experiments always get the same results, no matter who performs them, is one of the cornerstones of science's claim to objective truth. If a systematic campaign of replication does not lead to the same results, then either the original research is flawed or the replications are. Either way, something is awry." The *Economist* goes on to say that because some experiments are extremely difficult, the statistics are difficult to understand, and there are huge expenditures involved in making observations or measurements. Falsification is no longer a significant activity. The *Economist* describes the current state of falsifiability as essentially irrelevant.

Bruce Alberts (the brilliant and prolific scientist mentioned earlier, who was both the editor of *Science* magazine and the president of the National Academy of Sciences) is quoted in the *Economist* as saying, "Scientists themselves . . . need to develop a value system where simply moving on from one's mistakes without publicly acknowledging them severely damages, rather than protects scientific reputation." The *Economist* finishes the discussion by saying that "this will not be easy. But if science is to stay on its tracks, and be worthy of the trust so widely invested in it, it may be necessary."

Science is done by people. Often these people are extremely careful and painstaking; more often, these people are only as careful and painstaking as they feel it is necessary to be. Mistakes are made, and in various fields of science those mistakes can be falsified quite quickly—if a new molecule is made in a particular way and the preparation is published, other scientists can try to reproduce it—and if they can't, the originator almost certainly has made an error. The search for novelty in science and the nature of the support of scientific research guarantee that game-changing ideas will be examined but do not guarantee that these ideas can be falsified or will be examined from the viewpoint of falsification. So the definition of truth in science will be based on the acceptance by scientific peers and not whether the idea can be falsified.

Science is certainly a healthy and growing subculture within society. Per the National Science Board, the United States publishes more science and engineering articles than any other country, although the combined output of the European Union is larger than that of the United States. Asia's research article output is approaching parity with the United States and the European Union. Between 1997 and 2011, Asia's output more than doubled, led primarily by China. In 2011, China produced 11 percent of the world's science and engineering articles, more than any country except the United States. Publication of such papers shows no signs of stopping, but it eventually must. I feel that it will slow down substantially over the next twenty-five years and become a crucial but no longer growing aspect of our global society.

The discovery of life outside of Earth will be (in my view) the greatest scientific/technological event ever, and there is a strong possibility that this will happen by 2040. There also might be a year in which humanity, by working hard to make this century different from all previous centuries, will conquer poverty and starvation, and control the nature of climate change. We have the science and technology to feed, clothe, and maintain all the people on Earth (provided the number of people on Earth doesn't grow rapidly and eventually becomes constant). That would be an accomplishment which we would happily brag about to the new life that we have discovered in a different part of the galactic universe.

The 2015 world of experimental science will be completely revolutionized in the next four decades by a combination of robotics and computer simulation. Robots will do all sorts of things, ranging from complex chemical synthesis to materials testing, from manipulation of objects to tedious repetitive labors. They will do essentially all of the maintenance and machining necessary in physics and chemistry laboratories and in the commercial world, and they will use 3-D assembly to create (based on computer input) samples of materials, composites, blends, glasses, arrested relaxation materials, and hybrid organic-inorganic entities. Light manipulation and lasers will also be used by robots and by the devices that they will prepare.

One prediction of which I'm reasonably sure is that coffee (or, in exotic situations, espresso) will remain the fuel of science in 2040 and well beyond.

In life sciences, astonishing new knowledge will have been created. But major challenges will still remain, and new questions will be asked. Professor Cees Dekker of the University of Delft in the Netherlands is a distinguished physicist who, at the start of the twenty-first century, became deeply interested in biology. He suggests that by 2040 brain scans will be routine and perhaps allow even science fiction–type abilities such as reading thoughts. This is a bit frightening. While information technology and governmental slipperiness have essentially removed the right to privacy in most countries in 2015, the last bit of privacy—thinking to ourselves, talking to ourselves, and letting our brains invent and discover new things—will be no longer be limited to ourselves but might be read by using brain scans.

How to connect the concepts of the "mind" and "brain" will be unresolved, and the Sisyphean quest for understanding consciousness and mind will continue and remain one of the foremost questions in science (and in philosophy).

"Synthetic biology" will be a daily commodity, and microorganisms (because of their adaptive abilities) will be used for many practical applications, from sanitation to coloring paint to soothing mosquito bites to creating food. Synthetic biology will have provided artificial cells, whose major applications in the areas of drug delivery and regenerative medicine will have (together with robotics and new materials) completely changed the face of surgery and many other parts of medicine.

Some Thoughts to Consider

Erwin Schrödinger, one of the founders of quantum mechanics, wrote a book in 1944 entitled *What Is Life?*[7] He decided the simplest way that life could reproduce itself would be a solid material that is not periodic (that is, in which the same structure was not repeated next to itself time and again). This was one of the original thoughts that led to the development and understanding of DNA in the 1950s. The fundamental entity in biology, the cell, will be built using synthetic biology. This capability to construct arbitrary cell structures will tremendously deepen our understanding of cellular phenomena and our ability to prolong life.

According to the "many worlds" theory/interpretation of quantum mechanics, each motion or selection or choice made by an entity results in at least two different universes being instantaneously created. The created universes evolve in space-time for whatever short period elapses before yet another motion is made, another bifurcation into two universes is caused, and we keep going on multiple, noncommunicating paths, less traveled by. This "many worlds" interpretation is one of many suggestions as to how time evolution occurs in systems with coherent quantum mixing. If that theory is right, then between 2015 and 2040, the number of new universes created will have increased exponentially. Indeed, your reading of this chapter will, according to this model, cause multiple new worlds to separate from one another, lost in space-time.

Given these possibilities for creating new worlds, I am somewhat emboldened. The unruly, brilliant offspring of this science is capable of amazing feats, of repetitive motions that seem useless, and of lightning-like understandings and predictions, whose grandeur and intellectual sharpness are as exciting as going over the falls in a barrel.

So this short piece on what science—both physical and biological—might be like four decades from now is both detailed and playful, both serious and silly, both understood and questionable. Montaigne, in the third book of his *Essays*, said it better than anyone:

> The lines of my portrait are never at fault, although they change and vary. The world is a perpetual see-saw. Everything goes incessantly up and down—the earth, the rocks of the Caucasus, the pyramids of Egypt—both with the universal motion and with their own. Constancy itself is nothing but a more sluggish movement. I cannot fix my subject. He is always restless, and reels with a natural intoxication. . . . It is a record of various and variable occurrences, an account of thoughts that are unsettled and, as chance will have it, at times contradictory, either because I am then another self, or because I approach my subject under different circumstances and with other considerations . . .

I do not teach, I tell.

Afterword

Northwestern University is in the Midwest, and its faculty members are noted not only for their academic distinction and superb teaching but also for openness, candor, imagination, and a willingness to share. I asked some of my colleagues about what the world of science might be like in 2040, and I got a number of quite striking responses. They're reproduced here because we've already established that essentially nobody has any real clue as to what will have happened by then.

1. My vision for twenty-five years from now is truly grim. I fear that the current environmental crisis will have exploded into worldwide calamity. Coupled with human-induced atmospheric change, the alteration

of the earth's oceans expands the threat to a global one. Humanity may be struggling to survive. So science in twenty-five years will be focused on survival and damage control. (Donna Jurdy, Earth and Planetary Science)

2. Stem cells will be viable for disease treatment. There will be more reliance on human tissue for testing compounds as there has been little or no translation from animal models to human disease in neurodegenerative diseases or cancer. More industry partnerships will form to attack diseases without treatments. (Richard Silverman, Chemistry)

3. A big question about what life will be like in twenty-five years is how good is simulation technology, as we can all imagine that this will be used before any experiments are done, at least in most fields. There is much that we might expect concerning designer devices and biomolecules. Many structural and device materials could be more interesting if we can make them without defects on the micron scale—this is unheard of in nature. (George Schatz, Chemistry)

4. Despite considerable research investment we will not achieve the dream of a practical computer based on quantum mechanics. Such computers are predicted to have enormous power and efficiency. Nonetheless, from the effort we can anticipate a leap in scientific achievements generating spin-offs of new electronic devices for processing information with applications to smart health care and facile forms of communication. (Bill Halperin, Physics and Astronomy)

5. We will understand the design and operation of complex systems, whether those systems are signaling networks in cells, many-reagent chemical reactions, the air traffic control problem, or anything else. We will grow organs in the lab for transplantation, enabled by more understanding of the biology and material scaffolds. The protein folding problem will be solved, and we will be able to design from first principles enzymes that catalyze any given reaction. Our understanding of chemical reactivity will allow us to create machines that both plan and perform synthesis of any molecule. (Milan Mrksich, Chemistry and Life Sciences)

6. Scientists will start to measure with some precision the cosmic neutrino background, which provides a snapshot of the universe when it was one second old. The explosion of a nearby type 2 supernova in 2037 will lead to the observation of hundreds of thousands of neutrino events at gigantic neutrino detectors located in the United States, Japan, and

Chile/Argentina, finally providing enough information to allow us to understand in great detail how stars explode. (André Luiz de Gouvêa, Physics and Astronomy)

7. A major theme in science will be complexity. We'll continue to better understand complex systems as presented by biology and the environment. We will assemble or synthesize complex systems with greater control over the structures that combine to make an overall complex system. Catalysts will be made this way using strategies similar to what is now done in microelectronics. (Peter Stair, Chemistry)

8. I predict that dark energy and dark matter will become as laughable as phlogiston and aether. We will have found exoplanets with life on them. We will have figured out how the first stars, galaxies, and massive black holes (greater than 10^5 x solar mass) formed and reionized the universe. (Melville Ulmer, Physics and Astronomy)

These visions from active and thoughtful scientists show how prescient and spot-on Montaigne was. Science in 2040 will be powerful and vibrant, asking new questions, supporting and challenging society, making mistakes, and following the shaky path toward greater knowledge.

Notes

1. P. A. M. Dirac, "Quantum Mechanics of Many-Electron Systems," *Processing of the Royal Society of London* Series A, 123, no. 792 (1929): 714–33.

2. D. Hoffman, "The End of Science: A Book Review." *Notices of the American Mathematical Society* 45, no. 2 (1998): 260.

3. P. W. Anderson, "Why Do They Leave Physics?" *Physics Today* 53, no. 9 (1999): 11.

4. J. Stickland, *The Men of Manhattan: Creators of the Nuclear Era* (Lulu Enterprises Incorporated, 2011).

5. B. Alberts, *Molecular Biology of the Cell* (New York: Garland Science, 2014).

6. R. Gregory, *Discovery, or The Spirit and Service of Science* (London: Macmillan, 1918).

7. E. Schrödinger, *What Is Life? The Physical Aspect of the Living Cell* (1944, repr., New York: New York University Press, 2012).

CHAPTER 8

Technology

The Era of Answers

John Kelly III
Senior Vice President and Head of IBM Research

Nobody would be shocked to hear that technology can change radically in twenty-five years. All you have to do is look back twenty-five years from today to see the distance we have traveled. In 1989, cell phones were a new phenomenon and could only make static-filled voice calls, and almost no one bought anything online. In 2013, a billion smartphones were sold.[1] They have become the door to a vast parallel landscape of commercial, personal, and societal life. Among millennials, these devices are used for only the occasional phone call.

Over the coming twenty-five years, from 2015 to 2040, technology will change more radically than ever before. Information technology is just beginning a historic transformation. We're about to move to computers that work differently from the way computers have worked since the 1950s. They won't be programmed—they'll learn on their own, and through data they will have an awareness of the world and events around them. More important, they will enable a new wave of digital services that fill gaps in our perception, improve our judgment, and magnify our cognition.

Data is about to become a vital commodity, a raw material—the next natural resource.

We're about to evolve beyond the information age to enter the age of insight. In 2040, value will come from readily surfacing connections, insights, and answers buried deep in a universe of data—natural and human-generated—as limitless, emergent, and difficult to penetrate as the physical universe.

The shift will gain momentum, so that by 2040 technology will play a role we can barely comprehend today. (Who in 1990 could have grasped that something called Twitter might help organize rebels in Libya so they could overthrow a dictator?) In the coming era, technology will allow us to see more clearly using data and to think completely differently about age-old problems both large and small.

The economic implications will be significant. Among them will be a changed purpose for the corporation. In the 1930s, the economist Ronald Coase famously argued that corporations existed to reduce transaction costs—the costs of putting together the right set of suppliers and people and facilities to produce something. That was the very reason for the rise of the large-scale, vertically integrated company. The rise of programmable computers supported that. Over the past twenty-five years, computing and networks have crushed transaction costs, speeding the dismantling of vertical companies and blowing up business models of entire industries.

If transaction costs no longer matter so much, why will next-generation enterprises exist?

The answer is answers. We will dramatically lower the cost and reduce the time to get answers or the insights that lead to them.

Already in 2015, we see a glimmer of this in the world of online search, social networks, and retailing. Their value comes from knowing things about customers and the market. It's why Facebook's insights are perceived as more valuable to the market than the massive operations of companies that produce more traditional products and services.

Over the next twenty-five years, this will no longer be the realm of the Internet start-up. Every industry and every profession will transform itself through data.

To explain the implications of the age of insight in a tangible way, I'll go deeper into three other industries where change is afoot as answers and insights are becoming more affordable and readily available.

Health

In twenty-five years, it will seem almost medieval that you would take a pill or any treatment without already knowing exactly what it will do to your body. We will have systems that essentially build a virtual model of you, based on data ranging from your DNA, your family history, and medical records to your eating habits, sleep patterns, and work. Before taking any new medication, your doctor will be able to ask your virtual self: what will it do to you?

You will benefit from everything we know about the right treatment before you ingest anything—not after.

Education

In twenty-five years, it will seem mind-boggling that education was based mostly on time served—four years of college gets you a bachelor's degree, another two gets you an M.B.A. Instead, technology will make it possible to build a lifelong education around every student individually. The technology will be smart, persistent, and aware enough to act as a tutor and adviser for every person, always knowing what the student is learning or not learning—and what he or she needs to study to reach specific goals.

A student will have personalized support, and educators will have a more nuanced view into whether a student is learning before that student takes any tests.

Management

In twenty-five years, no decision maker will walk into a meeting without his or her cognitive apps, or "cogs"—much as he or she would look to spreadsheets and reports today. Cogs will ingest millions of pages of documents related to the decision maker's domain—more information than any human could ever get through in a lifetime. Cogs could act as an executive assistant or a sophisticated decision support system offering appropriate material, constructing scenarios, and helping model alternative arguments and evidence relevant to such complex questions as whether a firm should acquire, organically develop, or partner to enter a new business segment.

Cogs will exist in the cloud, interact easily as in dialogue, and be accessible through anything from a mobile device to a smart tabletop or a tiny embedded earpiece.

They will help managers understand the possible outcomes of decisions before those decisions get made.

Cognitive Computers

Technology is approaching a breaking point.

Torrents of data are flooding systems. Billions of people around the world are on the Internet, making transactions, posting on social networks, listening to music, and doing work—all of it generating data. By 2013, there were more than six billion mobile phone subscriptions globally, more than two billion of them with broadband capability adding more data.[2]

On top of that, the physical world is becoming packed with sensors that digitize life—water flow in rivers, traffic on city streets, and the movement of goods and people and animals. There are already about a trillion connected devices generating data.

Computers won't be able to keep up—at least not the programmable computers that have dominated for fifty to sixty years. Even if we can make those computers fast enough to crunch all that data, the software will be too inflexible to deal with the volume, speed, diversity, and uncertain veracity of it all. As a result we will often get answers after they're no longer valuable. We are like drivers of a car in a snowstorm who only have a sense of what we're not seeing through the windshield.

Fortunately, we're entering a new technology era. Let me explain.

The first era of computing—the tabulating era—began in the nineteenth century and continued into the 1940s. Tabulating machines were made up of a series of mechanical switches and were essentially elaborate adding devices, helping tally up a national census or a company's payroll. This was an enormous advance, and it made possible the rise of the modern bureaucratic nation-state and the modern corporation.

The second era emerged in the 1940s—the programmable computing era. At first these machines relied on vacuum tubes, then transistors, which got smaller and smaller and packed into microprocessors. The machines operate on an architecture described by mathematician John von Neumann: software programs tell the machines to carry out calculations in a series of steps, pulling in data stored separately from the programs. This is how most computers work today. While computers have gotten faster and faster, the von Neumann architecture means that all the work has to be lined up in the right steps as it flows through a machine's processors.

This, too, was a major advance in technology, business, and society. It made possible the multinational corporation—providing a common platform for everything from back office accounting to supply chains, ATMs, and travel reservation systems.

When the data is highly structured in understandable formats, such as tables in a database, programmable architecture does the job very well. But today, structured data is becoming a smaller and smaller fraction of what we are capturing. Most of what is known as "big data" looks more like life itself—full of images, sounds, patterns, language, and uncertainty.

The new era of computing, just emerging, will be one of cognitive systems. Instead of being programmed by humans, computers will "learn" from their interactions with data and people, and they will adapt, like the brain, to many parallel connections among data streams at once, generating patterns, observations, and insights. These systems will draw on unimaginable amounts of information and also take into account what they "know" about the people asking the question and the environment around them. The machines will, for the first time, interact with us in ways that are almost human, bringing order to the chaos of free-flowing and diverse information—and do so in something like real time.

IBM's Watson represents a starting point for a cognitive system.[3] It shows what this kind of technology can do today, which helps us imagine what it will do tomorrow.

The original Watson, built on software called DeepQA and running on a room-size computer, beat two human champions on the TV game show *Jeopardy!* in 2011. The system ingested hundreds of millions of pages' worth of material, from poems to Wikipedia entries to textbooks. The algorithms in the software broke down the material into categories and learned how words are used in various contexts. In this way, Watson started "learning" from the data rather than processing it through a set of instructions. In a sense, it became expert in a domain—the game of *Jeopardy!* It arrived at answers by coming up with numerous possibilities and ranking the certainty of each. Not only could Watson arrive at answers, it could leave a trail of breadcrumbs behind, showing how it came to the answers. And it became better through experience.

In the years since, Watson has been exploring applications in many domains from retail to financial services. But health care, where it has become impossible for physicians and even researchers to keep up with information, has become our grand challenge. Medical literature doubles in size every few years, yet doctors say they have little time to read medical journals each month. For physicians, incorporating hundreds of thousands of articles into their practice and applying them to patient care—together with seemingly unlimited patient-specific information, as we plumb the possibilities of genomics—is a significant challenge.

Today, the first of these systems are being "trained" with data in real environments, essentially advising professionals by bringing an immense store of knowledge to bear on a problem. These machines can "understand" spoken questions in natural language and logically arrive at possible answers. Watson in three seconds can sift through information equivalent to roughly two hundred million pages of data in natural language and analyze it to help a doctor identify the most likely diagnosis and treatment options in complex cases.

But there is much work still to be done in many domains, which will contribute to cognitive computing—from voice-based interaction with smartphones to deep exploration in "artificial intelligence." At the Massachusetts Institute of Technology, for instance, Rosalind Picard is studying the role emotions play in making more efficient decisions, working toward eventually building helpful emotions into cognitive machines. And in Silicon Valley, Jeff Hawkins, who invented the Palm computer, runs Numenta, which is developing software that can learn the way the brain learns.

The pace of development is breathtaking, and it's impossible to predict the future with confidence, based on the work we do today. But our experience from working with clients and universities at IBM Research tells me that by 2040, we will have exponentially greater computing power and a new cognitive software model that will be trained with data. The systems will gorge themselves on nearly infinite data.

Then the question is: what will we do with such magnificent technology?

Modeling a Human

Soon after computers were invented, scientists realized the machines could be used to simulate aspects of the physical world as a way to get faster or more cost-effective answers to difficult questions. During World War II, von Neumann and another mathematician, Stanislaw Ulam, developed a simulation method—the Monte Carlo method—that helped them understand the behavior of neutrons. That was pretty impressive, considering the day's computers could do only about four hundred calculations per second. The chip in a modern digital watch would put that to shame.

By the 1950s, scientists in the United States and Sweden began using computers to model, simulate, and predict weather, giving birth to the sophisticated meteorological predictions behind every TV weather reporter's forecasts today. Modeling exploded in the 1960s, applied to everything from inventory control to industrial systems design to the Apollo moon missions. In the 2010s, the world couldn't operate without simulations. Computer models test nuclear bombs without exploding any real ones, govern the traffic in the skies, and even keep Segway scooters from tipping over.

The Segway helps illustrate an interesting turning point in modeling. Modeling uses data to represent something that happens in the real world. Usually, it requires a lot of data, which means the simulation requires complex computations that, typically, take much longer than the actual event. When simulating a nuclear explosion, for instance, the simulation doesn't happen as fast as a real explosion. And that's OK for research. There's enough time to run the computations and study the answers.

However, magic happens when you can compute a model at the speed of nature. Inside a Segway, a small computer runs a model of the physics involved in balancing the scooter on its two wheels. It can do this as fast as the physics happen in nature, constantly predicting exactly what the Segway's machinery has to do to counter weight shifts and keep the scooter upright. The time to right answers is crucial—a split-second too late and the Segway's rider would be flipped onto the pavement.

As the next twenty-five years progress, technology will increasingly be able to compute accurate models of complex events in real time. One of the more stunning outcomes is that we'll all be able to access a real-time model of our own bodies.

Scientists at Lawrence Livermore National Laboratory are working with IBM to start down that path. The project, called Cardoid, is aimed at modeling the human heart. If we can accurately simulate the behavior of a heart down to the cellular level, we'll be able to test surgical procedures and medications on computers instead of on people. But the heart is so complex that until recently it took forty-five minutes of computation to simulate a single heartbeat. At that rate, the time to test a single drug would be years or decades—not a helpful span of time to get to a right answer.

Livermore tackled the problem by using a supercomputer with 1.5 million computing cores that can operate in parallel. By 2013, it could replicate nine heartbeats in one minute of calculations. It could model an hour of heart activity in about seven hours. That's an astounding improvement.

The pace of development has taken off over just a couple of years, and it will not be long before a supercomputer will be able to model a heart in real time. Watching such a computer model react to a drug or surgical procedure will then be the same as watching a real heart. And you can see where this is heading. A heart model that today runs on a supercomputer in a research lab will soon be delivered as a service accessed through the cloud on a tablet or smartphone.

While the cost and computation time go down, the complexity, customization, and accuracy will go up. In ten to fifteen years, your doctor will be able to access a model of your heart. You won't wait until you have heart trouble to use it. You might even access your model to experiment with the impact of a daily two-mile run or a low-fat diet.

Advanced computer science and medical science are merging in myriad ways. We'll be able to marry such high-performance computing capabilities with the knowledge and learning power of cognitive systems like Watson to assist doctors in providing quick, detailed assessments of a procedure or a drug for a specific individual.

In parallel, DNA sequencing is getting faster and cheaper. Over the next decade, knowing your genetic makeup will become as common as knowing your blood type, another valuable form of data. Today organizations such as the New York Genomic Center are already exploring the potential of cognitive systems to improve outcomes for the most aggressive cancers—those that spread because they mutate rapidly.

This is all about the time value of insight. Understanding a patient at the genomic level and finding precise treatments among thousands of possible combinations will need to occur in a window of maybe a few weeks or a month, otherwise there is no value to the patient. We should be able to do such analysis in hours or minutes.

By 2040, all this varied work will have begun to come together. Researchers will soon be able to economically and expediently explore the entire human body, collecting data that can inform simulations of particular brains, nervous systems, muscles, cells, proteins, and other body systems. We'll have enough data and computing power to start to model the entire human body as a system.

And as with search engines and cell phones today, we will wonder how anyone lived without this capability.

Personal Lifelong Tutor

In the 1930s, in the worst of the Great Depression—at the same time that Ronald Coase was developing the ideas for which he would later win the Nobel Prize in Economics—a Columbia University professor named Ben Wood asked for a meeting with IBM's longtime CEO, Thomas Watson Sr. Wood had been pioneering standardized testing as a way to measure students across schools and geographies. But scoring the tests by hand was a long and tedious process. Wood convinced Watson to donate IBM's tabulating machines so Wood could greatly speed the test-scoring process and make standardized testing a reality. For the first time, machines could know what a student had learned.

Over the following eighty years, computer analysis of standardized tests has surfaced information that has been valuable for educational institutions. But because the information is not part of a true system—at least not one that senses and responds in real time—it has not mattered much to individual students' actual learning or growth. It takes weeks or months to identify a student veering off track. Too often these insights are not fully grasped by the students or their support system when they have the most value.

The insights generated by a cognitive system could tell us not just what a student is learning but how he or she is best able to learn, and how fast. Such a system might then help the teacher tailor lessons and support specifically for that student. In fact, a smart system could become a lifelong educational adviser, guiding each student to courses, subjects, colleges, even jobs, that are a good match.

In 2015, a couple of developments are merging to help create this education technology. A very important one is the rise of massive open online courses (MOOCs)—digitized educational content widely available to anyone with an Internet connection. As more students use MOOCs, often as a supplement to classroom learning, the courses generate a tremendous amount of data about student behavior, such as how long students stay engaged with certain kinds of content or where and when they access content. This is the beginning of developing a more real-time data model of the way an individual student learns.

This is quite a flip in the world of education. Until now, students had to learn the courses; now we see courses beginning to "learn" the students.

In 2013, schools in Gwinnett County, Georgia—a district of 140,000 students—started working to analyze digital learning of individual students. The schools began to find, for instance, that the data can identify a student who is at risk of doing poorly before he or she takes a test. By intervening and helping, a student who might have failed a test and become discouraged would have a chance to correct course, get better grades, and have more positive feelings about school.

By 2040, this shift will have a more fundamental impact, altering the way we think about educational achievement in general. Learning today is mostly time based—students get a diploma for completing twelve years of school, then a degree for completing another four, and so on. By 2040, measures of achievement will be competency based. Students will get degrees or certifications that reflect not how long they have studied but what they know.

This, in turn, will change the role of the teacher. Instead of being a one-way delivery vehicle for information—or, even worse, a test proctor or disciplinarian—the teacher will be more like a tutor or mentor, valued as a source of wisdom and as a provider of individual counseling. The teacher will be able to draw on the system, which will "know" what the student knows.

Finally, because the classroom is no longer an arena of regimented socialization or one-way information transfer, it will become a more collaborative space where teachers help and advise individual students or small groups and where the group itself creates positive feedback loops of mutual knowledge and support. In 2040, the one-size-fits-all classroom lecture will seem as archaic as the twentieth-century television broadcast tower.

And because the system will "learn" along with you, it will not abandon you after college. If you want to go after a particular skill set or change careers, the digital assistant will help sustain focus on your objectives, the core requirements, and alternative pathways to proceed. It will act as a guide—an adviser and advocate for skills and learning. In fact, it will become the embodiment of "lifelong learning." By 2040, students will be surprised to find out learning wasn't always lifelong.

Cognitive Business Apps

At IBM's Thomas J. Watson Research Center, we built what we call the Cognitive Environments Lab. It's a way for us to work on the interactive environments of the future and to create cognitive applications that will help people make better decisions.

The entire room is lined with ultra-high-resolution screens. With the wave of a wand, a user can move data around the room. A natural language system recognizes spoken questions. This is the beginning of embedding cognitive computing in the environments we inhabit (whether our offices, our meeting rooms, our cars, or our homes) and utilizing such capability in our daily lives. These new cognitive environments will improve the work flow of experts and teams engaged in complex decision making.

By 2040, a manager may walk into a cognitive room at his or her company. The manager's personal cognitive agent will interface with the room, allowing him or her to plug into and interact with all the elements of the system. The personal agent will connect with other agents and people and help the manager generate hypotheses, gather evidence for and against, and generate possible answers when they are most valuable—before taking action.

Since the tabulating era of computers, machines have helped managers make decisions. They've tallied up financial numbers, analyzed performance, identified potential customers, and looked for trends in social media. Spreadsheets of old have given way to sophisticated analytics that can look for patterns no human would ever find. Hedge funds run detailed models of the global economy to spot risk and to try to know where to invest as early as possible. Computers have constantly marched toward providing enterprises with better answers and more detailed scenario models, in shorter time frames.

The cognitive computing era will take decision support to an entirely new level. The kinds of cognitive systems that will build models of the human body could certainly build models of a lot of things businesses care about. By 2040, a company might build a model of a target market and test a product before manufacturing it. A company could even build a model of itself, constantly learning from all the company's trial and error, success and failure, generating ideas and solutions unbiased by any individual human perspective or groupthink and giving the CEO a way to try out decisions before implementing them.

As in education, a company's cognitive system will be able to get to know individual employees, understanding their strengths and weaknesses and work patterns, intervening before failure, and helping guide their careers. By 2040, an employee's human resources file will likely be a sophisticated model of that employee's work and knowledge.

Ultimately, by 2040 we believe an executive will have a readily available, naturally interactive set of tools to model his or her business—a digital model always evolving as new information is drawn in. We call this emerging idea cognitive business apps, or "cogs."

A personal cog will "learn" from our experience and even anticipate what we need. It will "learn" through interacting with other people, other cogs, and other data sources, becoming more helpful, capable, and precise over time. It will "understand" and model its user. The personal cog will interact with many other domain-specific cogs that specialize in market information, news feeds, supply chains, patents, and regulations, and in the organization itself. It will interact with these other cogs as needed to answer questions, explore strategies, and anticipate issues.

We picture a businessperson in 2040 walking into a meeting space in which cogs that reside on a phone or tablet can be deployed in the room. Meetings will have another dimension, whether in a cognitive room or out for coffee with a smartphone. Businesspeople will have interactive access to data and expertise, along with a better understanding of the alternatives.

This will no doubt lead to new kinds of corporate structures and strategies, just as lowering transaction costs led to the development of the vertically integrated company in the mid-twentieth century.

It will also give rise to a new kind of executive. In a world of cogs and sophisticated computer models, the most successful decision makers will always be exploring. They will differentiate themselves not by knowing all the answers, but by knowing the right questions to ask. It will be easy and economical to bring in new perspectives, to challenge intuition and raise evidence. You can imagine that the economics and speed of insights and answers will drive a new kind of creativity in questioning, a bias toward agile approaches and openness to continual transformation.

2040

It remains daunting to make predictions about technology twenty-five years out. But, extrapolating from what we know now, I can be quite sure that by 2040 we'll be well into the era of cognitive systems that will fuel incredible innovation, just as the first computers and then the Internet did before them.

The technology will impact almost every facet of life and work.

We're quite sure the technology will completely change the way we approach health care, education, and management. We've already begun working on applying cognitive technology to those fields.

The real-time nature of these cognitive models will play out even more in purely digital domains. One such area is a very current concern, cybersecurity. In protecting people and assets, these systems watch over networks that operate at speeds limited often only by physics. In 2040, these systems will be targeted and even personal, adept at detecting patterns buried in billions of network log files and emerging models, developing, in a sense, "gut instincts," so they can react to a threat in a split second—the way a human instinctively ducks when an object comes at him or her.

When scientists in our labs at IBM think about the coming era of answers, we can think of a wide variety of other ways cognitive computing could be applied. This is not about "perfect" knowledge—whatever that might be. It's about good-enough confidence with appropriate timeliness. This is what we mean by "the right answer": the medical treatment that can halt a cancer before it metastasizes; the educational intervention that can set a young child's learning on the most individually tailored path at a point when the child's brain is still being formed; the business decision about an emergent market space that can anticipate and avoid "the innovator's dilemma."

But how exactly this will play out is, frankly, a bit of a challenge for a technologist. Perhaps it is better suited to the imaginations of science fiction writers, particularly as the application of technology becomes less and less linear. This era of systems will always be questioning, adapting, and changing, such that no model will be frozen in time. In fact, time will be a rich dimension in cognitive systems, as it is in the natural world. And the nature of prediction itself will change.

How will such cognitive systems and data models emerge in our lives? How will they be monetized? How will such a rich world of readily available insight and answers change the economy, society, and standards of living? Will it change how we actually think? Will it open a door to more fluid, imaginative, emergent—more fully intelligent—habits of mind? This goes beyond the familiar idea that technology throughout human history has freed us from lower-level physical or routine work, has freed us to apply ourselves to higher-order thinking. This suggests a change in what we mean by "higher-order thinking."

Technology always affects the global economy and society. Cognitive technology will be no different. From where I sit, the time value of answers and insights will drive the most profound changes. We're entering an age when raw information will be a resource, a commodity. The most valuable thing on earth will be knowing what to ask.

Notes

1. "Gartner Says Annual Smartphone Sales Surpassed Sales of Feature Phones for the First Time in 2013," Gartner, Inc., last modified February 13, 2014, http://www.gartner.com/newsroom/id/2665715.

2. "Global Mobile Statistics 2014 Part A: Mobile Subscribers; Handset Market Share; Mobile Operators," mobiForge, last modified May 16, 2014, http:/

/mobiforge.com/research-analysis/global-mobile-statistics-2014-part-a
-mobile-subscribers-handset-market-share-mobile-operators.

3. The Watson technology is named for IBM's founder, Thomas J. Watson Sr., as well as being an allusion to Sherlock Holmes's fictional sidekick, Dr. John Watson.

CHAPTER 9

The Environment

Bridging the Gap between Knowing and Doing: The New Environmental Governance

Mark R. Tercek

President and CEO, The Nature Conservancy

Jimmie Powell

Energy Team Lead, The Nature Conservancy

Our planet is at a critical inflection point. The standard of living of the world's seven billion people has significantly improved and is projected to get better. But, as we reach nine billion people and three billion new middle-class consumers in the next twenty-five years, society will experience an unprecedented increase in the demand for food, water, and energy. We will need to produce 50 to 100 percent more of these necessities from environments that are already strained. Our increased demands have the potential to push fragile, natural systems beyond the brink to collapse.[1]

Yet there is reason for cautious optimism. Thanks to advances in science, technology, and communications, we know more about the environmental challenges we face than ever before. And for the most part, we know how to address these challenges, barring unforeseen catastrophes from the climate system, infectious diseases, or human violence. The state of our environment in 2040 will largely hinge on one critical question: can we create the governmental institutions and processes needed to take full advantage of what we know needs to be done, and get it done before it is too late?

In this chapter, we answer this question with a tentative yes. By combining smart science with smart new systems of governance, we should be able to close the gap between knowing and doing and put ourselves on a path toward a diverse and sustainable planet in 2040, one that integrates conservation values and human development.

Living in the Anthropocene

Traditionally, threats to the environment have been viewed as singular events—isolated by geography, as with Love Canal, or tied to an event, such as the BP Deepwater Horizon oil spill. These types of threats will always remain. However, nature is increasingly at risk from ongoing human activity and the "by-products" of economic development. Agriculture, fishing, forestry, mining, energy production, manufacturing, and urban development are now the dominant forces shaping virtually every natural system across the earth. Population growth, wealth, trade, and technology will continue to accelerate the rate of change in fundamental natural processes affecting our climate, our food, our freshwater, and our oceans.

Human impacts may be magnified by tipping points, time lags, or feedback loops that are often unanticipated. For example, increases in temperature and sea level rise caused by carbon dioxide emitted this year will continue to be experienced for many decades or even centuries into the future. Loss of sea ice in the Arctic amplifies the warming impacts of the greenhouse gases that first caused the ice to melt, as newly open waters absorb rather than reflect the sun's energy. And if a warming Arctic releases the billions of tons of methane—a potent greenhouse gas—stored under its permafrost, our climate system could rapidly shift to a radically new equilibrium.

Complexities such as these and changes in technology and society make it hard to predict the future of our environment. For example, few people expected the shale gas revolution—and the associated risks and opportunities of horizontal drilling and hydraulic fracturing (also known as fracking)—even five years ago.

The geographic scope of environmental challenges adds further complexity. The impacts of some of our activities are global in reach and will require global solutions. Warming and ocean acidification caused by carbon dioxide emissions from power production, transportation, and deforestation will not be prevented unless we work together globally in some way.

On the other hand, environmental impacts such as water scarcity, biodiversity loss, and overfishing occur in similar form in many places around the globe but require primarily local actions to fix. Although national and international institutions may provide knowledge and leadership in addressing these threats, it will be the people farming in the watershed, cutting the forest, or fishing the bay who must find the path to sustain the resources upon which their livelihoods depend.

Finally, our capacity for harmful impact on nature is increasing dramatically. The global population has nearly doubled since 1970. At the same time, rising global incomes and increased consumption have combined to further magnify our impact as global economic output has quadrupled over the same period.

But there is good news. Our scientific capacity to anticipate the environmental impacts of our actions has increased even more dramatically. As the following case studies on ozone protection and global fisheries illustrate, developments in science and environmental governance allow for a future where we can better anticipate and avoid the threats to natural services essential for human well-being.

After describing these two cases, we examine three of the greatest threats from human activity: water scarcity, biodiversity loss, and climate change. Surely good science and new technology will play major roles in understanding and addressing each of these threats. But an equally important challenge in each case is governance. Can we apply the lessons learned from addressing the ozone crisis and the collapse of some fisheries to develop and implement new institutions that will guide our behavior so that these threats can be avoided?

In this chapter, the concept of environmental governance reaches well beyond the regulations of governmental agencies and regimes based on international treaties. It includes mechanisms and institutions that make use of market incentives and consumer information. It includes cooperatives and trade groups where industry participants help design regulations and monitor compliance. And it includes long-standing community institutions, especially in developing countries, that use social norms to cooperatively manage rangelands, irrigation and drainage systems, and small fisheries.

These new forms of governance may take shape as water funds that pay fees collected by cities to farmers to keep drinking water reservoirs clean; forest and bioenergy certification systems that ensure the use of sustainable practices in fiber and feedstock production by providing information to consumers; fisheries cooperatives that manage catch share systems; industrial trade associations that develop best practices and codes of conduct; and networks of nongovernmental organizations that play major roles in shaping national policy and international treaties.

Two hallmarks of success among the new environmental governance institutions are adaptive management—learning by doing—and network maintenance. An adaptive institution may change its form and function over time to reflect the changing nature of environmental threats and the most successful strategies to protect human and natural systems. Success also depends on "bridging" organizations that foster communication across stakeholder communities and across government agencies at various levels.[2]

We Can Get It Right: Two Case Studies

Lessons from the Ozone Crisis

In 1974, Mario Molina and Sherwood Rowland published a paper theorizing that chlorine and bromine in some widely used chemicals could damage the ozone shield—the layer of oxygen molecules in the upper atmosphere that prevents most of the sun's harmful ultraviolet radiation (UV-B) from reaching the earth's surface. The main culprit: chlorofluorocarbons (CFCs), nontoxic, highly stable, and relatively inexpensive chemicals used in refrigeration, aerosol sprays, and a number of industrial applications.[3]

Molina and Rowland's theory of ozone destruction was controversial.

There were no measurements showing that ozone in the stratosphere was declining. And there was no evidence that UV-B radiation reaching the earth's surface was increasing. Nevertheless, the nature of the potential risk was extraordinary. The U.S. Environmental Protection Agency (EPA) projected that ozone depletion could lead to 150 million cancer cases with three million deaths and twenty-five million cataract cases over the next century, if Molina and Rowland proved right.

In 1978, the EPA and the U.S. Food and Drug Administration (FDA) banned the use of CFCs as propellants in aerosol sprays. There was broad public support for this step, and many major personal care and household products manufacturers quickly moved to alternative formulations. But only Sweden, Canada, and Norway followed the U.S. lead; some governments, including that of the United Kingdom, expressed doubts about the science.

The EPA continued its study of CFCs and persuaded President Ronald Reagan to press for international action, resulting in the 1985 Vienna Convention for the Protection of the Ozone Layer. The treaty called for monitoring, additional research, and the development of a protocol at some point in the future that might regulate the production and use of CFCs.

That same year, the ozone hole was discovered. The hole—a decrease of 40 to 60 percent in the amount of stratospheric ozone extending over a very large region (10.6 million square miles at its largest in 2006) of the Southern hemisphere—quickly captured public attention.[4] The hole and the subsequent science proving that industrial chemicals were the culprits in its formation quickly built support for the regulation and phaseout of CFCs. The companies that made and used the chemicals promised to develop substitutes on an expedited schedule.

The promised protocol came quickly and was negotiated in Montreal in 1987. It called for a 50 percent reduction in all CFC production by 1998. It has been modified many times since to reflect new science, to accelerate production bans, and to add other chemicals. Today, 197 nations—virtually the entire world—have ratified the protocol. Global production of ozone-depleting substances has been reduced by 98 percent.[5]

Several governance innovations contributed to the protocol's extraordinary success:

- Developing countries with low levels of ozone use were granted a ten-year grace period during which use could actually increase before the phaseout period would begin.
- A multilateral fund was created to assist developing countries in converting their industries to substitutes.
- A trade regime was set up to prevent importation of CFCs from countries that declined to join the protocol.

In 1989, the U.S. Congress enacted an excise tax on ozone-depleting substances. As the tax rate increased over time, it eventually tripled the cost of CFCs and made substitutes economically competitive. Congress put a price on ozone depletion. The European Union also imposed its own excise tax.

The ozone crisis is not only a story of good science but of rapid technological innovation and new mechanisms of environmental governance that made the solution to a potentially catastrophic environmental disaster relatively painless.[6] Though it will take many decades for the ozone shield to heal—CFCs may stay in the atmosphere for up to one hundred years—the risk has been averted. By the mid-twenty-first century, ozone depletion will be a threat of the past.

Fixing Our Fisheries

Marine fisheries are an important part of today's global food system. They provide 20 percent of the animal protein in the diets of more than three billion people. They are also a significant part of the global economy. In 2010, fisheries and aquaculture produced 148 million metric tons of fish and shellfish worth $217 billion. Capture fisheries provided direct fishing jobs for an estimated thirty-eight million people in 2010, with another seventeen million employed in fish farming (aquaculture). The industry also includes processors, distribution systems, gear manufacturers, and vessel construction and maintenance workers. An estimated six hundred million people—10 percent of the world's population—depend on the industry for some part of their livelihoods.[7]

Overfishing has been a chronic problem. It occurs when the catch of a particular marine species in a specific geographic area is so large that the population cannot recover. The problem can be so severe that the fish stock collapses to near extinction and the ecosystem changes in ways that prevent recovery even if the fishing pressure is removed. Overfishing prevents fishers from realizing the full economic reward for their efforts. One estimate puts the global revenue loss at $50 billion per year.[8]

A key factor that has contributed to overfishing since the 1960s is improving technology. The size and power of vessels in the global fishing fleet has increased dramatically. More powerful vessels can pull more gear, and sonar has made finding fish easier. As fish populations decline, fishers have responded by further increasing capacity, often with subsidies from governments that are estimated at nearly $30 billion per year.[9]

Perhaps the most dramatic example of overfishing is the collapse of the cod fishery off the coast of Newfoundland. Overfishing in this three-hundred-year-old fishery began in the 1960s when foreign factory fleets entered the coastal waters of the United States and Canada and the fishery was severely damaged. When the foreign vessels were banned, the Canadian government provided significant subsidies to launch a fleet of Canadian-owned vessels fishing for cod. Scientific projections for the amount of fish that could be caught sustainably were overly optimistic, and the fishery soon began to decline. In 1992, the Newfoundland cod fishery collapsed. The region took a huge economic hit requiring $1 billion in government assistance to those who lost their jobs. Despite removal of the fishing pressure, cod have not recovered.[10]

Today, the Food and Agriculture Organization (FAO) estimates that 57 percent of all assessed fisheries are fully exploited—meaning that no growth in harvesting is possible. Approximately 30 percent of assessed stocks globally are overfished—up from 10 percent in 1974. And the outlook may be worse than the assessments imply. Only 450 stocks are regularly assessed out of an estimated ten thousand fisheries globally. A recent paper suggests that unassessed fisheries (which account for 80 percent of the global catch) are likely to be poorly managed and more likely to be overfished.[11]

Yet there is reason to hope that the trends have begun to reverse. Recent changes in fishing regulations in several countries are showing signs of success. Some of the most promising measures for avoiding economic and environmental disasters like the collapse of New England's cod fishery include the following:

- *Comanagement* brings fishers into the decision making and implementation of fishery regulations. Not only does this give the fishers a heightened sense of ownership, it also makes good use of their local knowledge.
- *Marine protected areas* take a wide variety of forms. Some areas are closed for a time to some types of fishing to let stocks recover. Marine parks and reserves are permanently set aside to protect important features such as coral reefs or spawning grounds.
- *Ecosystem-based management* sets total allowable catch by considering potential impacts of fishing on the entire marine system. In the past, government regulations have ignored the impacts of fishing on other aspects of the ecosystem such as food web interactions and the destruction of seafloor habitats.
- *Catch shares* give each licensed fisher a specific portion of the total allowable catch for a fishery. The fisher is guaranteed a right to catch that amount and can match the capacity of his or her gear to a sustainable level of fishing. If the right is permanent and transferable, the fisher has an interest in seeing the fishery managed sustainably because success will increase the market value of his or her share.

Just as we solved the global threat of ozone depletion, smart science combined with improved governance offers the prospect of dramatically better management of marine fisheries in the coming decades.

Global Challenges and Opportunities

Water Scarcity

Before looking to the future, it is important to note that today more than a billion of the world's poorest people lack access to safe drinking water and perhaps twice that number do not have access to sanitation services (safe toilets and sewage disposal). Illnesses caused by microbes in drinking water kill two million children each year and are the principal cause of infant mortality.[12]

The water we drink is only a fraction of the water we use. Agriculture accounts for approximately 71 percent of water withdrawals. Energy production and other industries account for another 16 percent, and municipal water supply systems withdraw the remaining 13 percent. While most of the water used by industry and municipalities is returned to surface water courses after use, much of the water used in agriculture evaporates from irrigation systems or transpires to the atmosphere from crops before people can use it again.[13]

The Challenge

Driven by a growing population and the changing diets of billions of people moving from rural poverty to urban prosperity in developing countries, global freshwater withdrawals are expected to increase by 40 percent over the next three decades. Meeting these new demands will be further complicated by changing precipitation patterns caused by climate change. The combined effects of population growth, urbanization, and climate change may soon subject a large portion of the global population to water shortages.[14]

Water scarcity takes three forms:

1. *Physical scarcity* is an imbalance between the size of the human population in a region and its annual freshwater resources. There is simply not enough water to meet human needs.

2. *Economic scarcity* occurs in regions where investments in water infrastructure such as reservoirs or groundwater pumping could meet human needs but the investments have not been made because they are not affordable. The world's poor, whatever their rainfall endowment, will be more likely to experience water scarcity than the rest of us.

3. *Environmental scarcity* can occur even in areas with adequate water flows to meet human needs. However, that supply comes at the expense of nature, including dams that block fish passage, withdrawals that cause rivers to dry up, and groundwater pumping so extensive that streams and wetlands no longer recharge in summer months. Although few regions in developed countries would be categorized as physically or economically water stressed now or even in the next few decades, many of these regions (e.g., the western United States and Mediterranean Europe) are already experiencing environmental scarcity.[15]

Today, two billion people live in regions with dry, fragile climates that are threatened by periods of water scarcity. One often cited measure of water scarcity developed by Falkenmark and others[16] finds that meeting all human needs including water for agriculture requires seventeen hundred cubic meters of water per person per day. By 2040, two-thirds of the global population will be in areas suffering from water stress (between five hundred and seventeen hundred cubic meters of water flow per person per day) and 1.8 billion people will live in areas of absolute water scarcity (less than five hundred cubic meters of water flow per person per day). Regions most likely to suffer water scarcity in 2040 are northern Africa and the Middle East, South Africa, India, Mexico, northern China, Chile, Australia, and small island nations, especially in the Caribbean.[17]

Many regions follow a similar pattern to meet the water demands of a growing population. First, either a river or a groundwater aquifer is tapped to meet needs. As demand begins to approach the limit from those supplies, the water agency will create storage reservoirs by damming local rivers and streams. If demand continues to outstrip supply, the supplier may look to transfer water from distant reservoirs to meet local needs.

These infrastructure investments are often subsidized by governments to keep water and food prices low. The subsidies mask the true cost of water, spurring even greater demand. Only when demand finally exceeds the capacity of storage and interbasin transfers will users begin to adopt water conservation practices.

Many of the steps along this pathway have negative consequences for nature. Areas rich in aquatic wildlife habitat such as wetlands and river deltas may shrink in size as water is diverted to human use. Some rivers—even great rivers such as the Colorado—are taxed so completely that water no longer reaches their deltas in most years. As underground aquifers are depleted and water tables drop, the water that would normally discharge to springs and seeps is lost. Dams may alter a river's cyclical rise and fall necessary for the breeding and reproductive behaviors of fish, wildlife, and plants. Dams also block the movement of fish, closing off spawning grounds and segmenting species into small populations that may not survive other threats. As flows in streams and rivers are reduced to build reservoirs, pollution concentrations and water temperatures increase, killing aquatic life adapted to different conditions.[18]

It's no wonder that aquatic species face a greater risk of endangerment and extinction than comparable organisms living on the land.

The Opportunity

A majority of the regions that will experience water shortages in the next few decades have one thing in common. If there is more water available to prevent scarcity, it will most likely be found in agriculture. Although the most effective water conservation strategies will vary widely across regions, reducing agricultural water demand will be key to meeting growing water needs. Strategies include more efficient irrigation systems, changes in tilling practices so that less soil moisture is lost through evaporation, shifts to crops requiring less water, and the development of new hybrid plants that can produce good yields in drier conditions.

One of the most promising ways to reduce agricultural water use involves new partnerships that channel payments from city water agencies and other large industrial water users to agricultural producers who put water back into the river. Freshwater is the most valued service that nature provides. Users are willing to pay for it, if institutions can be created that allow agriculture producers to deliver reliable water supply to cities and industries.

Market institutions like this now exist, especially in South America, to prevent pollution of urban water supplies. More than a dozen cities, including New York, Quito, Bogotá, and São Paulo, have created water funds that pay farmers upstream to adopt agricultural and ranching practices that reduce sediment pollution in the river. Cleaner water allows the city to avoid expensive investments in treatment that would otherwise be necessary to remove pollutants.

We should fully expect that similar voluntary and market-based arrangements between farmers and cities will be developed to meet water supply needs as cities struggle with growing scarcity. Properly structured voluntary institutions could avoid a great deal of human conflict as scarcity moves in. Complex questions related to water ownership and assuring that the needs of the poorest are met will require further innovations. New forms of environmental governance—in addition to new science and technology—will be required to enable many cities to meet their water needs.

Biodiversity Loss and Alteration

Biodiversity is the variety of living things on earth. Most people think of biodiversity as the wide range of plant and animal species. But biodiversity also includes genetic variations within a species—think about all the different kinds of dogs—as well as the variety of natural communities that form ecosystems such as tropical rain forests, coral reefs, prairie grasslands, and mountain meadows. Diversity makes these biological communities and their members more resilient, better able to survive disturbances such as changes in climate or the introduction of invasive species and new diseases.

Human well-being is highly dependent on biodiversity, especially in rural areas of the least developed countries. As mentioned earlier, the value of global fisheries exceeds $200 billion per year. The insects and birds that pollinate our crops provide nearly $200 billion per year in value. Forests provide timber for construction and firewood, capture and filter drinking water, and provide food for rural populations. Wetlands and coastal mangrove forests protect human communities from storm surges and river flooding. People living in the poorest nations receive as much as 30 percent of their livelihood from local biodiversity. And everyone benefits from the innate wonder of nature. Imagine what life would be like if there were only a few species that existed everywhere and all places looked the same.[19]

The Challenge

Human activities are having a profound effect on biodiversity; its loss is one of the major environmental challenges of this century. There are many drivers of this loss, including the conversion of natural areas such as forests and grasslands to urban and agricultural use; the unsustainable use of resources such as fisheries and freshwater as discussed previously; the intentional or accidental transfer of species from one region to another; overuse of nitrogen fertilizers that create imbalance in freshwater ecosystems; and the growing threat of carbon dioxide pollution causing changes in climate, sea level rise, and ocean acidification.

Of the roughly 1.9 million known species, the International Union for the Conservation of Nature has listed sixteen thousand species as declining, threatened, or endangered. Among those, 30 percent of amphibians, 23 percent of mammals, and 12 percent of birds are threatened with extinction within the next century. Those depending on freshwater and tropical rain forest habitats generally face the greatest risks.[20]

Some scientists believe that human activities are causing extinction rates to increase to more than one hundred times the natural background rate. Some predict that over the next few centuries that number may increase to one thousand or even ten thousand times the natural rate. These projections are based on models that relate drivers such as habitat conversion and climate change to estimates of species abundance. If these trends are correct, a huge percentage of species may be lost in a few millennia. Over the past five centuries a few hundred species are known to have been lost. Fortunately, many species on the brink of extinction have actually been recovered through human intervention.[21]

Extinction is usually a slow event. Large areas of forest cover may be lost to agriculture, but some remnant of the species population that depended on the forest habitat may hang on for many generations in the altered habitat, may evolve and adapt, or may relocate to new areas. We may be setting in motion an extinction crisis that will occur over the next few millennia, but it is not occurring in the next twenty-five years. We still have an opportunity to change the narrative on species extinctions.

Two major trends will affect that narrative. Although habitat conversion—most importantly from forests to croplands—has been the major source of biodiversity loss over the last century, the pattern is likely to change in the coming decades. Conversion of natural systems to crops and pasture will continue to be the most important driver in the least developed African and Asian countries, but it will no longer play the dominant role in Europe and North America nor in emerging economies including China, Brazil, Russia, South Africa, India, and Indonesia. In some of the most developed countries, agricultural land will continue to be abandoned, and ecosystem recovery and regeneration will occur on a significant scale. In addition, recent trends indicate that deforestation rates may be slowing in the Amazon and that some depleted fisheries are recovering.

The other major development will be the increasing role of climate change in biodiversity loss. It may account for 40 percent of the decline in the population of many species by 2040.[22] The impacts will reach across both developed and developing countries. Unchecked, climate change will emerge as the major driver of global biodiversity loss in this century.

The Opportunity
Again, one key to protecting biodiversity is in the quality of human governance institutions, whether global (i.e., the Convention on Biodiversity), local (e.g., parks, national forests, wildlife refuges), or in the private sector (individual business commitments to avoid or offset biodiversity losses). Although there are examples of tremendous success at each of these levels, our governance arrangements to protect biodiversity are falling far short of the need, and loss is likely to continue largely unabated over the next quarter century. Unlike water, where optimism for governance solutions is warranted, biodiversity is not currently treated as an urgent human need.

In response to global biodiversity loss, many governments have created protected areas, parks and wildlife refuges set aside and managed for the benefit of biodiversity. The number of protected areas around the globe has exploded over the past forty years, increasing from approximately ten thousand in 1970 to more than one hundred thousand today. Twelve percent of the earth's land area now has a protected designation, and 188 nations have committed to extend protection to 17 percent of all terrestrial habitats by 2020. Some countries have also created marine protected areas (although they cover only 7.5 percent of global coastal zones). Yet these formal commitments, while impressive, are not a panacea. Many areas are not effectively managed due to a lack of resources. In fact, 14 percent of designated protected areas lack any management measures at all.[23]

Many nations have also adopted regulatory measures to protect biodiversity and human welfare. One important tool to protect habitat is land-use planning that requires formal environmental assessments before major new projects or policies are implemented. Nevertheless, many of the values associated with biodiversity are not properly accounted for in the market and policy decisions that drive biodiversity losses. For instance, some of the most serious threats to biodiversity are actually driven by governmental subsidies for economic sectors including agriculture, fisheries, and bioenergy development. In this case governance is the problem, not the solution. Repeal of some particularly harmful subsidies would be an important reform.

Another example is climate change policy. Many observers believe that the most effective policy to reduce greenhouse gas pollution would be to put a price on carbon dioxide emissions from burning fossil fuels. But the policy would be much more effective—both for reducing global warming and for enhancing biodiversity—if it also paid (or provided a tax credit) for the sequestration of carbon in soil, forest, and grassland systems. Although much of the discussion about sequestering carbon in natural systems has been about preventing deforestation and restoring forestlands that have been lost to agriculture and urban development, it is important to understand that much more of the carbon now causing global warming was originally stored in soils rather than vegetation and was lost to the atmosphere by conversion of forests and prairies to croplands. Returning these hundreds of billions of tons of carbon to soils through practices that are also good for agricultural productivity is a high priority.

Consumer information is another recent innovation in governance that is increasing attention to the value of biodiversity in the marketplace. Certification systems for forest products, fisheries, and bioenergy now encourage consumers to insist on sustainable practices including biodiversity protection in crop and harvesting activities. This new tool for governance that operates outside of formal governmental channels may be especially important to protect deep-sea fisheries that are located outside territorial waters and tropical forests in the least developed nations.

Finally, many businesses are beginning to consider the role of nature in their supply chains and the impact of their plant and capital investments on natural systems. Biodiversity offsets for development impacts have been included in the laws of some countries including Brazil, Canada, China, France, Mexico, and South Africa. In addition, many leading global corporations, especially in mining and oil and gas production, are implementing biodiversity offsets to ensure that their activities have no adverse impact on land and water habitats. Public policies and grassroots activism should encourage these new practices to expand rapidly across many industrial sectors and should insist that biodiversity values get increased attention in corporate decision making over the next quarter century.

Climate Change

Human activities—principally the combustion of fossil fuels and the conversion of forests to other land uses—are increasing the concentration of carbon dioxide (CO_2) and other greenhouse gases in the atmosphere. CO_2 concentrations are now more than 40 percent greater than they were in 1750.[24] This trend has already led to warmer temperatures, more severe storm surges, and changes in rainfall patterns, weakening the natural systems on which we all depend. Yet despite an array of potential strategies, the world has yet to tackle CO_2 emissions in a coordinated fashion.

The Challenge

There is some uncertainty about the impact of greenhouse gas concentrations on temperature increases. The best current estimate is that each doubling of CO_2 concentrations will increase temperatures by approximately three degrees Celsius (or 5.2 degrees Fahrenheit). CO_2 concentrations in the atmosphere at the beginning of the Industrial Revolution were approximately 275 parts per million (ppm). If current emissions trends continue, a doubling to 550 ppm would occur by 2050. Some observers fear that CO_2 concentrations may double again by the early 2100s, producing a temperature increase of more than ten degrees Fahrenheit—but not immediately and not everywhere.[25]

Those are average temperature increases, and they will only develop over the long run. There will be great variability in temperature changes around the world; some areas may even get cooler before heating up. Regions in high latitudes such as the Arctic will see much greater temperature increases than tropical regions. Temperatures in winter seasons and at night will increase more than temperatures in the summer and during the day. And temperatures over land surfaces will increase more than temperatures at the surface of the ocean.

Global warming will also alter patterns of precipitation, as a warmer atmosphere can also hold more water vapor. Again, high-latitude areas may see increased rainfall while some areas in the subtropics and temperate zones may experience drier climates.

Although we can already measure some of these changes—global average temperatures have increased by 0.8 degrees Celsius over the twentieth century[26] and severe precipitation events are 5 percent more frequent in the United States[27]—the changes over the next twenty-five years are not likely to be dramatic. So why the urgent need for action?

For a variety of reasons, global warming is a very slow event. First, 90 percent of the sun's energy captured by the earth is stored in the planet's massive oceans, which take a long time to heat up.[28] Once heated, they will release that excess energy back to the atmosphere and land for millennia.

Second, positive feedback loops such as sea ice loss described previously may add to the warming caused directly by CO_2 pollution—even if carbon pollution is greatly reduced.

Third, while a large portion of the CO_2 emitted today will be absorbed by the oceans over the next century, as much as 20 percent of today's emissions will be in the atmosphere for centuries.[29] This long atmospheric residence will continue to push temperatures higher and higher each decade for many centuries into the future.

And finally, the investments that we make in power plants and industrial facilities have long lives of their own. Some coal-fired power plants in operation in the United States today are more than sixty years old. Hundreds of additional coal-fired power plants are expected to be constructed in the rapidly developing countries, especially China and India, over the next twenty-five years. They are likely to continue emitting billions of tons of carbon dioxide each year for many decades.

Once the climate change train is fully in motion, it may rumble down the tracks for centuries no matter what we do; thus the urgency to act now. Pundits have often used the "boiling frog" metaphor to shine a light on human behaviors that fail to act on gradually developing catastrophes until it is too late. Presumably, if you put a frog in a pot of cold water, put the pot on a burner, and heat it up gradually, the frog will fail to jump and will eventually be boiled to death. In the case of our impact on the climate system, the pot has long been on the burner. If we do not dramatically change our ways in the next twenty-five years, it will no longer be possible to remove the pot or turn the burner off—even if the water is yet to boil and the frog is still alive. Our planet is the frog.

In another respect, global warming may also be too sudden. If current trends in emissions continue for many more decades, the rate of temperature increase may become so rapid by the end of the twenty-first century or early in the twenty-second that a large portion of the earth's biodiversity would not be able to adapt fast enough to survive. The rate of temperature change is already greater than at any time in the last five hundred thousand years; a significant acceleration may leave species with slow reproductive cycles or with small populations trapped in isolated patches with nowhere to go.

Beyond the loss of biodiversity, continued carbon dioxide pollution will have far-reaching effects on human well-being. If current trends continue, by 2040 we can expect to see more frequent severe weather events with loss of life and property, sea level rise, growing water scarcity, lower agricultural productivity, and the spread of diseases into new regions.

The Opportunity

We know what we need to do. Global greenhouse gas emissions need to peak before 2020 and be reduced by at least 50 percent below 1990 levels by 2050.

And we know how to do it. In the developed world more than 60 percent of greenhouse gas emissions come from two sources—power plants and vehicles.[30] As industrial production and household wealth increase in the rapidly developing economies, emissions are likely to assume the same pattern there. We need to reduce CO_2 emissions from coal combustion at power plants and petroleum combustion in cars, trucks, planes, and ships.

Over the next twenty-five years, emissions reductions will be far more likely and more cost-effective in the power sector than in transportation. Although there will be some benefit from greater fuel economy associated with extensive use of hybrid technologies in cars and trucks, this is likely to be overwhelmed by the rapid growth in ownership and use of personal vehicles in developing countries. It is unlikely that zero-carbon-emissions technologies such as fully electric or fuel-celled vehicles will make any substantial penetration in the transportation sector even in highly developed countries by 2040.[31]

But significant changes are possible and would be cost effective in the power sector. Some combination of these four options is most likely: (1) increases in the efficiency of lighting, heating, and insulation of appliances, motors, and compressors in residential and commercial buildings;

(2) substantial power generation from wind and solar energy sources, accompanied by new technologies to store the intermittent power from these sources; (3) the conversion of coal-fired power plants to natural gas, drawing on the new abundance of shale gas resources; and (4) the use of carbon capture and storage systems that reduce emissions by up to 90 percent at fossil-fueled plants.

Some observers assert that it would be possible to generate a significant portion of our electricity from renewable sources such as wind, solar, geothermal, and biomass. But in many countries seeking rapid development, use of their domestic fossil resources will continue to be the preferred source of power. A large portion of the world's coal reserves are concentrated in a few countries, including Russia, China, India, Australia, the United States, and Kazakhstan.[32] Other countries have other high-carbon fossil resources such as heavy oil and tar sands that they would also like to use or export. It is unlikely that we will persuade these countries to turn away from their dirty fuels. Therefore, research and demonstration on carbon capture and storage systems for the continued use of fossil fuels must be an urgent priority.

The most efficient way to drive changes in the power sector would be to impose a price on carbon. This could be accomplished either through a carbon tax or with cap and trade programs such as those implemented by several states in the U.S. Northeast and in California (that includes credit for sequestering carbon in natural systems). Although partisanship has undermined climate policy at the national level in the United States, more than forty countries and many state and provincial governments have adopted and are successfully implementing carbon pricing policies.

Because the need for coordinated global mitigation policy, at least among the developed and rapidly emerging economies, is so urgent and because carbon pricing policies make so much sense from so many different perspectives, we should be confident that they will be in almost universal use by 2040. But it is harder to envision the diplomatic and governmental mechanisms needed to bring trade harmony and full participation in an international carbon pricing regime. It is unlikely to look like the Kyoto Protocol, with a cap on every nation's emissions. And unlike the Montreal Protocol, it may come too late to prevent significant damage. As noted earlier, a pricing system that fully incorporates the value of carbon sequestered in natural systems would help compensate for weaknesses in international policies—and would be of tremendous benefit to biodiversity.

Global warming is the most important challenge of our time. Science has already made a compelling case for the goals we must adopt. New technologies to get us there affordably are emerging every year. What we lack are the leaders, organizations, and governing instruments that will let us act effectively, confidently, and together across the globe. Whether and how we solve this problem in governance will define our environment in 2040 and for many centuries after.

The Reason for Hope

Without much attention, there has been a tremendous change in the structure of global environmental governance over the past forty years. It has moved out of regulatory bureaus and international tribunals into a legion of organizations and informal arrangements that have become the essential glue that holds the agenda for nature protection together and moves it forward across the globe. The new forms of governance involve actors of many types, including landowner associations, resources user groups, indigenous communities, nongovernmental advocacy organizations, academics and scientists, and philanthropists and foundations.

These new institutions are important and effective not so much because of their legal authority or their size but because of their shared knowledge, the trust built from long-standing personal interactions, their reach across scales to achieve local, national, and global coordination, and their commitment to transparency to maintain legitimacy.

This new environmental governance is what we do at The Nature Conservancy. We are a "bridging" organization. Our job is to build and maintain the connections between players—governments, scientists, investors, users, producers, and consumers—who have more traditional roles. We facilitate outcomes across scales, using new tools and adapting to new information to achieve change that would otherwise not be possible.

There are many examples of this work in our portfolio: creating water funds in South America; developing certification schemes for forest products and bioenergy; supporting fisheries comanagement; creating markets for investment in forest carbon; designing biodiversity offsets for energy and mining development; and mapping marine protected areas in coastal zones around the world.

It is necessary to have good science on environmental trends and the technologies offering sustainable alternatives. But that is not enough. What we more often need today is better understanding of the governance and institution-building processes at all scales so that we can turn science and technology into nature protection.

None of us can predict the new environmental challenges we will experience between now and 2040. But we can be sure that we are getting better at building and managing the governance institutions necessary to sustain nature on a planet now defined by our development.

Notes

1. OECD, "Environmental Outlook to 2050," Paris, 2012, www.oecd.org/dataoecd/41/4/50523645.pdf.

2. Fikret Berkes, "Evolution of Co-Management: Role of Knowledge Generation, Bridging Organizations, and Social Learning," *Journal of Environmental Management* 90 (2009): 1692–1702.

3. Mario J. Molina and F. S. Rowland, "Stratospheric Sink for Chlorofluoromethanes: Chlorine Atom Catalyzed Distinction of Ozone," *Nature* 249, no. 5460 (1974): 810–12.

4. David W. Fahey and Michaela I. Hegglin, "Twenty Questions and Answers about the Ozone Layer: 2010 Update," Earth System Research Laboratory, National Oceanic & Atmospheric Administration, accessed December 10, 2014, www.esrl.noaa.gov/csd/assessments/ozone/2010/twentyquestions.

5. Council on Environmental Quality, "Celebrating the 25th Anniversary of the Montreal Protocol," September 17, 2012, accessed December 10, 2014, http://www.whitehouse.gov/blog/2012/09/17/celebrating-25th-anniversary-montreal-protocol.

6. "The major difference between the success of Montreal and the failure of Kyoto is the low cost of implementing the Montreal Protocol due to technological innovations." Stephen Polasky, personal communication, February 7, 2014.

7. Food and Agriculture Organization of the United Nations, *The State of the World's Fisheries and Aquaculture 2010* (Rome, 2010).

8. World Bank, *The Sunken Billions: The Economic Justification for Fisheries Reform* (Washington, D.C.: 2009).

9. Food and Agriculture Organization of the United Nations, *The State of the World's Fisheries and Aquaculture 2010*.

10. William E. Schrank, "The Newfoundland Fishery: Ten Years after the Moratorium," *Marine Policy* 29 (2005): 407–20.

11. Cristopher Costello et al., "Status and Solutions for World's Unassessed Fisheries," *Science* 338 (2012): 517–20.

12. A. Pruss, K. Day, L. Fewtrell, and J. Bartram, "Estimating the Global Burden of Disease from Water, Sanitation and Hygiene at a Global Level," *Environmental Helath Perspectives* 110, no. 5 (2002) 537–42.

13. 2030 Water Resources Group, "Charting Our Water Future: Economic Frameworks to Inform Decision-Making," Washington, D.C., 2009, accessed December 10, 2014, www.2030waterresourcesgroup.com/water_full/Charting_Our_Water_Future_Final.pdf.

14. 2030 Water Resources Group, "Charting Our Water Future."

15. The terms "physical scarcity" and "economic scarcity" were first used in a comprehensive 2007 study: David Molden, ed., *Water for Food, Water for Life: A Comprehensive Assessment of Water Management in Agriculture* (International Water Management Institute, 2007). The concept of "environmental scarcity" is added here.

16. Malin Falkenmark, "The Massive Water Scarcity Threatening Africa: Why Isn't It Being Addressed," *Ambio* 18, no. 2 (1989): 112–18, and Charles J. Vorosmarty, Ellen M. Douglas, Pamela A. Green, and Carmen Revenga, "Geospatial Indicators of Emerging Water Stress: An Application to Africa," *Ambio* 34, no. 3 (2005): 230–36.

17. Frank R. Rijsberman, "Water Scarcity: Fact or Fiction?" Proceedings of the 4th International Crop Science Congress, Brisbane, 2004.

18. Brian D. Richter et al., "Tapped Out: How Can Cities Secure Their Water Future?" *Water Policy* 15 (2013): 335–63.

19. OECD, "Environmental Outlook to 2050," 2012, and United Nations Environment Programme, "GEO 4: Global Environment Outlook," Malta, 2007, accessed December 10, 2014, http://www.unep.org/geo/GEO4/report/GEO-4_Report_Full_en.pdf (December 10, 2014).

20. Julia Marton-Lefèvre, "Biodiverity is Our Life," *Science* 327 (2010): 1179.

21. Peter Kareiva and Micelle Marvier, *Conservation Science: Balancing the Needs of People and Nature* (Colorado: Roberts and Company, 2011), 33–42.

22. OECD, "Environmental Outlook to 2050."

23. Ibid.

24. Intergovernmental Panel on Climate Change, *Climate Change 2013: The Physical Science Basis. Contribution of Working Group I to the Fifth Assessment Report* (New York: Cambridge University Press, 2013).

25. IPCC 2013.

26. IPCC 2013.

27. Jerry M. Melillo, Terese (T.C.) Richmond, and Gary W. Yohe, eds., *Climate Change Impacts in the United States: The Third National Climate Assessment* (Washington, D.C.: U.S. Global Change Research Program, 2014).

28. IPCC 2013.

29. IPCC 2013.

30. World Resources Institute, "CAIT 2.0: Climate Analysis Indicators Tool," accessed December 10, 2014, cait2.wri.org.

31. Energy Information Administration, "Annual Energy Outlook 2014," Washington, D.C., 2014, accessed December 10, http://www.eia.gov/forecasts/aeo/.

32. World Energy Council, *2010 Survey of Energy Resources* (London, 2010).

PART FOUR

Education,

Communication,

and

Society

CHAPTER 10

Education

The Future of Higher Education in the United States (and the World)

Gary Saul Morson
Frances Hooper Professor of the Arts and Humanities,
Northwestern University

Morton Schapiro
Professor of Economics and President,
Northwestern University

There is a long-standing tradition of making bold, and spectacularly mistaken, predictions about U.S. higher education. So it is with caution and modesty that we hazard a few of our own.

While economists tend to be overly optimistic about growth and prosperity, education experts tend toward unjustified pessimism. Around 1900, the founding president of Stanford, David Starr Jordan, predicted the imminent demise of the liberal arts college as research universities took their place. Tell that to Williams, Amherst, Pomona, and other top liberal arts colleges, now more selective and richer than ever. For other forecasters, the Great Depression portended the end of higher education as they knew it, with crumpling endowments and reductions in state funding and private giving supposedly leading to long-term educational disaster. The GI Bill, now celebrated as one of the most important pieces of legislation, was at the time resisted by some prominent university presidents who feared the end of excellence associated with educating the masses. Next, educators warned that the large baby boom generation would threaten the nature of institutions unable to expand enrollment quickly enough without wreaking havoc. After that, baby bust pessimists foresaw massive excess capacity leading to fiscal disaster. In fact, college enrollment rose.

Today you can't open the paper without hearing about impending doom. There are no jobs for college graduates; loan burdens are prohibitive as graduates or dropouts struggle to pay off $100,000 in college loans on barista-level salaries; and new technologies are driving the traditional four-year, nonprofit, residential model into oblivion. Either tenure will bankrupt the few institutions retaining it or "contingent" faculty with short-term contracts will replace tenured faculty. Exorbitant sticker prices have created a bubble resembling the tulip market of seventeenth-century Holland. Only the foolhardy will major in anything other than science, engineering, math, business, or economics. What's more, the days of substantial federal research support are numbered. Public flagship universities will continue to lose stature, while the United States will surrender its domination in rankings of the world's universities.

In short, if this is the golden age of American higher education as some say, by 2040 it will be long gone.

To address these points, we first establish today's facts, some of which will likely prove surprising.

Higher Education Today

Higher education in the United States is a big business.[1] There are around forty-seven hundred "firms"—about sixteen hundred public institutions, seventeen hundred private nonprofit ones, and fourteen hundred private for-profit schools. Because public institutions are typically much larger than private ones, they enroll almost three quarters of all students. The annual budgets of these forty-seven hundred institutions add up to around $500 billion, 3 percent of the U.S. gross domestic product (GDP). These schools attract a total of twenty-one million "customers," eighteen million undergraduates and three million in graduate or professional schools. More than eight hundred thousand come from outside the United States (half from China, India, and South Korea), making the United States the world's largest net exporter of higher education services. Various international rankings agree that the most prestigious institutions are disproportionately in the United States.

Nevertheless, the United States is falling behind other industrialized countries in college attainment. Each fall the Organization for Economic Cooperation and Development (OECD) releases its ranking of the percentage of twenty-five- to thirty-four-year-olds with a higher education degree, and each year the United States seems to lose a spot.[2] At 42 percent, we are at our all-time high, but because other countries have been increasing attainment rates more quickly, the United States currently ranks only fourteenth among thirty-seven developed countries. South Korea, the OECD leader, is at 65 percent.

It may be surprising to learn that of the forty-seven hundred schools in the United States, fewer than 10 percent could be considered "selective." At most institutions, students are free to enroll having met limited (if any) requirements. Consumers are used to being able to buy a product without proving their worth as potential purchasers. It is thought that colleges and universities are different—with a much larger group of willing purchasers than are allowed to buy. But except for a few schools, that is untrue.

Many of the 150 or so "national" colleges and universities (those drawing from the top students in the United States and abroad) have increased their draw—and their pricing power—over the past few decades. Some are major research universities, including the sixty U.S. members of the Association of American Universities (the AAU), the exclusive group of universities receiving the lion's share of federal research dollars. Some are prestigious liberal arts colleges.

Also surprising is that the "$50,000 a year price tag" is far from the norm. The latest count shows that only 149 of the forty-seven hundred charge that amount, including room and board.[3] They enroll fewer than six hundred thousand of the eighteen million or so undergrads—with more than half receiving a substantial discount. That leaves at most three hundred thousand students and their families actually paying $50,000 a year, far fewer than media attention suggests.

Why pay such an amount? Another surprise is that the return to a college degree is at or near record levels.[4] There used to be a cycle of high returns inducing an oversupply of college-educated workers, thereby reducing the college premium (the ratio of earnings of college graduates to those whose highest degree is a high school diploma) until market adjustment led to a new rise in the premium. The nadir of the cycle took place in the mid-1970s, but then the college premium took off. Even after decreasing in the wake of the massive economic downturn of 2008, it quickly rebounded. By 2012, it reached a new high for women and was only slightly behind the 2008 record level for men. So even after the worst of economic times, the college premium recovered and set out again on its long-term upward path.

Clearly, the transfer of blue-collar jobs offshore has contributed mightily to this new phenomenon. More than half the increase in the college premium over the past several decades results from a decline in the denominator (wages for high school graduates). But even if a college education has become more of a defensive move, it is still an extraordinary financial investment.

There are unfortunate people with $100,000 or more in college loan debt working away at jobs that pay little and do not require a college degree.[5] But around 30 percent of college students graduate with no loan debt at all, and the rest average around $30,000, an amount the college premium covers before long. Sure, there are exceptions, but the data speak for themselves. And at the most selective private colleges and universities, the majority graduate without any loans at all, while the rest average under $20,000. We repeatedly hear that total college loan debt exceeds a trillion dollars, more than credit card debt! But credit card debt usually reflects consumption choices, while a college degree is an investment—for most, the best of a lifetime. Moreover, there is lots of evidence that college leads to more satisfying and healthier lives. Well-educated people tend to exercise more, vote and volunteer more often, and engage in more activities with their children. The graduate benefits, and so does society, one reason for government to cover some of the expense.

Finally, students who attend a top private institution might wind up paying less than they would at a public institution closer to home. The *San Jose Mercury News* reported in March 2012 that a family of four earning $130,000 a year would be asked to pay—taking into account financial aid grants—$24,000 a year at California State University at East Bay, $33,000 at the University of California at Santa Cruz, and only $17,000 at Harvard.[6] At institutions with the resources to enroll the most qualified students regardless of ability to pay—or at other schools that discount according to "merit"—the sticker price does not come close to indicating what the actual cost would be. In fact, only 29 percent of all undergraduates pay the sticker price, a number that falls below 15 percent for those attending private four-year colleges and universities.

Nevertheless, some significant headwinds may mean more difficult days ahead.

For three decades public universities have been receiving a declining share of state expenditures (with those dollars diverted mainly to health care). Most of the for-profit sector operates under increased government scrutiny because of high student loan default rates. And private nonprofit higher education is more stratified than ever—with the most prestigious colleges and universities benefiting from increasing cachet in global markets, while, at other privates, rapidly rising discounts off the sticker price have eroded tuition revenues, their principal income source.

Predicting the Future

So, where does higher education go from here?

We focus on seven topics relating to the pedagogy underlying the educational experience and to the economics governing it.

We categorize our predictions based on Supreme Court Justice Felix Frankfurter's 1957 classic ruling in *Sweezy v. New Hampshire*, laying out the four essential freedoms of a university—"to determine for itself on academic grounds who may teach, what may be taught, how it shall be taught, and who may be admitted to study."

Who May Teach?

One trend is clear: the prevalence of tenure in American higher education has been reduced dramatically. In 1975, 57 percent of all full-time and part-time faculty (other than graduate students) were in the tenure system, but by 2011 there were only 29 percent.[7] Following the end of mandatory retirement for faculty on January 1, 1994, non-tenure-track professors at Ph.D.-granting public universities went from 24 percent of all full-time faculty to 35 percent and from 18 percent to 46 percent at private nonprofit ones.[8] Some discern a potential blow to academic freedom; others anticipate declining efficiency resulting from a changed distribution of authority.

Do undergraduates taught by faculty outside the tenure system learn as much? A recent analysis based on Northwestern data indicates that faculty outside the tenure system (most of whom are full-time) actually outperform tenure-track/tenured professors in the classroom, at least when considering introductory classes taken during freshman year.[9] Non-tenure-line faculty not only inspire undergraduates to take more classes in a given subject but also lead the students to do better in subsequent coursework. We applaud the increasing attention being paid to the work conditions of non-tenure-line professors, especially those with full-time positions. Should they be treated in a manner commensurate with their value, the rise of designated teachers at U.S. colleges and universities may be less of a cause for alarm than some people think.

That gets us to our first question:

In 2040, what percentage of American faculty will be in the tenure system?

Some observers predict that tenure-track/tenured professors will bottom out at 15 to 20 percent of all faculty, with tenure largely limited to flagship public and private research universities and the wealthiest liberal arts colleges.[10] A key question concerns attempts to institute posttenure review. The University of Texas Board of Regents, for example, has proposed that tenured faculty members be evaluated annually, with two unsatisfactory reviews leading to possible dismissal. Not surprisingly, the American Association of University Professors regards this proposal as an assault on tenure.

Unless such resistance abates, or Congress restores a mandatory retirement age for professors, the downward trend is sure to continue. Neither change is likely. As tenured professors retire, they will continue to be disproportionately replaced by faculty outside the tenure system. By 2040, our guess is that only around 10 percent of positions will be held by tenure-track/tenured professors.

Where will professors teach? Will the financial problems inflicting public colleges and universities finally abate, or will more and more professors leave publics for privates?

That leads to our second question:

Will public research universities continue to be able to attract a world-class faculty and student body?

Will the federal government restore the growth rate in sponsored research at public and private universities? And will states restore the historic percentage of their expenditures to higher education?

While some observers think that the current decrease in research support marks a new reality, we believe we are merely at a down part of a long cycle. There have been downturns before, but then federal research support resumed its long-term upward trend, with Congress and the public recognizing the contribution of research to scientific breakthroughs and economic growth.

On the other hand, public universities will still struggle to replace state appropriations with other revenues. The days when public higher education attracted a stable share of state expenditures—once 7 percent, now 5 percent—are long gone. These two lost percentage points amount to $30 billion, more than a third of current state appropriations to higher education.

If we expect the federal government to see the light, why wouldn't states? Almost all of that $30 billion has gone to health care, specifically to Medicaid. Harvard economist Tom Kane concluded that the future of public higher education depends on the containment of Medicaid costs. Our best hope is that the 1990s repeat themselves and state budgets rise faster than the higher education share of the pie declines. That would take robust economic growth along with reining in not just health expenditures but also state pension obligations.

Around three out of four college students attend public institutions, and we don't expect that to fall much by 2040. But we do expect that recent funding troubles at public institutions will not go away. Top public research universities have been losing stature and, regrettably, we foresee that trend continuing.

What May Be Taught?

Understandably, in times of uncertain economic growth prospects, politicians focus on skills translating fairly directly to employment. The

STEM fields (science, technology, engineering, and mathematics) are today's darlings, with the humanistic social sciences, the arts, and the humanities either forgotten or worse. Several governors have expressed skepticism about the wisdom of states supporting students studying the humanities given their presumed poor earnings prospects.[11]

This approach is shortsighted. No one should confuse starting salaries with ultimate earnings. Looking a decade or so out beyond graduation, humanities majors generally have low unemployment rates and, in some cases, salaries mirroring those of workers with more technical training.[12] To be sure, data from the U.S. Census Bureau show that the lifetime earnings of engineering majors exceed those of arts majors by $1.4 million. But work-life earnings of students who study the arts are nonetheless a robust $1.9 million. And, of course, the payoff to higher education isn't limited to finances.

Still, the market test is whether students themselves are leaving the humanities in increasing numbers. Humanities skeptics are quick to point out that in the late 1960s nearly 18 percent of all bachelor's degrees were earned in the humanities. By 2010, it was only 8 percent.[13] However, that decline took place many years ago, with the percentage in the humanities being quite stable since the early 1980s. On the other hand, a recent study of Harvard undergraduates shows a continuing downward trend, from 1954, when 36 percent of all majors were in the humanities (including history) to 20 percent in 2012, with the slide showing no signs of ending. At Stanford, around 45 percent of faculty members in its main undergraduate division are in the humanities; but only 15 percent of its students are.

Some observers cite the fact that student demand in the humanities is adversely affected by the disproportionate share of non-tenure-track instruction in those fields (the Northwestern results call this hypothesis into question). Others point out that the gap between professorial salaries in the humanities and other academic disciplines has been growing, leading perhaps to declining relative quality among faculty. Still others say the lack of student interest reflects changes in the field itself.

That brings us to question three:

Will anyone ever major in the humanities, arts, and nonquantitative social sciences again?

The decline in interest in the humanities likely reflects, at least in part, what humanists themselves have been doing. For the last three decades, predominant trends in critical theory have been teaching that there is no such thing as objective literary value and that Shakespeare is considered to be better than John Grisham (or a laundry list) only because of social power relations. (Of course, not everyone subscribes to this view of value.) As the editors of *The Norton Anthology of Theory and Criticism* observe when paraphrasing the position of cultural studies, "Literary texts, like other artworks, are neither more nor less important than any other cultural artifact or practice. Keeping the emphasis on how cultural meanings are produced, circulated, and consumed, the investigator will focus on art or literature insofar as such works connect with broader social factors, not because they possess some intrinsic interest or special aesthetic value."[14] In that case, why should great literature be studied at all? Students who come to this conclusion can hardly be said to be irrational. It has also become common to teach literature by measuring how enlightened the author was in terms of current values, which are presumed correct. But if current beliefs can only be confirmed, why should students put in the considerable effort to read difficult texts?

The future of the humanities would seem to depend on a shift, which may already be under way. Great literature does what no other university subject can. Sensitively read, it offers practice in empathy with people unlike oneself.[15] When readers identify with a character from another social class, period, culture, or gender, they experience a new sense of the world. To do so, they must bracket, not presume, the values and social beliefs usually taken for granted. Other disciplines may recommend empathy, but only great literature offers constant practice in it.

In retrospect, it seems obvious that critical theory's doctrines compromise the very reasons for studying the humanities. Within the profession, dynamics leading to status have gone one way, while external pressures have led in the contrary direction, toward making the humanities ever more important. Increasing globalization and social diversity put a premium on being able to understand other people from within.

Both trends will continue, but, at least for a while, the trend toward empathy will grow in relative strength. One sign this is happening will be a different understanding of "world literature," a term that now usually means Western literature plus the literature of other countries responding to Western dominance and oppression. It is as if non-Western cultures were producing nothing of value before they encountered Europeans. Instead, world literature will include not primarily "postcolonial" literature but demand more attention to earlier non-Western classics, such as *A Dream of Red Mansions*, the *Bhagavad-Gita*, and *The Tale of Genji*. The Persian *Shahnameh* (*Epic of Kings*) will be widely known, along with classics from the Arab world when it was the hegemonic power invading Europe. To be sure, it requires more effort to grasp Confucius and Lao-Tzu than a contemporary English or French novel from the Third World, but the study of such authors, along with Shakespeare and Dostoevsky, will indicate that it is important to transcend the perspectives American academics easily take for granted. In that case, the future of these fields will be brighter.

Other nations are figuring out what some here want us to ignore—that training in the liberal arts does create economically viable citizens.[16] Why did Singapore invite Yale to open a liberal arts college? Why in China and India is the adoption of a liberal arts curriculum very much on the table? How ironic if in our panic to match those countries in the production of engineers, they pass us by in the education of students with broader, less technical backgrounds!

That leads us to our fourth question:

Even if those subjects are still taught at research universities in 2040, will there be liberal arts colleges around to teach them as well?

More than two decades ago, the economist David Breneman made the startling discovery that the number of "liberal arts" colleges was far smaller than popularly believed.[17] In 1990, schools without large numbers of graduate students were lumped together as liberal arts colleges. But Breneman took a close look at the 540 private schools with few or no graduate programs and found that fewer than half—only 212—had even a large minority of students majoring in the traditional arts and sciences fields. A recent study applying these criteria found that number had fallen to only 130.[18]

The others had not closed but had added more and more preprofessional subjects, and graduate programs, to their curriculum. This is not to say that students studying accounting, management, and nursing at small baccalaureate colleges might not benefit from seminar-size classes and an undergraduate focus, but don't think that there are large numbers of philosophy and English majors at these schools.

The elite of the 130 remaining liberal arts colleges are stronger than ever, but others are undergoing substantial economic distress. Will they go under? Absolutely not. But they will probably introduce business majors and the like. Majoring in philosophy or art history at a world-renowned college (or research university) may not be thought to be all that risky in terms of job prospects. But elsewhere, market changes will make the true "liberal arts college" more of a rarity.

How Shall Courses Be Taught?

Massive open online courses (MOOCs) will supposedly replace the pedagogical model of a faculty member giving a lecture to, or leading a discussion with, physically present students. Some educators feel that soon most students will learn microeconomics—or Russian literature—from the world's greatest experts, signing up as one of hundreds of thousands who access the lectures at their leisure, relying perhaps on local instructors to answer their questions and run discussion sessions. There is something attractive about being taught by the very best and going at your own pace, and that model might supplement traditional pedagogy in a productive way. But replace it?

Think of it like this: could you do psychotherapy this way? Or learn to play the violin? If the humanities teach a skill such as empathy, they will require *presence*. For the student and professor, it will be important to put oneself on the spot (in all senses) with someone who is actually there. To be sure, if the humanities devolve into memorizing approved interpretations or confirming already held beliefs, MOOCs may play a relatively large role. But if the humanities change from current trends, they will not. Experience with MOOCs trying to teach literature may itself provide impetus for change in the humanities.

Even in a large lecture class, successful professors can truly engage and put themselves on the spot. Then they don't just provide information but model the process of thinking about literature, much as a physically present violin instructor or musician differs from a recording. After all, if presence did not matter, and a mere recording of a great performance would do, why do people still go to live concerts?

Whatever their use as a supplement, online technologies will not replace traditional courses. Despite their rhetoric, top colleges and universities act as if they agree. The premier schools are active MOOC producers. And yet, they seldom give the same credit for such courses to their own students. Such courses usually qualify for "alien" credit, the sort given to high school advanced placement courses and classes taken at summer or study-abroad programs run by other institutions. MOOCs rarely count toward the major, go toward the college residency requirement, or figure in a student's overall grade point average. In short, there is something of a bait and switch here.

Even the most traditional of teachers—and that includes us—use technology in meaningful ways. There are excellent classroom management platforms that save teaching time while enhancing student learning. Long gone are the days when ten minutes of every eighty-minute class were spent on course mechanics. Plus, what a joy it is to be able to show a short video illustrating an important point or to bring in an off-campus expert for a real-time contribution to a class. But these changes enhance, rather than replace, the traditional course. They do not alter the very nature of learning, as MOOCs usually do.

This discussion suggests question five:

Will the residential undergraduate experience be replaced by MOOCs and other online teaching?

We don't see the residential experience much imperiled by remote learning, especially at the nation's selective colleges and universities. Faculty may be blissfully unaware that much learning takes place outside of the classroom: during discussions in common rooms or cafés; with friends on a team; or while running a community service organization or an a cappella group. Students reflecting on their treasured educational experiences cite favorite courses and the camaraderie of an intramural team. It is hard to believe they will ever cite beloved MOOCs.

Who May Be Admitted to Study?

College enrollment rates in the United States are the highest ever: 70 percent of high school graduates enroll at a two- or four-year college within twelve months of graduation. But gaps in enrollment by income and race have persisted. OECD data show that the enrollment prospects for children of parents with educationally disadvantaged backgrounds are worse here than in almost all other developed countries.[19]

Moreover, not all college attendance is the same. Of students from families with income below $60,000 who attended college in 1999, only 6 percent enrolled at elite institutions, compared with 26 percent from families earning above $200,000.[20] More recent data suggest this disparity has been growing.

While college access for black and Hispanic students has been increasing, it has primarily been at open-access institutions. The sad news is that there are significant numbers of academically qualified minority students who would thrive at selective colleges if they chose to enroll there. A small subset of Chicago Public Schools (CPS) high school graduates have the records and standardized test scores for access to a very selective college.[21] But only one in three of these match appropriately. The others wind up attending underresourced, nonselective institutions, where they cannot develop their talents as well and where their graduation rates are less than half as high as they would have been had they attended elite schools.

That leads us to our sixth question:

Will college enrollment rates in the United States continue to rise and will gaps by income and race attenuate?

We must first ask: will the college premium remain at record levels? And how will sticker and net prices change?

Many jobs that provided good wages to workers without college degrees still exist but are now located in Bangalore, Jakarta, and Shanghai rather than in Atlanta, Chicago, and Cleveland. Some such jobs will remain in the United States, but not many. On the other hand, generations of college graduates could expect to become richer than their predecessors, but those days may be over. Still, the college premium will continue to rise and so demand for higher education will grow.

That, however, will not translate into robust growth for college and university revenues. Tuition increases will continue to be eroded by increases in financial aid. As mentioned earlier, only 29 percent of all undergraduates pay the sticker price—with the percentage at private colleges and universities now down to under 15 percent. The number of families paying the sticker price will fall further, especially without federal antitrust protection allowing college presidents to end highly costly merit aid wars.

Even schools with the pricing power to increase sticker prices proportionate to the richest Americans' increase in income face increasing political pressure not to do so. For the past century, sticker prices have increased around three percentage points above inflation, but those days are about to end. Public scrutiny is putting the brakes on tuition increases even if the market is not. We expect that schools at the very top of the pecking order will disrupt price increases even further. When you have a $4 billion operating budget and you only net $150 million from undergraduate tuition, you might eventually question the entire sticker price/financial aid model. Why not let anyone who can meet your admissions standards come to college for free? That is already the norm in Ph.D. programs. If, say, Princeton did this for undergraduates, wouldn't Harvard, Yale, and Stanford follow? How would this affect the many other schools who couldn't possibly forgo all undergraduate tuition revenue? While the current funding model is not a bubble about to burst, a range of economic, political, and competitive pressures imply that net tuition revenues will become a smaller and smaller portion of all institutional revenues.

Might that lead to greater enrollment by low-income students? Evidence suggests that this is more a matter of sociology than economics. Recall the curious case of top CPS high school students eschewing selective institutions in favor of open enrollment ones. It is as much about not wanting to leave the local community, and not recognizing that colleges differ from one another, as it is about not realizing the net price most would face would be well below the sticker price. The focus on "going to college" obscures the fact that college is not a commodity— that is, not a good undifferentiated by quality.

We saw that where you go to school has a profound effect on your graduation prospects. But assuming you do graduate, does the higher selectivity of a school increase earnings?

Some observers point to the well-known study showing that many students attending the University of Pennsylvania would have had a similar earnings stream if they had attended Penn State.[22] But the addition to earnings from attending a more selective institution is greater for students from low-income backgrounds and still greater for students of color. And don't forget that Penn State is not your typical public—it is one of the nation's thirty-four public universities in the AAU (out of a total of sixteen hundred public colleges and universities).

We think that the many college outreach programs put into place in recent years will begin to have a positive impact. More of those CPS students will take advantage of the opportunity to attend an elite institution. As it is, some changes in K-12 education are beginning to pay dividends. Longer school days, school choice, and charter schools are leading to higher graduation rates and at least modest increases in some test scores. Right now only 11 percent of the 130,000 undergraduates attending the most prestigious group of thirty-one private colleges and universities come from families in the bottom two-fifths of the income distribution, with fully 69 percent coming from the top fifth.[23] We predict that by 2040 those numbers will change dramatically for the better.

We come now to our seventh and final question:

Will the United States continue to attract large numbers of students from throughout the world, enticed by the prominence of top colleges and universities?

The eight hundred thousand foreign students among the twenty-one million students studying at U.S. colleges and universities include both undergraduates and graduate students. International students bring to the most prestigious programs not only the best talent in the world but also tuition revenues. Even at the most heavily endowed schools, foreign students receive little or no financial aid either as undergraduates or as students in master's degree programs. Those dollars are even more important, and in some cases critical, at the many less-prestigious colleges and universities that rely heavily on tuition. If foreign students stayed home, much of American higher education would feel the blow.

The trend is worrying. While the United States remains the global leader by attracting around 16 percent of all students who study abroad, ten years earlier the figure was 24 precent.[24] As long as the overall number of students enrolling in a country other than their own continues its rapid climb, the declining share of the United States need not be a problem. But as other countries create new colleges and universities, and increase the prestige of existing ones, the attractiveness of studying at any U.S. institution without a global reputation will be reduced, and full-pay foreign students will be increasingly scarce by 2040. The drying up of this income stream will be one more in a long list of reasons contributing to the growing stratification in U.S. higher education over time.

Conclusion

Careful readers might now understand the reason behind the parentheses in our title around the words "(and the World)." This is not a review of worldwide higher education. Even with our knowledge of U.S. higher education, based not just on studying its finances and its curricular offerings, but on having spent all of our professional lives teaching in this country, we predict the course of change with great trepidation. It would be reckless for us to pontificate on Germany, India, and China. We do, however, consider the United States relative to worldwide higher educational developments. Will U.S. institutions continue to attract foreign students in great numbers and dominate world rankings? Will the United States be alone in the world in terms of a focus on the liberal arts? Will the United States continue to be passed by other countries in terms of college attainment and lag even further behind other nations in educating students coming from low-income backgrounds?

Contrary to the tenor of past predictions, we are optimistic about the state of American higher education in 2040. The best of today's liberal arts colleges will thrive—and will actually be teaching the liberal arts. Some faculty will still be in the tenure system, but the many others who are not will do a fine job with undergraduate teaching and be better appreciated and supported than they are presently. Public flagships will still be prominent, if not quite the world leaders they are today. U.S. colleges and universities will continue to predominate, even if international competitors take away some full-pay foreign students. Many schools will lose some pricing power, undermined by increased price responsiveness at all but the elite institutions, and all colleges and universities will face increasingly challenging political realities. But a college degree will continue to be a great economic investment, and so enrollments will increase to record levels.

As knowledge grows, the need for those who provide it will grow as well. Pressure on the system will lead to changes and adaptations, but the United States will continue to provide the model for the world.

Notes

1. An excellent source of data on U.S. higher education, from which the following numbers are drawn, is *Almanac 2014–15, The Chronicle of Higher Education*, August, 22, 2014.

2. OECD, *Education at a Glance: OECD Indicators 2012* (OECD Publishing, 2012), Chart A1.1, 26.

3. *Almanac 2013–14, The Chronicle of Higher Education*, August 23, 2013.

4. A comprehensive piece on changes over time in the returns to higher education is David H. Autor, "Skills, Education, and the Rise of Earnings Inequality among the 'Other 99 Percent,'" *Science* 344, no. 6186 (May 23, 2014): 843–51. Another illuminating look is provided in Sandy Baum, Jennifer Ma, and Kathleen Payea, *Education Pays 2013: The Benefits of Higher Education for Individuals and Society* (New York: College Board, 2013), https://secure-media.collegeboard.org/digitalServices/misc/trends/education-pays-2013-full-report-022714.pdf.

5. For an overview of college loan debt, see *Trends in Student Aid 2013* (New York: College Board, 2013). See also Sandy Baum, Charles Kurose, and Jennifer Ma, *How College Shapes Lives: Understanding the Issues* (New York: College Board, October 2013).

6. Matt Krupnick, "Believe It: Harvard Cheaper than Cal State," *San Jose Mercury News*, March 4, 2012.

7. The American Association of University Professors website presents its Contingent Faculty Index summarizing data from the IPEDS Fall Staff Survey. http://www.aaup.org/sites/default/files/files/AAUP-InstrStaff2011-April2014.pdf.

8. Ronald G. Ehrenberg, "American Higher Education in Transition," *Journal of Economic Perspectives* 26, no.1 (Winter 2012): 193–216.

9. David N. Figlio, Morton O. Schapiro, and Kevin B. Soter, "Are Tenure Track Professors Better Teachers?" (working paper 19406, National Bureau of Economic Research, September 2013).

10. See, for example, Robin Wilson, "Tenure, RIP: What the Vanishing Status Means for the Future of Education," *Chronicle of Higher Education*, July 4, 2010.

11. See, for example, Kevin Kiley, "North Carolina Governor Joins Chorus of Republicans Critical of Liberal Arts," *Inside Higher Education,* January 30, 2013.

12. Anthony P. Carnevale and Ban Cheah, "Hard Times: College Majors, Unemployment and Earnings," Georgetown Public Policy Institute, May 2013, distinguishes between the economic experience of recent college graduates and those who are a numbers of years from graduation.

13. See, for example, Jennifer Levitz and Douglas Belkin, "Humanities Fall from Favor," *U.S. News & World Report*, June 6, 2013.

14. Vincent B. Leitch et al., eds., *The Norton Anthology of Theory and Criticism*, 2nd ed. (New York: Norton, 2010), 2478. This collection, with its influential selections, copious introductions, and extensive bibliography, is a key starting point for any study of theory and criticism. It is worth noting that the discipline used to be called "literary theory" or "literary criticism"; the dropping of the qualifier "literary" from the title reflects the trends described in the passage quoted.

15. Empathy, social perception, and emotional intelligence have been linked explicitly to reading literary fiction. See P. Belluck, "For Better Social Skills, Scientists Recommend a Little Chekhov," *New York Times*, October 4, 2013.

16. See, for example, Gerald A. Postiglione, "China Weighs the Value of American Liberal Arts," *Chronicle of Higher Education*, August 29, 2013.

17. David W. Breneman, *Liberal Arts Colleges: Thriving, Surviving or Endangered?* (Washington, D.C.: Brookings Institution Press, 1994).

18. Vicki L. Baker, Roger G. Baldwin, and Sumedha Makker, "Where Are They Now? Revisiting Breneman's Study of Liberal Arts Colleges," *Liberal Education* (Summer 2012).

19. *Education at a Glance*, Chart A6.1, 102.

20. Michael S. McPherson and Morton Owen Schapiro, "Opportunity in American Higher Education," Reflections on College Access & Persistence, In Honor of the 40th Anniversary of the Higher Education Act, Proceedings & Papers from a Symposium Held in Washington, D.C., September 2005, Advisory Committee on Student Financial Aid, September 2006.

21. Melissa Roderick and Jenny Nagaoka, "Increasing College Access and Graduation among Chicago Public High School Graduates," in *College Success: What It Means and How to Make It Happen*, ed. Michael S. McPherson and Morton Owen Schapiro (New York: College Board, 2008).

22. Stacy Berg Dale and Alan B. Krueger, "Estimating the Payoff to Attending a More Selective College: An Application of Selection on Observables and Unobservables," *Quarterly Journal of Economics* (November 2002).

23. For an excellent analysis of this topic, see Catharine Hill, Gordon Winston, and Stephanie Boyd, "Affordability of Highly Selective Private Colleges and Universities," *Journal of Human Resources* (Fall 2005); Catharine Hill and

Gordon Winston, "How Scarce are High-Ability, Low-Income Students?" in *College Access: Opportunity or Privilege?* ed. Michael S. McPherson and Morton Owen Schapiro (New York: College Board, 2006); and Catharine B. Hill et al., "Affordability of Highly Selective Private Colleges and Universities II," January 1, 2010.

24. *Education at a Glance*, Chart C4.3, 364.

CHAPTER 11

Communication

Media of the Future

Arianna Huffington
Chair, President, and Editor-in-Chief,
Huffington Post Media Group

When it comes to the way we tell stories, the defining factor in the next twenty-five years of media will be the hybrid nature of news. When I heard that Jeff Bezos was buying the *Washington Post*, one of the first people who came to mind was a fellow countryman of mine, the Greek philosopher Heraclitus, who around twenty-five hundred years ago said, "No man ever steps in the same river twice."[1] Or, as James Fallows put it, the sale was "one of those episode-that-encapsulates-an-era occurrences."[2] But even as the sale encapsulated an era that is passing, it also has the potential to expand the era we are in. The combining of the best of traditional media with the boundless potential of digital media represents the media of the future.

It's time we move the conversation away from the future of newspapers to the future of journalism—in whatever form it's delivered. After all, despite all the dire news about the state of the newspaper industry, we are in something of a golden age of journalism for news consumers. There's no shortage of great journalism being done, and there's no shortage of people hungering for it. And there are many business models that try to connect the former with the latter.

The future will definitely be a hybrid one, combining the best practices of traditional journalism (fairness, accuracy, storytelling, deep investigations) with the best tools available to the digital world (speed, transparency, and, above all, engagement).

Though the distinction between new media and old has become largely meaningless, for too long the reaction of much of the old media to the fast-growing digital world was something like the proverbial old man yelling at the new media kids to get off his lawn. Many years were wasted erecting barriers that were never going to stand.

Among the benefits the Internet has brought is the ability to relentlessly stay on a story long after a lot of the big, traditional outlets have moved on. The participation enabled by the Web allows people to engage with the story, contribute to it, develop it in small ways, take it deeper, and keep at it until it gets the attention it deserves. We've had too many autopsies but not enough biopsies (most notoriously over the invasion of Iraq and the financial meltdown), and we need to change that.

In the debate over new media versus old media, the lament is often heard that one of the things we're in danger of losing from the heyday of old media is muckraking, crusading journalism. But by enabling participation, new media can actually help fuel stories that lead to real change.

Additionally, one thing that's often missing from traditional journalism is news about what's working. Yes, it's important to know what's broken and what's gone wrong, but if that's all we get, we won't have a true picture of what's really going on in our lives and our communities.

Too often news about things that are actually working is looked down on or saved only for Thanksgiving or the last five, feel-good minutes of a local newscast. The reason most often given? Because news about what's working isn't popular. But I can definitely say this is not true. At HuffPost, we've made a commitment to report on what's working in our communities and all over the world. Our experience shows that people are in fact hungry for these kinds of stories—they are always among our most shared, and we found out that advertisers love them too.

Truth 2.0

We may be drowning in spin, smoke screens, and lies, but people are longing to cut through to the truth.

So how can the Internet and technology help us find our way? By continuing to give people a place they can turn to uncover the truth. The Internet has shown great promise in this regard. YouTube, Twitter, email, and turbocharged search engines have made it easier to expose the lies our leaders continue to tell.

At the same time, this is a moment of economic anxiety. In times like these, people are more likely to be driven by their lizard brains and react in response to fear rather than facts, making it easier for demagogues to scapegoat and peddle conspiracy theories laced with violent undertones. In this kind of atmosphere, people sometimes refuse to believe their own eyes. And it becomes easier to perpetrate the latest big lie.

So, to fill this need, I would love to see a new online tool that makes it possible to instantly fact-check a story as you are reading it—or watching it on video. A companion tool in service of the truth would instantly provide historical context to a story you are reading or watching, as well as a narrative that helps put the facts into a larger framework.

In a compelling post, Jay Rosen writes about the need for journalists to revive the art of storytelling. The Internet has been great for putting masses of data at our fingertips, but it has too often sacrificed explanation, context, and narrative on the altar of speed because, as Rosen puts it, "all the day-to-day rewards go to breaking news."[3]

I would love to see a dot-com innovation that immediately provides a reader or viewer with the background knowledge needed to better understand the data and information being delivered as news. The powers that be—both political and corporate—have mastered the dark art of making information deliberately convoluted and indecipherable. For them, complexity is not a bug, it's a feature.

Our future tool will also automatically simplify needlessly complicated laws, contracts, and linguistic smoke screens. Speech replete with verbal gymnastics in an attempt to befuddle and bamboozle us will immediately be translated into clear and precise language. It will be Truth 2.0.

And just as our instant fact-checking, context-providing, and translation tools will bring us more truth, new dot-com innovations providing greater transparency will deliver a return of trust—the other great need we are facing today. The institutions that hold our democracy together have taken crippling blows in the last few years, leaving our country awash in disillusionment, anger, doubt, cynicism, and widespread wariness. Though disheartening, given all that has happened over the last decade—an economic crash based on greed, a bank bailout with no strings attached, and a gridlocked legislative process beholden more to special interests than the public interest—this breakdown is hardly surprising.

I would love to see an app that allows us to pull the curtain back on the corridors of power and see who is really pulling the levers. A great early iteration of this was provided by the Sunlight Foundation during a health care summit in 2010. During its live streaming of the discussion, the foundation offered a dose of transparency by showing, as each of our elected officials was speaking, a list of his or her major campaign contributors. It was simple, powerful, and it spoke volumes about the extent to which many players in the summit were bought and paid for.[4]

The future version of this kind of tech will allow us to see who is funding whom and who is carrying water for which special interest, in real time and across every imaginable platform. The Sunday shows will be a whole different animal when we are able to effortlessly and instantly follow the money—and connect the dots.

My final wish may at first sound counterintuitive, but my crystal ball shows that the future will bring us a dot-com innovation that allows us to disengage from the 24/7 connectivity that the first twenty-five dot-com years have led to.

Plotinus was a philosopher in the third century A.D. who studied the sources of knowledge, wisdom, and creativity. "Knowledge has three degrees," he wrote, "opinion, science, illumination. The means or instrument of the first is sense; of the second, dialectic; of the third, intuition."[5]

The Internet has contributed much to the first two kinds of knowledge—science (in the form of easy access to reams of data and information) and opinion—but has in many ways taken us further away from illumination and our inner source of wisdom.

Hence the growing need to pull the plug on our hyperconnectivity. To disconnect from all our devices in order to reconnect with ourselves. There are already a plethora of Internet sites, mobile apps, and high-tech tools that make it easier to do just that—everything from yoga sites that let you take classes via your computer to mobile apps that provide guided meditation to devices that allow you to monitor your stress level.

And at HuffPost we have developed a course-correcting, free smartphone app called "GPS for the Soul." It provides tools to help us return to a state of calm and balance. I know it's something of a paradox to look to an app to help us reconnect to ourselves, but there's no reason not to use technology we always have in our pocket or our purse to help free us from technology. Think of it as spiritual training wheels. "GPS for the Soul" connects you to a personalized guide, with music, poetry, breathing exercises, and pictures of your loved ones, which can help you destress and recenter and gives you access to the guides of experts, other users, or your friends.

Virality über Alles

Now that going viral has gone viral, social media have become the obsession of all media. It's all about social now: What are the latest social tools? How can a company increase its social reach? Are reporters devoting enough time to social? Less discussed—or not at all—is the value of the thing going viral. Doesn't matter—as long as it's social. And viral!

The media world's fetishization of social media has reached idol-worshipping proportions. Media conference agendas are filled with panels devoted to social media and how to use social tools to amplify coverage, but you rarely see one discussing what that coverage should actually be about. As Wadah Khanfar, former director general of Al Jazeera, told our editors when he visited our newsroom in 2012, "The lack of contextualization and prioritization in the U.S. media makes it harder to know what the most important story is at any given time."

"We are in great haste," wrote Thoreau in 1854, "to construct a magnetic telegraph from Maine to Texas; but Maine and Texas, it may be, have nothing important to communicate."[6] And today we are in great haste to celebrate something going viral but seem completely unconcerned whether the thing that went viral added one iota of anything good—including even just simple amusement—to our lives. The truth is that sometimes it does, but often it doesn't. It's not even a very complex question; the problem is that we seldom bother to ask this question before we dutifully hop on the algorithmic viral wave. We're treating virality as a good in and of itself, moving forward for the sake of moving. "Hey," someone might ask, "where are you going?" "I don't know—but as long as I'm moving, it doesn't matter!" Not a very effective way to end up in a better place.

So, the question remains: As we adopt new and better ways to help people communicate, can we keep asking what is really being communicated? And what's the opportunity cost of what is not being communicated while we're all locked in the perpetual present, chasing whatever is trending?

Social media are a means, not an end. And going viral isn't "mission accomplished," regardless of what it was that went viral. As James DeJulio put it, "It seems that overnight, the viral video has become some sort of badge of honor within advertising communities. CMOs without them are beginning to feel like the only kid in second grade without a Cabbage Patch [doll]."[7] Just Google "how to make a video go viral" and you'll find a trove of tips on how to hit the sweet spot, along with reams of analysis on why this video lit up the Internet and why that one was dead on arrival.

Fetishizing "social" has become a major distraction, and we're clearly a country that loves to be distracted. Our job in the media is to use all the social tools at our disposal to tell the stories that matter—as well as the stories that entertain—and to keep reminding ourselves that the tools are not the story.

Someday, historians will likely look back at this virality-über-alles age and wonder what we were trying to accomplish. The answer will be: not a whole hell of a lot. Our times demand a much better response. All these new social tools can help us bear witness more powerfully or they can help us be distracted more obsessively.

Three Megatrends

So, when we consider the future of our media landscape, including the ways technology is rapidly transforming it, three trends stand out. The first is the seismic shift from presentation to participation. The second is the paradox of using technology to disconnect from technology. And the third is the game-changing shift from using social media as a way to make our lives more fun to using social media to make the world better.

The shift from presentation to participation means that the days of the media gods sitting up on Mount Olympus and telling us how things are have long since ended. People are tired of being talked to; they want to be talked with. Ours is a global conversation, with millions of new people pulling up a seat at the table—indeed, nearly three billion people will join the Internet's community by 2020.[8] That conversation has fueled revolutions and allowed media to engage with readers in totally new ways.

The lines between amateurs and professionals are being crossed every minute. As Clay Shirky put it, the word "amateur" derives from the Latin *amare*—love.[9] The secret of anyone who successfully connects with the public, be they professional or amateur, is that they love to create, produce, and share. And when you love what you do, other people will love what you do.

So, if the first trend is a Garden of Eden blooming with engagement and self-expression, the second trend is about the snake in the garden—the temptation to stay connected to our 24/7 digital world, which actually disconnects us from the world around us, from our loved ones, and especially from ourselves. And millions of people are paying a heavy price, in terms of health, creativity, and ability to solve problems, for always being hyperconnected.

According to the Flynn Effect, intelligence quotient (IQ) measurements have been rising each decade since the early twentieth century. So, our IQs are getting higher, but our problem-solving ability is not keeping pace. We are surrounded by leaders with high IQs who make dreadful decisions despite great degrees.

Luckily there is a powerful, countervailing force—using technology to get away from technology. Of course, I realize there's a paradox in the idea that, of all things, an app can help deliver us from the snake in the garden, but the snake is very wily, so our solutions have to be just as clever.

The third megatrend is that people are going from searching for information and data to searching for meaning. People are using technology to connect with others, not just around similar passions and interests but around the causes that most resonate with them. New means of communication have given us the ability to widen the circle of our concern.

For all these reasons, I see the next twenty-five years of digital media as full of promise—combining the best of traditional journalism with the best of digital technologies.

Notes

1. "Heraclitus," *Wikiquote*, last modified October 18, 2014, http://en.wikiquote.org/wiki/Heraclitus.

2. James Fallows, "Why the Sale of *The Washington Post* Seems so Significant," *The Atlantic*, August 5, 2013, http://www.theatlantic.com/business/archive/2013/08/why-the-sale-of-the-washington-post-seems-so-significant/278383/.

3. Jay Rosen, "News without the Narrative Needed to Make Sense of the News: What I Will Say at South by Southwest," *PressThink* (blog), March 10, 2010, http://archive.pressthink.org/2010/03/07/what_i_plan_to.html.

4. Luke Rosiak, "SunlightLive Covers Health Care Summit," *Sunlight Foundation* (blog), February 25, 2010, http://sunlightfoundation.com/blog/2010/02/25/sunlightlive-covers-health-care-summit/.

5. "Plotinus Quote," Wisdom Quotes, accessed January 7, 2015, http://www.wisdomquotes.com/quote/plotinus.html.

6. "Respectfully Quoted: A Dictionary of Quotations," Bartleby.com, accessed January 7, 2015, http://www.bartleby.com/73/1540.html.

7. James DeJulio, "Here Are Ten Tips to Create A Viral Video," *Business Insider*, October 14, 2011, http://www.businessinsider.com/10-tips-to-create-a-viral-video-2011-10.

8. Peter H. Diamondis and Steven Kotler, *Abundance: The Future Is Better than You Think* (New York: Free Press, 2012), 149.

9. Megan Garber, "Clay Shirky's 'Cognitive Surplus': Is Creating and Sharing Always a More Moral Choice than Consuming?" Nieman Journalism Lab, June 25, 2010, http://www.niemanlab.org/2010/06/clay-shirkys-cognitive-surplus-is-creating-and-sharing-always-a-more-moral-choice-than-consuming/.

CHAPTER 12

Society

The Future of Fearmongering

Barry Glassner

Professor of Sociology and President of Lewis & Clark College

Americans will be fearful in 2040, often about matters of minor consequence. I cannot predict which dangers will preoccupy the populace. I'm confident, though, that while the fears of that era will appear to be a random assortment, ranging from misjudgments about young people to disinformation about disease, in fact they will be part of a larger story about the state of the nation.

I also have little doubt that the scaremongers of 2040 will propagate their scares to the public largely through three means: repetition, trend claiming, and misdirection.

Purveyors of fear will continue to sell their wares the same way discount stores make their profits: on volume. Consider a pair of statistics about crime from the late twentieth century. Between 1990 and 1998, the murder rate in the United States decreased by 20 percent. During that same period, the number of stories about murder on network newscasts increased by 600 percent. Frequent viewers of evening newscasts could be excused for mistakenly thinking the crime rate was skyrocketing.

This chapter is adapted from Barry Glassner, *The Culture of Fear* (New York: Basic Books, 2010), and Barry Glassner, "Narrative Techniques of Fearmongering," *Social Research* 1, no. 4 (2004). Please consult those sources for pertinent citations.

More than repetition is involved, however, in successful fearmongering. Fearmongers of the future will need to deploy narrative techniques to normalize what are actually errors in reasoning. I suspect the most common of these techniques will continue to be the christening of isolated incidents as trends, and misdirection.

Pervasive fearmongering about youth violence at the end of the twentieth century provides an instructive case in point of how these discursive maneuvers magnify risks. Beginning in the mid-1990s, the United States experienced a steep downward trend in youth crime, but in the face of comforting statistics year after year, fearmongers recast those statistics as "the lull before the storm," as a *Newsweek* headline in 1995 put it. "We know we've got about 6 years to turn this juvenile crime thing around, or our country is going to be living in chaos," President Bill Clinton asserted in his 1997 State of the Union address, even though the youth violent crime rate had fallen 9.2 percent the previous year.

Six years later the nation was not living with chaos, at least as a result of youth violence, but the bipartisan fearmongering that went on about juvenile crime had demonstrable effects on public perceptions. In surveys conducted during the second half of the 1990s, adult Americans estimated that people younger than age eighteen committed about half of all violent crimes, when the actual number was 13 percent.

The misperceptions were fueled largely by isolated incidents of school shootings that got portrayed as trends. After a sixteen-year-old in Mississippi and a fourteen-year-old in Kentucky went on shooting sprees in 1997, killing five of their classmates and wounding twelve others, fearmongers spoke of "an epidemic of seemingly depraved adolescent murderers," as news commentator Geraldo Rivera put it. And three months later, in March 1998, when two boys, ages eleven and thirteen, killed four students and a teacher in Jonesboro, Arkansas, *Time* magazine declared that it was no longer "unusual for kids to get back at the world with live ammunition." When a child psychologist on NBC's *Today Show* advised parents to reassure their children that shootings at schools are very rare, reporter Ann Curry "corrected" him. "But this is the fourth case since October," she said.

In point of fact, during the previous academic year (1996–97), violence-related deaths in the nation's schools had hit a record low—nineteen deaths out of fifty-four million children—and only one in ten public schools reported any serious crime. Yet *Time* and *U.S. News and World Report* both ran headlines that year referring to "teenage time bombs," and William Bennett, the former U.S. secretary of education, proclaimed in a book, "America's beleaguered cities are about to be victimized by a paradigm-shattering wave of ultra-violent, morally vacuous young people some call the superpredators."

The superpredators never arrived, and over the next several years, although school shootings were rare, they made big news. In May 1998, when a fifteen-year-old in Springfield, Oregon, opened fire in a cafeteria filled with students, killing two and wounding twenty-three others, the event felt like a continuation of a "disturbing trend," the *New York Times* reported. The day after the shooting, on National Public Radio's *All Things Considered*, criminologist Vincent Schiraldi tried to explain that the recent string of incidents did not constitute a trend, that youth homicide rates had declined by 30 percent in recent years, and more than three times as many people were killed by lightning than by violence at schools. But the show's host, Robert Siegel, interrupted him. "You're saying these are just anomalous events?" he asked, audibly peeved. The criminologist reiterated that "anomalous" is precisely the right word to describe the events, and he called it "a grave mistake" to imagine otherwise.

To speak of these events is to bring to mind for many adult Americans an incident of horrific school violence; namely, the killings at Columbine High School in Littleton, Colorado. Fourteen students and a teacher died, and twenty-four more students were injured. The Columbine incident, and its public reception, are worth reconsidering in the present context because they bring to light two realities that I suggest will persist well into the future: in a culture of fear, the perceived importance of extraordinary events diverges from their empirical reality, and so do the causal explanations for those events.

Nearly twelve months had passed between the killings in Oregon and the Columbine disaster. Yet after the shootings in Littleton, reporters, politicians, and pundits spoke as if the tragedy there were the continuation of a trend and further evidence of an epidemic, when in point of fact, the Columbine incident was unprecedented in American history. Moreover, the number of students killed in U.S. schools that academic year (1998–99) was half of what it had been in the early 1990s, when journalists and politicians seldom talked about school violence. During the period of the so-called epidemic of school violence, fewer than 1 percent of all homicides of school-age children occurred in or around schools. Most of the remainder occurred in homes and other domestic settings, a story seldom told on newscasts or in other public discourse.

In attributing causes to the Columbine shooting, journalists, politicians, and pundits employed another tool as well in fearmongering about youth violence, one that, as I have suggested, I expect will be prevalent for decades to come: misdirection. The term comes from the world of magic. If a magician wants to make a coin appear to vanish from his right hand, he may try to direct the audience's attention to his left hand while he gets rid of the coin.

A comparable form of misdirection occurs in political and media venues. Following the Columbine shootings, the public's attention was directed away from real trends and persistent dangers that confronted children and adolescents, such as the fact that tens of millions did not have health insurance, were malnourished for parts of each month, and attended deteriorating schools. There was misdirection as well from the most proximate and verifiable factor in the deaths at Columbine and elsewhere; namely, the ready availability of guns to people who should not have access to them.

A study published in the *Journal of the American Medical Association* the same year as the Columbine shootings documented that even though the number of youth homicides had been declining, guns were responsible for an increasing proportion of the killings. Yet, instead of a clear, focused discussion on keeping guns out of kids' hands, following the Columbine shootings, the public was treated to orations about all sorts of peripheral matters such as the Internet, video games, movies, trench coats, and recordings by Marilyn Manson (a musician popular with adolescents at the time), each of which pundits implicated in the Columbine tragedy.

A New Story Line for a New Century

The three techniques for fearmongering I have discussed—repetition, the depiction of isolated incidents as trends, and misdirection—continued to prove effective in the early twenty-first century, but with new targets and within a different story line. I anticipate the same will hold in 2040: the methods employed to exaggerate dangers and educe panic will remain reasonably constant, but the specific fears and the broader cultural narrative will change.

Radical changes in narrative and in choices of bogeymen can occur almost overnight in response to weighty events. The period following the terrorist attacks on the World Trade Center and Pentagon on September 11, 2001, demonstrate as much. In the weeks immediately following the far-too-real horrors of 9/11, counterfeit horrors that had occupied much of the popular media almost completely disappeared from public discourse. No longer were TV news programs and newsweeklies obsessed, as they had been just prior to the attacks, with dangers to swimmers from shark attacks and to Washington interns from philandering politicians. Gone were warnings about roller coaster accidents and coyotes prowling suburban neighborhoods.

Nor did the latest incident of violence in a school make headlines and provoke pundits to decry the sorry state of America's youth. Part of the reason is plain: the loss of thousands of lives and the threat of more terrorism overshadowed any such stories. Even producers at local TV news programs and cable news channels could not fail to understand that for some time, stories about bioterrorism, airport security, and hate crimes against Arab Americans would hold more interest and importance for viewers than the usual fare.

But I suggest there was a more important, longer-lived, and foretelling reason that some of the old scare stories did not occupy the public discourse post-9/11: a powerful and pernicious narrative of the previous decades largely lost its usefulness for fearmongers in the news industry and for the politicians and pundits they quote—what might be dubbed the "sick-society" story. In that account, the villains are domestic, heroes are hard to find, and the story line is about the decline of American civilization. Post-9/11, a new narrative came to the fore, one about national unity, villains from foreign lands, and the greatness of American society.

One result of this change was a shift in the putative dangerousness of some categories of people and behaviors. The demise of the sick-society narrative augured especially well for young American males in their late teens and twenties, who were portrayed in the media throughout the first decade of the twenty-first century as heroes in the New York City

Fire Department and in the military or, alternatively, as campaigners for world peace. The change marked a striking departure from how this age group was characterized in the 1990s. Post-9/11, talk of adolescent superpredators didn't fit the celebration of American society and its citizens or the appeals to young Americans to make wartime sacrifices. Nor did the supposed causes of youth violence I noted earlier fit into the new narrative. Suddenly it was no longer fashionable to disparage our popular culture. On the contrary, the culture was referenced not as an infectious agent that turns kids into killers but as a feature of American society that is wrongly reviled by our enemies. "We are battling a bunch of atavistic ascetics who hate TV, music, movies, the Internet (except when they're planning atrocities), women, and Jews," *New York Times* columnist Maureen Dowd put it.

The predominant foci for fearmongering following September 11, 2001, were foreign terrorists and dangers to the American homeland. I doubt there has been a phrase, at least in recent times, that was more effective at exploiting Americans' anxieties than "the war on terror." From late 2001 until they left office in early 2009, the Bush administration, their allies, and many people in the news media repeated the phrase incessantly. As former National Security Advisor Zbigniew Brzezinski noted in the *Washington Post* in 2007, "The little secret here is that the vagueness of the phrase was deliberately (or instinctively) calculated by its sponsors. Constant reference to a 'war on terror' did accomplish one major objective: it stimulated the emergence of a culture of fear. Fear obscures reason, intensifies emotions and makes it easier for demagogic politicians to mobilize the public on behalf of the policies they want to pursue."

In the first weeks after 9/11, when the homegrown scares of the previous three decades seemed trivial, obsolete, or beside the point, the nation's collective concern sensibly coalesced against a hard target: Osama bin Laden and his organization, Al Qaeda. The administration of President George W. Bush quickly redirected that concern, however, to what it dubbed the "worldwide war on terror," a war and associated enemies similar in their vagueness to those denoted in previous decades by the "war on drugs" and the "war on crime." From those earlier wars, American journalists and their audiences had been conditioned to treat more seriously than they ought shocking statistics that were not fully explained or verified, dire warnings that flared and faded, isolated incidents depicted as ominous trends, and testimony from self-appointed experts with vested interests in whipping up anxieties. Following 9/11 and throughout the subsequent wars in Afghanistan and Iraq, the same patterns ensued, only this time the statistics, warnings, and testimony came predominantly from the administration. A study found, for example, that more than 90 percent of news stories about Iraq on NBC, ABC, and CBS during a five month period in 2002 and 2003 came from the White House, Pentagon, or State Department.

Wearing flag lapel pins and crying on camera, journalists suspended even the pretense of objectivity as they affirmed the administration's claim that the attacks of 9/11 constituted a fundamental turning point in human history. "The world is different," another phrase repeated often in late 2001 and 2002, became a kind of password that opened the door for an extraordinary degree of fearmongering, as did its corollary, "9/11 can happen again."

From the beginning, the language of the administration was apocalyptic. "Americans should not expect one battle, but a lengthy campaign unlike any other we have ever seen," President Bush proclaimed in late September 2001. The following January, in his State of the Union address, he announced that our enemies were not only bin Laden and Al Qaeda, but an "axis of evil" consisting of Iraq, Iran, and Korea, as well as any nation that harbored terrorists. At home, Americans should brace themselves for attacks by members of Al Qaeda sleeper cells who lived among us, as the 9/11 terrorists had, and could strike at any moment.

The administration began warning of a far more distant danger as well. Throughout 2002, it claimed that Iraq had aided bin Laden and was building weapons of mass destruction (WMDs). Those claims proved false, but the administration used them to garner broad support from Congress, pundits, and the public for its 2003 invasion and occupation of Iraq. And over the next five years, as casualties mounted and the financial costs of the president's self-described "crusade" soared, it was crucial to the administration that Americans remain frightened about possible terrorist attacks on U.S. soil so that they would continue to support the Iraq war and the broader "war on terror."

As time passed and such attacks did not occur, skeptics began to ask the obvious questions: Why hadn't terrorists attacked freeways and bridges? Poisoned the water supply? Grabbed an automatic weapon and shot up a mall? Americans with no connection to foreign terrorist organizations do such things in their own homeland, but it became increasingly evident that sleeper cells full of impassioned, highly trained terrorists did not exist.

How, then, to keep the fears alive? In large measure, the Bush administration relied on an ingenious repetition device, a color-coded terror alert chart created by the newly established Department of Homeland Security that reflected what the department deemed the degree of risk at any given time. The color chart reminded the populace, graphically and continuously, that they were in danger. Sometimes the risk was greater, sometimes lesser, but always there was danger.

Government officials repeatedly issued "code orange" (high-risk) terror alerts. In each instance, a public official such as the attorney general or the director of Homeland Security appeared before the press, promised that the alert was based on "credible" or "reliable" sources, and offered no further information. No attacks occurred, but the Bush administration benefited from the scares. A study published in 2004 found that when the terror warnings increased, so did Bush's approval rating—an effect that was not lost on the administration. In a memoir published after Bush left office, Tom Ridge, the first director of the Department of Homeland Security, reported that senior members of the administration had pressured him to raise the terrorism threat level at key moments during Bush's reelection campaign of 2004.

Some of the warnings were laughable from the start, as when the government advised citizens in late 2001 to stockpile duct tape and rolls of plastic to seal their homes against chemical weapon attacks—despite the fact that experts knew these measures were probably pointless. (When chemical agents are released outdoors, they are almost immediately diluted by the wind.) Since the risk of dying in a chemical weapon attack is far less than a million to one, an American was more likely to die in a car accident en route to purchase the duct tape.

Therein lies a lesson from this era worth keeping in mind in future panics: when it comes to sustaining fear, one scare supports another, and risk assessment by the frightened populace gets distorted. When fearful people buy guns, drive instead of fly, or isolate themselves in their homes, their probability of accidental death or injury increases. In 2001, as a result of the attacks of 9/11, the number of deaths from terrorism in the United States was the highest in the nation's history. Yet even during that eventful year, relative to other hazards, the danger from terrorism was low. According to figures published by the State Department, the number of deaths from terrorist attacks worldwide was 3,547, more than three-quarters of which were on 9/11 in the United States. By comparison, nearly three times as many Americans died from gun-related homicides that year, and five times as many died in alcohol-related motor vehicle accidents.

Continuity and Change

The war on terror did not bring an end, however, to worries about all low-level domestic dangers. Even as some groups, such as young American males, received a partial reprieve, the culture of fear, rather than narrowing, expanded to include new scares along with such enduring ones as child snatching.

Consider a little experiment I conducted just months after the attacks, in the summer of 2002. Over the course of a couple of weeks, whenever I had the chance, I turned on the TV and flipped between MSNBC, Fox News Channel, and CNN to see what they were covering. Rarely did I have to wait more than twenty minutes to hear a report about one or more child abductions. Editors and journalists defended spending so much air time on child abductions through declarations of a "trend" or "epidemic," even as child abductions remained extremely rare, and they threw out bogus numbers. On his Fox News Channel show, Bill O'Reilly talked of "100,000 abductions of children by strangers every year in the United States," though an exhaustive study from the U.S. Office of Juvenile Justice and Delinquency Prevention (OJJDP) that year found only 115 cases a year of "stereotypical kidnappings" (children abducted by nonfamily members and kept for long periods or murdered). "The majority of victims of stereotypical and other nonfamily abductions were teens—not younger children—and most were kidnapped by someone they knew somewhat—not by strangers or slight acquaintances," a subsequent report in 2006 from the OJJDP noted.

The obsession with kidnapped kids showed no signs of slackening in subsequent years. When Madeleine McCann, just shy of her fourth birthday, went missing in May 2007 from a resort in Portugal, the story drew attention for a couple of years, well after the Portuguese police had closed the case. After another child, Caylee Anthony, disappeared in June 2008, her case also attracted extensive coverage. Combining two archetypes that have been frequently featured, and are likely to continue so, in the U.S. media—the missing child and the monstrous mom (Anthony's mother was eventually arrested for the murder)—Anthony's story became nearly an obsession for some cable TV hosts. Most notable, perhaps, was Nancy Grace, a former prosecutor who has relentlessly covered missing children on her nightly HLN (CNN's Headline News Network) program. CNN might as well rename HLN "CAN, as in Caylee Anthony Network, because HLN has been riding the toddler's demise for hours each day," *Los Angeles Times* media critic James Rainey noted after watching the network for a few days in 2009.

In public lectures and media interviews, when I mention examples such as those and the actual statistics about missing children, I am often asked: other than appealing to our baser appetites, what harm is there in the news media obsessing over missing children? My answer is, considerable harm, ranging from needless restrictions on children's ability to play and get exercise to expensive and ill-conceived legislation. The nationwide Amber Alert system, named for a child murdered in Texas in 1996, costs the federal government $5 million annually, the states many times that amount, and produces frequent notices on roadways and in the media about kidnapped children. But "the system does not typically work as designed (i.e., to save children who are in life-threatening danger) and might be generally incidental to the safe return of most of the hundreds of children for whom the alert system is said to have been 'successful,'" researchers concluded from their study of Amber Alerts over a three-year period.

As we look to the future, it behooves us to ponder long-term ramifications of recurring scares such as child abduction. Even were the Amber Alert system and others like it to become more successful than the research suggests, crucial questions would remain. As criminologist James Alan Fox of Northeastern University noted in an op-ed in the *New York Times*, "More important than the risk of ineffectiveness is the danger of misuse. What should the criteria be for determining reliable information? Who might get hurt in the process of hurriedly chasing down inaccurate leads and wrong suspects? What might happen, for example, if an incorrect license plate of a suspected abductor is displayed on electronic highway signs? Might some poor motorist be pulled over by authorities or, worse, chased down by a group of vigilantes? These concerns are especially salient in the climate of fear and hysteria that surrounds what many have accurately called a parent's worst nightmare."

For children, too, fear and hysteria about stranger danger are harmful in ways that can have lasting effects on individuals and the larger society. While children should certainly be taught commonsense rules about interacting with strangers, too many warnings can lead to what some scholars have dubbed the "mean world syndrome." Children raised to view every adult with distrust might have little desire to become engaged in civic life when they are adults.

Here, as in other instances I've reviewed, a focus on bizarre and uncommon cases misdirected attention from common dangers. In a UNICEF study in 2007 that looked at factors including poverty, health, safety, and education, children in the United States were found to be at greater danger than anywhere else in the developed world.

America's Most Serious Social Problem?

For some scares—child kidnapping being a case in point—the particulars do not vary much from one year to the next. In others, the specific behaviors, subpopulations, alleged causes, and purported effects differ over time. Fearmongering about teen motherhood is an illustrative example, as a quick comparison of two recent periods—the 1990s and the years following September 11, 2001—point up.

Within the sick-society narrative of the 1990s, teen mothers were portrayed as much more ominous and plentiful than they were. Although only about one-third of teen mothers were younger than eighteen years old, and fewer than one in fifty was fourteen or younger, one would not have imagined as much. Numerous TV programs and print media promulgated the fiction of an epidemic of pregnancy among very young teens. These included not only hyperbolic programs of the Ricky Lake and Maury Povich genre but also more highbrow fare. In an interview on National Public Radio's *Morning Edition* in 1995, for example, Gary Bauer of the conservative Family Research Council intoned, "It was not many years ago in this country when it was not common for thirteen-year-olds and fourteen-year-olds to be having children out of wedlock. I'm enough of an optimist to believe that we can re-create that kind of a culture." The interviewer, NPR's Bob Edwards, failed to correct this misleading statement. Nowhere in the segment did he indicate that it remained extremely uncommon for thirteen- and fourteen-year-olds to have children. Nor did Edwards note that, until relatively recently, most thirteen- and fourteen-year-olds were *unable* to bear children. As recently as a century ago the average age for menarche was sixteen or older, whereas today girls typically have their first menstrual period by age thirteen, and some as early as age nine.

Scores of journalists, politicians, and social scientists gave intricate explanations for why adolescents get pregnant and ignored the obvious. As the British sociologists Sally Macintyre and Sarah Cunningham-Burley noted in an essay, "Ignorance about contraception, psychopathology, desire to prove adulthood, lack of family restraint, cultural patterns, desire to obtain welfare benefits, immorality, getting out of school—a host of reasons are given for childbirth in women under 20, while 'maternal instinct' is thought to suffice for those over 20."

The causes of teen motherhood had to be treated as distinct and powerful during this period. Otherwise, it would have made no sense to treat teen moms themselves as distinct and powerful—America's "most serious social problem," as President Bill Clinton called them in his 1995 State of the Union address. Nor would it have made political sense for legislators to include in the 1996 Federal Welfare Law $250 million for states to use to persuade young people to practice premarital abstinence. In what may well qualify as the most sweeping, bipartisan, multimedia, multidisciplinary scapegoating operation of the late twentieth century, at various times during the decade of the 1990s, prominent liberals including Jesse Jackson, Joycelyn Elders, and Daniel Patrick Moynihan and conservatives such as Dan Quayle and William Bennett accused teen moms of destroying civilization. Journalists, joining the chorus, referred to adolescent motherhood as a "cancer," warned that teen moms "breed criminals faster than society can jail them," and estimated their cost to taxpayers at $21 billion a year. Newspaper and magazine columnists called out-of-wedlock births from young mothers "the smoking gun in a sickening array of pathologies—crime, drug abuse, mental and physical illness, welfare dependency" (Joe Klein in *Newsweek*) and "an unprecedented national catastrophe" (David Broder in the *Washington Post*). Richard Cohen, also of the *Post*, asserted that "before we can have crime control, we need to have birth control" and deemed illegitimacy "a national security issue."

That an agglomeration of impoverished young women, whose collective wealth and influence would not add up to that of a single Fortune 100 company, do not have the capacity to destroy America seemed to elude the scaremongers. So did the causal order. Teen pregnancy was largely a response to the nation's educational and economic decline, not the other way around. Girls who attended rotten schools and faced rotten job prospects had little incentive to delay sex or practice contraception. In the mid-1990s at least 80 percent of teenage moms were already poor before they became pregnant. Journalists put up astounding statistics such as "on average, only 5 percent of teen mothers get college degrees, compared with 47 percent of those who have children at twenty-five or older" (*People*, in an article bleakly titled "The Baby Trap"). Yet the difference is attributable almost entirely to preexisting circumstances—particularly poverty and poor educational opportunities and abilities. Studies that compared teen moms with other girls from similar economic and educational backgrounds found only modest differences in education and income between the two populations over the long term.

The panic over young mothers points up another enduring reality about a culture of fear. Warnings can become self-fulfilling, producing precisely the negative outcomes that the doomsayers warn about. Exaggerations about the effects of unwed motherhood on children stigmatize those children and provoke teachers and police, among others, to treat them with suspicion. Why do so many children from single-parent families end up behind bars? Partly, studies find, because they are more likely to be arrested than are children from two-parent households who commit similar offenses. Why do children from single-parent families do less well in school? One factor came out in experiments where teachers were shown videotapes and told that particular children came from one-parent families and others from two-parent families. The teachers tended to rate the "illegitimate" children less favorably.

While fearmongering of the 1990s about young women focused largely on low-income adolescent mothers, after September 11, 2001, the targets expanded to include young women from other income groups and even nonpregnant girls—indeed, even girls who had yet to have intercourse. Rather than the predominant metaphors being about a sick society, now they were about rapidity and about sexual practices adults found disturbing. As Katie Couric put it in 2005, the trouble was "kids growing up way too fast, having oral sex at ridiculously young ages."

Among the most widely reported teen sex stories in the news media in the first decade of the twenty-first century was a supposed "pregnancy pact" at Gloucester High School in Massachusetts. First publicized by *Time* magazine, the tale was about a group of seventeen girls, none older than age sixteen, who, *Time* reported, "confessed to making a pact to get pregnant and raise their babies together. Then the story got worse. 'We found out one of the fathers is a 24-year-old homeless guy,' the principal says, shaking his head." Numerous media outlets repeated the story, calling it "shocking" (CBS) and "disturbing" (CNN), wondering "shall we go to the mall—or get pregnant" (Salon.com headline) and "what happened to shame" (Fox News).

"The pact is so secretive," CNN said, "we couldn't even find out the girls' names," a difficulty that may have resulted from there being no such pact, as reporters who dug an inch deeper learned from other officials at the school and in the town, as well as from one of the pregnant students. The notion of a pact arose from stories about girls who had promised to help one another care for their children, she suggested. It was only *after* they'd learned they were pregnant, the student explained, that they made the promise.

In an op-ed after the pregnancy pact story had been roundly debunked, sociologist Mike Males proposed that politicians, reporters, and social scientists abandon the term "teenage pregnancy" altogether. Contrary to the misimpression that phrase conveys, in the majority of cases, the mother is not "a child herself," she's in her late teens, and the father isn't a teen at all. He is in his twenties.

That the term "illegitimacy," having largely disappeared from the lexicon, made a comeback at the end of the twentieth century, when nearly one in three children was born to an unwed mother, is not only paradoxical but underscores my principal prognostication about fearmongering.

While neither the targets of the predominant scares of 2040 nor the cultural narrative within which they'll be placed can be foretold, the culture of fear will thrive; the tools I have reviewed in this chapter for amplifying risks will be at play; and many of the bogeymen and bogey-women of that era will be considerably less dangerous than they're portrayed.

The World To Be

Gary Saul Morson and Morton Schapiro

In an article in the September 1934 issue of *Everyday Science and Mechanics* magazine, Walter Dill Scott, president of Northwestern University, was quoted as saying that technology would transform the college experience in dramatic ways: "The university of twenty-five years from now will be a different looking place, says President Scott of Northwestern. Instead of concentrating faculty and students around a campus, they will 'commute' by air, and the university will be surrounded by airports and hangars. The course will be carried on, to a large extent, by radio and pictures. Facsimile broadcasting and television will enlarge greatly the range of a library; and research may be carried on by scholars at great distances."

The accompanying cartoon depicted a student in bed studying in front of a large screen, with a loudspeaker blaring away. The caption reads: "The radio-television scholar of 1960 attends a morning lecture."

Apart from making library materials available much more widely, that turned out not to be the Northwestern of 1960, and despite the advent of the Internet and of the massive open online course (MOOC), it is not the Northwestern of today. If you believe our chapter on education, it is unlikely even to be the Northwestern of 2040, a century after Scott's bold prediction.

It wasn't that President Scott was some starry-eyed mystic; by all accounts, he was a serious and innovative thinker. But just as some of the smartest and most influential Americans as selected by *Fortune* magazine in the 1950s imagined a world in 1980 that was so different than the one we experienced, he was largely mistaken.

Will the predictions in this volume fare any better than the one written sixty years ago? At the risk of trying to appear wiser than our predecessors, there are reasons for us to hope. For one, compared with the *Fortune* book, our list of authors is considerably more diverse. A volume that more closely reflects the multiplicity of today's thinking might just turn out to more accurately anticipate the world to come. And while there is certainly less optimism about the future, history seems to suggest that a more balanced view of some things getting better and some worse makes sense.

Above all, there is less of a certainty that this, of all times, is the most critical one in world history. The one thing that does not change, in Marcel Proust's view, is that it always appears there have just been great changes. Sure, the next twenty-five years will be important in many regards—but the most important *ever*, in every single area? We doubt it, and compared with the earlier volume, so do our authors.

What will the world look like in twenty-five years? In what way do the predictions from our authors converge, and in what ways do they differ?

One of the gloomier forecasts in the book isn't about war, religion, or the environment—it is about the economy. A 2 percent annual growth rate (which has been the norm for some time in the United States) implies a doubling in economic output every thirty-five or so years; Robert Gordon's 0.8 percent annual growth rate in the U.S. future would mean it would take ninety years. The headwinds of demographic change, poor education, rising inequality, and soaring debt would make economic life in 2040 much worse than many observers expect and substantially poorer than a simple extrapolation of historical trends would imply. What a different world that would be, as for the first time in many generations, a large number of Americans would achieve lower levels of material well-being than their parents had.

We suppose that the good news is that, according to Richard Easterlin, personal satisfaction is largely unrelated to economic growth. So even if the economy were to continue to grow at historic rates, people wouldn't necessarily get any happier. For Easterlin, changes in satisfaction have much less to do with increases over time in household or individual income and much more to do with meaningful employment and the presence of a social safety net. Unfortunately, other chapters cast doubt on whether these and other noneconomic factors are likely to improve, bringing higher levels of satisfaction with them.

Eileen Crimmins fears that any ongoing increases in life expectancy are more likely to produce long years of physical and mental infirmity rather than golden years full of meaningful activity and pleasure. Perhaps new technologies will lead to a rosier health picture, but Robert Gallucci worries that technological change may also create unexpected vulnerabilities among nations, as countries lacking the ability to engage in large protracted fights may instead wreak havoc through cyber and space warfare. And if a newly intensified competition for resources leads to even faster climate change, environmentally challenged nations may be pushed into conflicts in greater numbers. And that isn't even considering the most destructive of the black swans—surprising events that could destabilize the world. The impact from a new plague, the disintegration of China as a national state, or the detonation of nuclear bombs in major world cities, for example, could make slow economic growth seem the least of our problems.

The emergence of new technologies could have other negative effects as well. Wendy Kaminer questions freedom's future. The diminution of privacy is a fact today, and what is left will be under assault in the coming years. Fear plus technology equals unprecedented surveillance and a gutting of the Bill of Rights. Mark Ratner foresees that the last bastion of privacy will disappear when our very thoughts can be read from outside, a truly horrifying prospect. We doubt this is what Easterlin had in mind when he hoped for a growth in nonmaterial sources of personal satisfaction.

But all is not gloom and doom.

Religion, according to Eboo Patel, could lead to increased respect and cooperation, at least in the United States. Interfaith activities will blossom and religious communities will work together to address great issues such as climate change and poverty.

Ratner points hopefully to an increase in the diversity of those practicing science, arguing that the breakdown in barriers of gender, race, age, residence, and social standing bodes well for the future of scientific success. While Kaminer worries that universal connectivity may trample human rights, Ratner optimistically expects that these connections will lead scientists and policy makers to work ever harder to conquer poverty and malnutrition. And when he talks of *universal* connectivity—he means just that, not just of the earth but life outside as well.

John Kelly is also hopeful that radical changes in technology in the years to come hold great promise, as we enter the age of insight. Economic, medical, educational, political, and other implications are astounding, and much of the news is good. Cognitive systems will fuel innovation and potentially transform the human condition. Further, according to Mark Tercek and Jimmie Powell, advances in science, technology, and communications might also help us understand and address environmental challenges in a new way. With the environment in danger, they are cautiously optimistic that we might just put ourselves on a path toward real sustainability. This depends on the quality of governance institutions, both globally and locally, and on the commitment of the private sector to protect biodiversity.

Education will continue to play a critical role, perhaps in a more traditional form than Kelly (and President Scott) assume. If successful, especially in using new technologies to enhance lifelong learning, perhaps one of the headwinds expected by Gordon will be countered, and the threat with regard to the demise of personal liberty feared by Kaminer will be thwarted by a better informed citizenry. And maybe a resurgence in the humanities, arts, and humanistic social sciences will not only enhance "subjective well-being" in Easterlin's terms, regardless of the dismal path of economic growth imagined by Gordon, but will also provide a cultural literacy and sense of respect that will bode well in terms of Patel's religious tolerance and Gallucci's prospects for world peace. Well, one can hope.

Will we ever address climate change, the dwindling of individual rights, and other great issues if we never even hear about them? Arianna Huffington points to a revolution in communication technology as a way to better uncover the truth. How nice would it be to be able to instantly fact-check a story you are reading? Instead, with social media and the like, it is easier than ever to perpetrate the latest big lie. According to Barry Glassner, focusing on the wrong fears has a long history in the United States and abroad, predating the recent revolution in communications. Fearmongering is a way of life, and while the particular worries will change, the methods employed to exaggerate dangers are expected to remain reasonably constant over the next quarter century. No wonder, as Kaminer argues, so many of us are scared to the point where we enthusiastically trade in civil liberties for the sake of "national security." If only Huffington's "Truth 2.0" app would be brought to market. In the meantime, we will likely obsess on topics that scare us needlessly, while spending insufficient attention on those that are worthy of our concern.

In sum, the optimistic contributors to this volume, while not as overwhelmingly dominant as in the earlier one, are still in the majority.

Will that better world they foresee actually come into being?

Almost forty years ago, one of us studied econometric forecasting in graduate school with Lawrence Klein, who went on to win the 1980 Nobel Prize in Economics for his work in creating models that predict economic trends. One day Professor Klein joked in class that the secret to successful forecasting is either to go very short, simply assuming that tomorrow will look very much like today, or to go very long, far enough in the future that when your bad predictions come to roost, you are but a distant memory.

Sage advice, which the authors here have bravely—or perhaps recklessly—ignored.

The year 2040 doesn't seem all that far away, but twenty-five years is ample time for the world to embark on dramatic new paths in health, economics, politics, religion, science, and the like. Will readers one day marvel that this volume contains Nostradamus-like predictions of the world to be? The *Fortune* book suggests that most of what we say here will be wildly off the mark. But perhaps, like the forty-handicap golfer, if you swing enough, one of your shots will inadvertently go straight, and readers will be amazed that someone actually got something right.

In any case, our most confident prediction is that if this book is read in 2040, people will learn less about how they got to that time and place and more about the world twenty-five years earlier—our greatest fears and our loftiest aspirations. That, we expect, will be our lasting contribution.

abortion, 68

Adventures of Huckleberry Finn (Mark Twain), 79

aging populations, 13–14, 19, 54–55, 56, 201

agriculture, 139, 141, 142–43, 146

Alberts, Bruce, 103, 106

Al Qaeda, 69, 72, 188–89

alternative energy. *See* renewable resources

Amazon.com, 11

Amber Alert system, 192

American Economic Association, 33

American Political Science Association, xxiii

Anderson, Philip, 101

Anthony, Caylee, 192

Arab Spring, 55

artificial intelligence, 12, 118

astrophysics and exoplanetology, 104, 107, 110–11

atomic power, xvii, xx, xxvi

automobiles: in China, 39; driverless, 12, 18, 102, 105; fatalities, 26; pollution and, 146; technological advances, 18, 146; Verne's predictions, 8

Autor, David H., 171n4

Bauer, Gary, 193–94

Baum, Sandy, et al., 171n4

Beck, Glenn, 69

Bell, Alexander Graham, 8

Bellamy, Edward, 99

Bennett, William, 185, 194

Benz, Karl, 8

Berlin, Isaiah, xxiv

Bezos, Jeff, 175

Bhagavad-Gita, 164

bin Laden, Osama, 72, 188–89

biodiversity loss, 131, 140–43, 146

biology, 103–4, 107–8

"black swans," 50, 56–58, 201

Bohr, Niels, 99

brain scans, xvi, 107, 108

Brandeis, Louis, 80, 92

Breneman, David, 164

Broder, David, 195

Brzezinski, Zbigniew, 188

Buddhism, 66

Bush, George W., xxiii, 188–90

Canada, 19, 135, 143

capital punishment, xx

carbon dioxide (CO_2) emissions, 130, 131, 140, 143, 144–46

Carter, Jimmy, 67

CATO Institute, 90

chemistry, 100, 102, 110

China, 39, 42–43, 141, 143; disintegration possibility, 56, 201; education, 157, 164; environmental issues, 143, 145, 147; growth, 7, 39, 53–54, 141; happiness, 40, 43, 44; research output, 106; "restructuring" of economy, 42–43; water scarcity, 138

chlorofluorocarbons (CFCs), 132–34

Church Committee, 82, 93n5

civil liberty, xvi, 83, 87–88, 91

climate change, xvi, xxv, 52, 107, 109, 130–31, 137, 141–42, 143, 144–48, 201

Clinton, Bill, 184, 194

cloud, the, 116, 120

Coase, Ronald, 114, 121

"cogs" (cognitive business apps), 115–16, 123–25

Cohen, Richard, 195

college affordability, 15, 19, 157

complex systems, 111

computer sciences, 7, 9, 10–11, 107, 110,

116–26; cognitive computers, 113–14,
117–19, 122–26, 202; modeling,
119–22, 124
confidence. *See under* prediction and
prophecy
Confucius, 164
contingency, xxi, 80; "contingent" faculty,
156; radical, xxiii
corporations, xviii, 12, 51, 124–25
Couric, Katie, 196
critical theory, 163
Curry, Ann, 184
cybersecurity, 125

Darwin, Charles, 101
data, 102, 113–14, 116, 121, 122, 177;
"big data," 11, 12–13, 100, 117–18
debt: credit card, 158; government,
17–18, 200; student, 15, 19, 156, 158
DeJulio, James, 180
Dekker, Cees, 107
demography, 13–14, 19, 24, 54
Denison, Edward, 14
Department of Homeland Security, 190
digitalization, 6–7, 10, 12, 116
Dirac, Paul, 100
DiTella, Rafael, et al., 40
DNA, 100, 101, 104, 108, 115, 120–21
Dostoevsky, Fyodor, xx, 164
Dowd, Maureen, 188
Dream of Red Mansions, A (Cao Xueqin),
164

Easterlin, Richard A., et al., 38
East Germany, 42, 43–43
Eck, Diana, 64
economics, xxviii n11, 5–20, 60, 114, 155,
161, 200; happiness and, 33–34, 37–39,
42–44
Economist, 105–6
Edison, Thomas, 8, 102
education, 14–16, 19, 20n11, 59, 115,
121–23, 202; enrollment issues, 156,
166–70; higher, 155–71, 199–200; hu-
manities decline, 162–65; massive open
online courses (MOOCs), 122, 165–66,
199; tenure system, 159–60
Edwards, Bob, 194
Ehrlich, Paul, xviii–xix, xxii, xxv
Elders, Jocelyn, 194
Eliot, George, xv
Ellison, Keith, 69
Ellison, Ralph, 74

email, xvi, 7, 11, 89, 177
employment, xvii, 34, 39–44, 201
endangered species, 140–41
environmental issues, 109–10, 129–49, 202
Environmental Protection Agency, 133
Esping-Andersen, Gøsta, 40
exceptionalism, 60

Fabulous Future: America in 1980, The,
xvi–xix, xxvi–xxvii, 5, 9, 19, 28–29, 34,
200, 203
Facebook, 11, 80, 114
Falkenmark, Malin, 138
Fallows, James, 175
Falwell, Jerry, 67
families, 16–17
Faraday, Michael, 105
fearmongering, 183–97, 203; misdirection
and, 186. *See also under* terrorism
Festinger, Leon, et al., xxii–xxiii
fishing and fisheries, 130, 131–32,
134–36, 140, 142, 143
Flynn Effect, 181
Food and Drug Administration, 133
food supply, xviii, xxii, 103, 107, 202
Ford, Henry, 12
Fortune. See *Fabulous Future*
fossil fuels, xvii, 143, 144–47
Fox, James Alan, 192–93
fracking, 130–31
Francis, Pope, 75–76
Frankfurter, Felix, 159
free speech issues, 55, 80, 82, 90–92
"futuribles," xvi, xxvii n4
"futurisms," xx–xxi
futurology. *See* prediction and prophecy

Galbraith, John Kenneth, xviii
Gandhi, Mahatma, 63
Gellman, Barton, 89
genetically modified organisms (GMOs),
xvi
GI Bill, 15, 155–56
Giuliani, Rudy, 92
Gladwell, Malcolm, xxvii n3
Gleeson, John, 86–87
globalization, 51
global warming. *See* climate change
Goldin, Claudia, and Lawrence F. Katz,
14, 15–16
Google, 11
Gouvêa, André Luiz de, 110–11
Grace, Nancy, 192

Graham, Billy, 68
Great Depression, 121, 155
Greenewalt, Crawford, xvii, xxvi
Greenwald, Glenn, 89
Grisham, John, 163
gross domestic product (GDP), 5, 10, 16, 19, 35, 36–40, 156
gun control, 186

Halperin, William, 110
happiness, 33–45, 201
Harrington, John, xxii
Harris, Sam, 71
Hawkins, Jeff, 118
health care and life expectancy, 23–32, 105, 115, 118, 120–21, 161, 201
Heckman, James, 15, 20n11
hedgehogs vs. foxes, xxv
Heraclitus, 175
Herberg, Will, 65
"higher-order thinking," 126
Hinduism, 63–64, 66
Hitchens, Christopher, 71
Hobbes, Thomas, 60
Hoffmann, David, 101
Hoover, J. Edgar, 82
Horgan, John, 101
HuffPost, 176, 179
Humphrey, George, xvii
hunger, 103, 107, 202
Huntington, Samuel, 69
Hybels, Bill, 76

IBM, 117, 120, 121, 125; Thomas J. Watson Research Center, 118, 123
income inequality, 10, 16–17, 18, 19, 59
India, 53–54, 141; education, 157, 164; pollution, 145, 147; religious diversity, 63–64; tension with Pakistan, 52–53, 64, 69; water scarcity, 138
industrial revolutions, 5–7
"inflection points," xvi, 129. *See also* "tipping points"
information revolution, xvii, 6, 10
information technology (IT), 12, 55, 89, 107, 113
insurance industry, 14, 27–28
Internet, 7, 11, 19, 116, 122, 125, 186, 199; journalism and the, 176–78, 181; universal connectivity, 105, 202
IQ measurement, 181
Islam, xvii, 58, 63–64, 66, 69–70, 72–74
iTunes, 11

Jackson, Jesse, 194
Japan, 26, 53, 56
Jeopardy!, 117–18
Jinnah, Muhammad Ali, 63
John Paul II, 68
Jordan, David Starr, 155
Jorgenson, Dale, 16, 21n15
journalism, 175–81, 202; old media vs. new, 176, 180–81. *See also* fearmongering
Journal of the American Medical Association, 186
Jouvenal, Bertrand de, xxvii n4
Judaism, 66–67, 71, 73
Jurdy, Donna, 109–10

Kagan, Elena, 89
Kane, Tom, 161
Kennedy, John F., 65, 68
Khanfar, Wadah, 179
Khomeini, Ruhollah, 68
King, Martin Luther, Jr., 66
Klein, Joe, 195
Klein, Lawrence, 203
Klotz, Irving, 104–5

Ladies' Home Journal, 8–9
Lao-Tzu, 164
La Rochefoucauld, François de, xv
Lawrence Livermore National Laboratory, 120
legal abuses, 85–87
libertarianism, 83, 90
life sciences, 103–4, 107
LinkedIn, 11
Lives of Others, The, xxvii n2
Ludlum, Robert, 80
Luxembourg, 21n21

Macintyre, Sally, and Sarah Cunningham-Burley, 194
Males, Mike, 196
Malthusianism, xix
management tools, 115–16, 123–25; adaptive management, 132
Manson, Marilyn, 186
marijuana legalization, 87
marketing, 12–13, 114
massive open online courses (MOOCs), 122, 165–66, 199
mathematics, 101, 103
McCann, Madeleine, 191–92
"mean world syndrome," 193
Meany, George, xvii

medical advances, 11–12, 18, 23, 105, 108, 118, 120–21; threats, 57, 107–8, 110
meteorology, 119
microorganisms, xv, 108
Middle East, 53, 58, 138
military policies, 50–51
Mill, John Stuart, 92
Milošević, Slobodan, 69
modeling. *See under* computer sciences
Molina, Mario, and Sherwood Rowland, 132–33
Montaigne, Michel de, 109, 111
Moynihan, Daniel Patrick, 194
Mrksich, Milan, 110
"murder by legal sentence," xx
Murray, Charles, 17
Murray, John Courtney, 66

nanotechnology, xvii, 100
National Public Radio, 185, 193–94
National Security Agency (NSA), xvi, 82, 83, 88, 92
Nature Conservancy, 148–49
Netflix, 11
Neumann, John von, xvi–xvii, xxvi, 117, 119
New Republic, xviii
Newsweek, 184, 195
New York Times, xxi, 9, 185, 188, 192
New York World's Fair, 9
9/11 attacks, 65, 69, 70, 81, 84, 187–89, 191
1984 (George Orwell), xvi, 88
Northwestern University, 109–10, 160, 192, 199–200
Norton Anthology of Theory and Criticism, The, 163, 172n14
nuclear weapons, xv, 53, 56–57, 69, 201
Numenta, 118

Obama, Barack, 64, 73–74
Oberhelman, Doug, 16
oil and gas, xv, xxii. *See also* fossil fuels
O'Malley, John W., 66
O'Reilly, Bill, 191
Organization for Economic Cooperation and Development, 33–34, 157
Orwell, George, xvi
ozone depletion crisis, 131, 132–34

Palestinian–Israeli conflict, 57–58, 69
pharmaceutical advances, 11–12, 29

physics, xix, 100–101, 103, 104
Picard, Rosalind, 118
Plotinus, 178
politics, xxiii–xxiv; American, 19–20, 58–60, 82, 92, 147, 178; international, 49–58, 147–48
Popper, Karl, 105
population growth, xviii, xxii, 10, 54, 129, 130, 131, 137
poverty, 17, 53–54, 107, 201–2
prediction and prophecy, xvi, xviii–xxvi, xxviii n11, 7–9, 99; assessments of, xxi–xxiv; Bohr on, 99; components of, xxiv–xxv; crying wolf tendency, xxvi; degrees and expressions of confidence, xv, xviii, xxv–xxvi, xxxvii, xxix n24, 23, 24, 28, 76, 118, 147, 183, 203; of disaster, xv–xvi, xxvi; Eliot on, xv; failure of, xviii–xix, xxi–xxiv, xxviii n11, 49; Greenewalt on, xxvi; Klein on, 203; La Rochefocauld on, xv; luck and, xxiii–xxiv; von Neumann on, xxvi
privacy. *See* surveillance
Proust, Marcel, 200
Pusey, Nathan, xvii
Putnam, Robert, and David Campbell, 67–68, 71–72, 76

quantum mechanics, 100, 101, 108, 110
Quayle, Dan, 194

Rabi, I. I., 101
Rabin, Yitzhak, 69
Rainey, James, 192
Rauf, Feisal Abdul, 70
Reagan, Ronald, 67, 133
religion, xvii, 63–76, 91, 201; apocalyptic, xxii; faith-fueled violence, 65, 69; "nones," 71–72, 76
renewable energy, 105, 147
Ridge, Tom, 190
Rivera, Geraldo, 184
Robertson, Pat, 67
robots, 12, 13, 18, 107
Rosen, Jay, 177

Saez, Emmanuel, 16
Sagan, Carl, 104
Sarnoff, David, xvii, xxvi
Scandinavia, 19, 21n21, 40–41
Schatz, George, 110
Schiraldi, Vincent, 185

school shootings, 184–86
Schrödinger, Erwin, 108
science fiction, 8, 99, 126
scientific advances, 99–111, 201; coffee
 and, 107; working methods, 105–7
Scott, Walter Dill, 199–200, 202
Scruggs, Lyle, 40–41
search engines, 121, 177
Segway scooters, 119
"self-help" politics, 50, 60n1
"self-perpetuating worldviews," xxiv
semiconductor technology, 18
sexuality, 68, 72, 74–75, 194–96
Shahnameh (Abolqasem Ferdowsi), 164
Shakespeare, William, 163, 164
Sharma, Ruchir, xxviii n11
Shirky, Clay, 181
"sick-society" narrative, 187, 193, 196
Siegel, Robert, 185
Sikhism, 63–64, 70
Silver, Nate, xxix n24, xxix n27
Silverglate, Harvey, 86
Silverman, Richard, 110
Simon, Julian, xviii–xix, xxii
simulation technology, 110, 119
Smith, Al, 73
Smith, Wilfred Cantwell, 63–65, 66
Snowden, Edward, 82–83, 85, 87, 88–89
social media, 80, 81, 85, 114, 116, 124,
 179–80, 202
social safety nets, 34, 39, 40–45, 201
"soft power," 51, 60n2
South Korea, 19, 53, 157
Soviet Union, 42, 55
Stair, Peter, 111
standardized testing, 121
"state of nature" view, 50, 60n1
stem cell technology, 110
Stevenson, Adlai, xvii
Storm P (Robert Storm Petersen), 99
subjective well-being (SWB), 38–41
Sunlight Foundation, 178
Supreme Court, 80, 89, 159
surveillance and privacy issues, xvi, xxvii
 n2, 55, 79–90, 92, 93n5, 107–8, 201

Tale of Genji, The (Murasaki Shikubu), 164
teen motherhood, 193–96
telephony advances, 6, 8, 11, 13, 19, 80,
 89, 113, 121

"telescreens," xvi
television, 10, 19, 199
terrorism, xv, 56–57; fears of, 81–85,
 87–88, 93n3, 188–91
Tetlock, Philip, xxii, xxiv
Theil, Peter, 9
Thoreau, Henry David, 179
3-D printing, 12, 107
Time, 184–85, 196
"tipping points," xvi, xxvii n3, 130
Today Show, 184
Tutu, Desmond, 68
Twitter, 9, 80, 114, 177

Ulam, Stanislaw, 119
Ulmer, Melville, 111
"ultimate resource" (ingenuity), xix
unemployment, xxiii, 14, 19, 39–40,
 42–43
unmetered air, xvii
urbanization, 54, 137
U.S. News and World Report, 185

Verne, Jules, 8, 9
Vijg, Jan, 11
viral videos, 180

Wall Street Journal, xxi
warfare, 51–53, 59, 201
"war on crime," 188
"war on drugs," 81, 87, 188
"war on terror," 87, 188, 189, 191
Warren, Earl, xvii
Warren, Rick, 76
Washington Post, 84, 88, 89, 175, 188, 195
water scarcity, 52, 131, 136–39, 146
Watson (computer), 117–18, 120, 127n3
Watson, Thomas, Sr., 121, 127n3
Watt, James, 6
"welfare state" policies. *See* social safety
 nets
Whewell, William, 105
Wiener, Norbert, 9
Wikipedia, 11, 117
Wilson, Charles E., xxvii
Wood, Ben, 121
World Values Survey, 38–39
workweek, xvii, xx

YouTube, 177, 180